Teaching Ninetee... Literature

Teaching nineteenth-century literature can be an incredibly rewarding experience, resulting in lessons which are exciting and engaging and enable amazing levels of student progress. This essential handbook guides teachers through the key events of the period, offering theoretical approaches and a wealth of practical ideas for teaching nineteenth-century fiction and poetry in the secondary classroom.

Supporting and inspiring teachers as they introduce nineteenth-century texts to their students and nurture their interest and enthusiasm for the genre, *Teaching Nineteenth-Century Literature* provides a grounding in the major historical events of the nineteenth century, describes pedagogical approaches to teaching fiction and poetry, and offers step-by-step guidance on the use of literary resources. Chapters offer advice on overcoming the particular challenges of the genre, including unwieldy plots, complex vocabulary and unfamiliar sentence structures, and illustrate how texts from the period can be made fully accessible to even the youngest pupils. With a range of detailed activities, photocopiable lesson plans, case studies and extracts for use in the classroom, teachers will be able to quickly and easily build a scheme of work that is stimulating and beneficial for children of varying abilities.

Equipping teachers with the knowledge, understanding and resources they need to teach nineteenth-century literature in an engaging, inspiring and intellectually stimulating way, this practical and accessible text will be an invaluable resource for secondary school English teachers, students and trainees.

Rachel Fenn is Head of English at École Jeannine Manuel in London, UK.

Anna McGlynn is a teacher of English at Weald of Kent Grammar School, UK.

Teaching Nineteenth-Century Literature

An Essential Guide for Secondary Teachers

Rachel Fenn and Anna McGlynn

Routledge
Taylor & Francis Group

LONDON AND NEW YORK

First published 2019
by Routledge
2 Park Square, Milton Park, Abingdon, Oxon OX14 4RN

and by Routledge
52 Vanderbilt Avenue, New York, NY 10017

Routledge is an imprint of the Taylor & Francis Group, an informa business

British Library Cataloguing-in-Publication Data
A catalogue record for this book is available from the British Library

Library of Congress Cataloging-in-Publication Data
Names: Fenn, Rachel, author. | McGlynn, Anna, author.
Title: Teaching nineteenth-century literature : an essential guide for secondary
    teachers / Rachel Fenn and Anna McGlynn.
Description: Abingdon, Oxon ; New York, NY : Routledge, 2019. | Includes
    bibliographical references and index.
Identifiers: LCCN 2018046082 (print) | LCCN 2018060621 (ebook) |
    ISBN 9781351066426 (eb) | ISBN 9781138479166 |
    ISBN 9781138479166(hb :alk. paper) | ISBN 9781138479173(pb :alk. paper) |
    ISBN 9781351066426(ebk)
Subjects: LCSH: Literature, Modern—19th century—Study and teaching
    (Secondary)
Classification: LCC PN67 (ebook) | LCC PN67 .F46 2019 (print) | DDC
    809/.034071—dc23
LC record available at https://lccn.loc.gov/2018046082

ISBN: 978-1-138-47916-6 (hbk)
ISBN: 978-1-138-47917-3 (pbk)
ISBN: 978-1-351-06642-6 (ebk)

Typeset in Melior
by Swales & Willis Ltd, Exeter, Devon, UK
Printed by CPI Group (UK) Ltd, Croydon CR0 4YY

Contents

Introduction

On teaching nineteenth-century literature

Teaching literature from the nineteenth century can seem a mixed blessing for many teachers. While many are Literature graduates, who will have encountered the classics throughout their own studies and retain a fondness and enthusiasm for them, there is a sense that teaching these seminal texts to students in secondary school, particularly in Key Stages 3 and 4, is quite an undertaking. Students can feel intimidated by the often complex vocabulary and unfamiliar sentence structures found in nineteenth-century literature, and many are put off by stories that they feel are old-fashioned, boring and irrelevant. The drive to include more contemporary fiction across the curriculum over the past few years has made English lessons much more appealing to students who don't enjoy reading, but this does mean that many have never read any novels that are older than they are. Used to pacey and exciting action, adventure or dystopian fiction that contains unchallenging vocabulary and a familiar setting, the leap to the dense and often convoluted plots of Victorian novels that take place in a seemingly foreign world can seem one that is simply too far. Many teachers, understandably, are in agreement with this, and have been vocal in the press about nineteenth-century literature being inappropriate for the pre-Key Stage 5 classroom. However, we couldn't disagree more.

The experience of teaching fiction, poetry and non-fiction from the nineteenth century can be an incredibly rewarding one, and result in lessons which are exciting and engaging and enable amazing levels of student progress. With a little creativity, the process of familiarising your students with the work of Georgian and Victorian authors can begin as soon as they start secondary school, and through this regular exposure to the syntax and language of the period, a later introduction to more challenging texts will hold little fear. After all, students in Key Stage 3 are used to being exposed to a bewildering variety of new educational experiences across the curriculum, so the introduction of non-contemporarily written literature will simply be another new experience for them. If you, as a teacher, approach this as another great opportunity to learn and acquire knowledge, then you will frame the introduction of nineteenth-century literature as an enjoyable and enriching part of their English classes. By building on this during their studies, you will be able to create confident and competent readers who will be well prepared for the demands of GCSE and beyond.

This book begins with a summary of the major historical events of the nineteenth century, with a focus on those that will tie in with key themes in the literature commonly found on school syllabi. This will provide you with an excellent grounding to ensure you are able to weave context effortlessly into your lessons as you study key texts with your students. By explaining the rapid pace of industrial, scientific and societal change in the nineteenth century, you will be able to make them appreciate that the window into this time is through the literature of the period. It has shaped our understanding of our national history and, through permeating our culture, created a sense of self, even without our realising it. What would gentle Sunday night television viewing be without a costume drama adaptation of Austen? How would our idea of a 'real' Christmas look without the mental images created by Dickens? Thinking about how much impact these nineteenth-century novels still have on the world around us shows us how significant they still are. By ensuring your students see *why* the literature of the period is to be valued, you will make sure that their study of the texts becomes relevant to them.

The chapters on teaching poetry and fiction provide a guide to nineteenth-century literature and how to teach it in an engaging and innovative way, spanning from Key Stage 3 to Key Stage 5. With a range of suggested activities and lesson plans, you can use these chapters to build a scheme of work that is both engaging for students and easy to plan for you. For Key Stage 3 specifically, there are innovative methods for introducing literary texts from the period in a way that students will find engaging and thought provoking, catering for those of all abilities. This section of the book shows you how you can use contemporary neo-Victorian texts as a way into nineteenth-century literature if you feel teaching a whole nineteenth-century text will be too much of a challenge for your class, while also giving advice on how to gently introduce traditional nineteenth-century texts to younger students.

Using non-fiction can be a fantastic way to ease students into nineteenth-century language and context, and we have a whole chapter advising you on the best ways to find resources and incorporate these into your teaching; a case study of using non-fiction with *Jane Eyre* will give you a starting point. In addition, a chapter covers how to teach the doorstopper novels that tend to fill teachers with fear, giving practical advice on different ways to cover large amounts of reading and unwieldy plots with ease.

Finally, we recognise that obtaining resources to use in the classroom can be tricky for busy teachers, and so the last chapter contains a variety of extracts from nineteenth-century fiction and non-fiction texts, arranged by theme, ready for you to photocopy and use in class.

Essentially, what this book aims to do is equip you with the knowledge, understanding and resources to ensure that you can teach engaging, inspiring and intellectually stimulating lessons with confidence. Whether you are reading this book because you are about to embark upon your first foray into the literary canon of the nineteenth century, or you are already a self-professed fan of the period, we hope that it will offer you a fresh perspective on teaching nineteenth-century literature that makes the prospect of teaching it a delight!

The nineteenth century in a nutshell

It is not necessary for either you or your students to become experts in nineteenth-century history in order to access its literature meaningfully. However, a good understanding of the major events and ensuing debates of the period will enable you to spot cultural, historical and ideological references in texts with more ease, and allow you to draw inferences and meaning from them that you may otherwise have missed.

What is important for students to understand, first and foremost, is that generalisations about 'Victorians' and how they thought and felt about the world around them need to be avoided. Just as someone growing up in the 1980s would have experienced an entirely different lifestyle to someone growing up in the 1940s, such would have been the difference for those living in the 1880s as opposed to the 1840s. Therefore, we must encourage students to view the nineteenth century as a period made up of ten separate decades between which quite distinct changes happened, and not as a single unit of time populated by homogenous 'Victorian' people with beards and hats and big dresses. For over a third of the nineteenth century, after all, Queen Victoria was not even on the throne, and the largely rural, unindustrialised, provincial Britain of 1800 had become a cosmopolitan, metropolitan centre of the world's largest empire by 1900. Nineteenth-century texts, therefore, need to be looked at within the context of their decade rather than as part of a loosely generalised 'nineteenth century', and the timeline provided in this chapter will help you to see at a glance what events and ideas will be most relevant to discuss when talking about your specific text. As the concept of this chapter is to give a brief, essential overview of the period, we will not go into enormous depth on any of the topics of importance to nineteenth-century society, but merely give you the nutshell knowledge you will need in order to support your students. Suggested reading on the period is given throughout the chapter should you wish to find out more about any of the topics discussed.

BRIEF NINETEENTH-CENTURY TIMELINE

1789 – French Revolution begins

1792 – Publication of Mary Wollstonecraft's *Vindication of the Rights of Women*

1798 – Malthus' *Essay on Population* published – this influenced Darwin and many nineteenth-century thinkers – said that world population was growing faster than our ability to produce food, and that unless something was done to check the growth in population, terrible poverty and want would result

1805 – Battle of Trafalgar – Nelson defeats French and Spanish fleets

1807 – Slavery is abolished in the British Empire (but not the slave trade)

1815 – Battle of Waterloo – defeat of Napoleon and peace in Europe; passing of the Corn Laws, which set the price of corn at an inflated rate to protect British producers against imports, raising prices of basic foodstuffs

1819 – Peterloo Massacre – eleven people killed and hundreds wounded at a mass meeting agitating for political reform

1830 – Opening of the world's first passenger railway, the Liverpool and Manchester railway

1832 – Great Reform Act is passed, abolishing 'rotten boroughs', creating new boroughs to take into consideration the expansion of small towns into cities as industry developed, and widening political representation (amongst men only)

1833 – Slave trade is abolished in the British Empire; Factory Act – abolished child labour under the age of nine

1837 – Queen Victoria comes to the throne

1838 – The People's Charter calls for democratic reform – becomes the most significant political pressure group, particularly amongst working people, over the next decade. Its supporters are called 'Chartists'; opening of the London–Birmingham railway line – precipitates the 'railway boom' of the 1840s

1840 – The penny post is introduced, making it much cheaper to send letters

1845 – Irish Potato Famine begins – it lasted four years, killed about 1 million people and caused the emigration of a million more

1846 – Corn Laws abolished

1848 – 'Year of Revolutions' across Europe

1851 – The Great Exhibition takes place in London

1854–6 – The Crimean War

1858 – India Act, giving control of India to the British Crown

1859 – Publication of Charles Darwin's *On the Origin of Species*

1861 – Prince Albert dies, plunging Queen Victoria into deep mourning

1866 – Second transatlantic cable laid between Britain and US (the first, in 1858, failed after a few months and it took eight years to raise the funds to lay another)

1867 – Second Reform Act, extending the vote to the male working classes and doubling the electorate

1870 – Married Women's Property Act – allowed women to retain wages earned and property inherited during marriage independently of their husbands (this was extended in 1882 to all property a woman owned or acquired regardless of when it was obtained); Elementary Education Act – it becomes compulsory for all children between the ages of five and thirteen to attend school

1876 – Queen Victoria declared Empress of India

1885 – Partition of Africa to European powers at conference of Berlin

1886 – First Irish Home Rule bill for Ireland introduced to parliament

1898–1902 – Boer War

1901 – Queen Victoria dies

Political reform

The nineteenth century saw a considerable amount of political changes that would transform Britain and take it from a society ruled solely by aristocratic elites to being a democratic nation where – as long as you were a man – your class did not prohibit you from having a say in how your government was run.

The call for reform started in the eighteenth century, with the French Revolution triggering a desire for change across Europe. After the Napoleonic wars at the beginning of the nineteenth century, there was much dissent amongst the working classes, who had been hit badly by rising unemployment, famine and the introduction of the **Corn Laws**, which raised the price of food by restricting imports to benefit British producers. The industrial north of England, home to many of England's largest towns and cities, had hardly any political representation as boroughs had not been changed to reflect the huge shifts and growths in population over the latter half of the eighteenth and beginning of the nineteenth century. In 1819, a demonstration agitating for political reform in St Peter's Field, Manchester led to tragedy when many were killed and injured after troops stormed the protestors – this became known as the **Peterloo Massacre**. Initially this caused a crackdown on reforms by the government, who were terrified of further uprisings and facing their very own French Revolution, but this only fanned the flames of discontent even further. In 1832 the government relented and introduced the **Great Reform Act**, which abolished many 'rotten boroughs' (boroughs where there were hardly any eligible voters and which were usually controlled by a prominent family), established new boroughs to reflect the changing population distribution of the country and allocated a greater number of MPs to boroughs with larger populations. This Reform Act also extended the franchise to men under certain financial and property conditions, which widened the electorate considerably but still effectively excluded the working class. Obviously there was no question at this point of widening the franchise to women.

The **Chartist** movement developed out of this Reform Act, and was instigated by a group of working-class men who wrote 'The People's Charter', agitating for universal male suffrage (again, no concern for women!), and, amongst other things, the property qualification for MPs to be abolished and a salary introduced for the role, allowing anyone to stand as a member of parliament rather than only those who could afford to do so. The Chartists hosted demonstrations and caused a great deal of anxiety to the government, who feared violence and unrest would spread throughout the working classes. However, in reality their movement did not have enough popular support to truly cause a threat. Even so, the government did take notice of their demands and recognised the need to give more working-class men the vote; this was addressed fully in the **Second Reform Act of 1867**, which considerably extended the franchise to the working classes and doubled the male electorate overnight.

The issue of securing **votes for women** started to develop alongside the Chartist movement, and the first formal organisations formed to lobby for female suffrage were created in the 1860s. However, it was only really with the creation of the National Society for Women's Suffrage, founded by Millicent Fawcett in 1897, that a real movement developed, with many smaller organisations joining under this umbrella, allowing for a more strategic and effective campaign. The real fight for votes for women happened in the Edwardian period, and so falls outside the scope of this book. What students should realise about the nineteenth century is that it was a time when women had very few political rights and freedoms and this was something that was not actively challenged or considered to be problematic by the Establishment. The reason why women were not given votes was because they were considered too feeble-minded and emotional to make a choice, and if they did vote, they would only vote as their nearest male relative instructed them anyway. Even Charles Darwin's works advocated the belief that women's brains were smaller and intellect less well developed, and it was only due to petitioning from upper-class women, who were threatened with losing their dowries and children if they wanted to divorce their abusive husbands, that the Married Women's Property Act was passed in 1870.

Aside from franchise reform, another major political issue throughout the mid- to late nineteenth century was **Ireland**. Ireland became part of Great Britain after the 1800 Act of Union, and was problematic from the start, for obvious reasons. From the 1860s there was call for **'Home Rule'**: an Irish parliament with responsibility for its own domestic affairs, while Westminster would continue to make decisions in foreign affairs. Fenians, however, wanted complete separation, with Ireland becoming fully independent of the rest of Britain once more, whereas Unionists didn't want a separate parliament at all, as they feared it would become dominated by the Catholic Church. William Gladstone's Liberal Party saw Home Rule as the best option, whereas the Conservatives wanted a Unionist approach. This caused a great deal of conflict inside the Houses of Parliament, and the wrangling dominated newspaper headlines. Gladstone tried repeatedly to push through Home Rule, after being impressed by the leader of the Home Rule Party, Charles Parnell, but he was defeated several times and lost power because of it. Ireland dominated the political scene for much of the latter nineteenth century, but continual infighting and blocking of bills by the House of Lords meant that Home Rule was not passed until 1920, and remains a contentious issue today.

Political literature

Middlemarch (1871) by George Eliot is set around the time of the Reform Act and provides an interesting commentary on contemporary attitudes to reform.

The less well-known *The Semi-Attached Couple* (1860) by Emily Eden, great aunt of Prime Minister Anthony Eden, contains a very interesting section on a pre-Reform Act election, revealing the corruption of the process.

Sensation novels, particularly those of Wilkie Collins, deal very well with the political position of women in nineteenth-century society, with many of Collins' female characters, such as *The Woman in White*'s Laura Fairlie and *No Name*'s Norah and Magdalen Vanstone, used and abused by men due to having no legal recourse to keep their own property.

Anthony Trollope's *Palliser* series (1864–79) charts the rise of the ridiculously named politician Plantagenet Pallister and is a wonderfully witty and surprisingly contemporary-feeling commentary on political life.

Foreign policy

The Victorian era is commonly viewed as one of peace and prosperity, but the reality is that almost constant wars were being fought throughout the nineteenth century to either gain or maintain foreign territories. Once the wars were over with the European powers at the beginning of the century, much of the other battles going on across the Empire have disappeared from public memory, with the Crimean and Boer Wars in particular no longer being matters of general knowledge. However, they were certainly defining events to Victorians, and feature heavily in their literature.

At the peak of the Empire, in the 1870s, when Queen Victoria was given the title Empress of India, British-controlled lands made up a quarter of the world's surface. **Imperialism** was an enormous driving factor in foreign policy decisions. There was an overriding belief that the Empire was not just about gaining land, but about civilisation. Victorians saw the main purpose of Empire as taking the moral values of a very British form of Christianity to 'uncivilised' cultures. There was a genuine belief that it was in the best interests of the colonised nations to come under the protection of the British flag, and though in our postcolonial times it is difficult to view this attitude with anything other than criticism, it must be remembered that many Victorians saw their actions as benevolent and characterised them as such.

Britain's position as a benevolent and civilising force no doubt stemmed from the smugness many British people felt (particularly towards America) at Britain being one of the first nations to **ban slavery in 1807**; this was followed by a total ban on the slave trade in 1833. This was very much a popular movement in Britain, with it becoming a passionate *cause célèbre* across all sectors of society, particularly amongst women. Though much anti-slavery literature of the period is American, with *Uncle Tom's Cabin* (1852) by Harriet Beecher Stowe being the most famous example, Jane Austen's use of a slave plantation being the source of income for the Bertram family in *Mansfield Park* (1814) provides an intriguing insight into British attitudes towards slavery.

India came fully under control of Britain in 1858 after the passing of the India Act, which dissolved the East India Company, who had been governing India in the name of the British government, and gave power over India directly to the British Crown. This was a result of the Indian Mutiny in 1857, when many British soldiers were killed and around two hundred British women and children savagely murdered while under hostage in Cawnpore. This massacre of innocents, with them being labelled 'The Angels of Albion' by the British press, was responded to with outrage and horror in Britain, and crops up repeatedly in literature of the period. The mutiny was so shocking in many ways because India was very much seen as the jewel in the crown of the Empire; its seemingly benign exoticness appealed enormously to the Victorian public, and to Queen Victoria herself, who brought servants over from India and insisted on them wearing their traditional dress. As such, Indian influences abound in literature of the period, with Rudyard Kipling's novels being the most famous examples.

The Crimean War started over complicated reasons to do with religion between the Ottoman and Russian Empires; an in-depth knowledge of this is certainly not important for our purposes! Britain tried to be a peacemaker but ended up being drawn into the conflict after both the Ottoman and Russian Emperors refused to back down. The war itself is most significant to students of the nineteenth century due to its depiction in the press and literature. The Crimean War was widely denigrated as an example of gross mismanagement, largely due to an old-fashioned army ruled by aristocrats who had bought their commissions rather than earning them with any particular talent, and most of the casualties were not caused by conflict, but infection. **Florence Nightingale** rose to fame as the 'lady with the lamp' while nursing soldiers in the Crimea, and her reforms to nursing and medical care in general were a direct consequence of her experience there. The Crimean War was the first to make use of modern technology, and the telegraph allowed reportage from the front lines to make it back to Britain with incredible speed, allowing for extensive, detailed and up-to-date coverage in the press. This enabled an intense level of public involvement in the war, and this legacy is seen in the name of many Crimean places in the English language – balaclava and cardigan being two – and in literature, with Tennyson's 'The Charge of the Light Brigade' (1854) probably the most famous example, functioning as an exposé of the poor leadership of the campaign.

The **'Scramble for Africa'** began in the 1870s as a result of King Leopold II of Belgium (a cousin of Queen Victoria), who claimed the Congo as his personal fiefdom and began extracting incredibly profitable ivory and rubber, with devastating consequences for the native population. Britain already had a foothold in Africa at this time, in Egypt and part of modern-day South Africa, though the Dutch Boer population in South Africa were incredibly resistant to British rule, which led to the First and Second Boer Wars in the latter part of the century. However, the untapped potential of the rest of the 'dark continent' was incredibly tempting, and with huge swathes of land ripe for the taking, the British government was keen to take more territories. They were not alone; with a number of European powers becoming interested in Africa in the wake of King Leopold's claiming of the Congo, a conference was held in Berlin in 1884–5, when the European powers negotiated the fair terms in which 'effective occupation' of territory could be claimed and trade routes left open to enable free trade throughout the continent. This led to what has been termed the 'Scramble for Africa', when most of Africa was colonised by European powers over a twenty-year period, either through making deals with African leaders or through bitter fighting.

Britain managed to secure a number of colonies in Africa, including the Sudan, Nigeria and eventually most of what we now consider modern-day South Africa and Zimbabwe. This Imperial strategy was not received with universal praise; many in Britain were uncomfortable with the treatment of the native populations and disliked the focus on profit rather than civilisation. **Cecil Rhodes**, who was Prime Minister of the Cape Colony and founder of the diamond company De Beers, was a highly controversial figure whose ceaseless desire to add territory to the existing colony and brutal treatment of the native population led ultimately to the Second Boer War. Towards the end of the century, the jingoistic Imperialist sentiments of earlier times had become somewhat tempered by a more liberal questioning of the ethical implications of colonisation, which is exemplified in Joseph Conrad's *Heart of Darkness* (1899). However, plenty of novelists did tap into the more imaginative elements of Imperialism, with Africa proving to be a popular setting in boys' adventure stories such as those of H. Rider Haggard. The lush, exotic landscapes of Africa, the 'primitive' nature of its tribes and the element of the unknown treasures yet to be found within its unmapped interior provided irresistible material for endless stories of British men adventuring into the 'darkness' and getting up to all sorts of derring-do that proved their pluck and courage under adversity. It is interesting to consider that these sorts of novels were the diet of schoolboys who would go on to view the First World War as a similar sort of adventure.

The Boer War (technically the Second Boer War, as there was another brief war in the territory a decade earlier) took place between 1898 and 1902 and, like the Crimean War, was followed very closely in the press. Caused by, amongst other tensions, the backfiring of a manoeuvre by Cecil Rhodes to gain more power, it was a long, drawn-out, bloody conflict that went from being enthusiastically supported by the British public – the mass celebrations on Mafeking night in 1900 to celebrate the relief of the British troops sieged there were the largest ever seen in London – to a source of shame and embarrassment, especially after the introduction of concentration camps where Boer women and children were forcibly moved to enable the army to carry out its 'scorched earth' policy of destroying farms and lands to prevent Boers from resupplying their troops. The shocking conditions in these camps, leading to the deaths of thousands of women and children, were reported in the newspapers back in Britain thanks to a campaign by British woman Emily Hobhouse, and this caused a wide sense of outrage among the public, leading to an enquiry run by another woman, Millicent Fawcett. This use of women as respected campaigners and political advisers represents a real change in how women were involved in public affairs as the century came to a close. The war limped on and was eventually won, but it shook British confidence in its military and in its power as an Imperial force.

Peace was largely maintained with Europe during the nineteenth century, and Britain was one of the only monarchies not challenged during the revolutions across Europe in 1848. Queen Victoria became known as the 'grandmother of Europe' after her children and grandchildren married into the monarchies of Prussia, Russia, Germany, Greece, Romania, Denmark, Norway and Spain, and she had an active policy of marrying her descendants strategically as part of her and Prince Albert's vision of creating a united, liberal Europe. Evidently this did not prevent the First World War from breaking out, but while Victoria was on the throne at least, peace reigned between Britain and her immediate neighbours (with the brief exception of the Crimean War).

Foreign policy literature

Heart of Darkness (1899) by Joseph Conrad looks at the negative impact of the Scramble for Africa.

Rudyard Kipling's *Kim* (1901) is a classic novel depicting the life of a boy growing up in British-ruled India.

H. Rider Haggard's novels, such as *King Solomon's Mines* (1885), are boys' own adventure stories set in 'darkest Africa'.

Jane Austen's *Mansfield Park* (1814) gives an insight into British attitudes to the slave trade.

Religion

It is tempting to believe that everyone in Victorian Britain was deeply religious and went to their local **Church of England** (Anglican) church every Sunday, but this is a bit of a myth. There was actually a considerable decline in Anglican church attendance amongst the working classes that became progressively worse as the century drew to a close; this was for a number of reasons, but largely because the Church, in many ways, failed to adapt itself to a rapidly industrialising society. With cities swelling and the traditional rural heartlands of the country emptying, the Church of England was left behind as non-conformist (i.e. not Anglican) churches, such as Baptists, Methodists and the Salvation Army, set up meeting houses and relief work in the impoverished slum neighbourhoods of the cities, seeking to reform and convert the working classes.

Non-conformism and the development of interest in **Roman Catholicism** amongst an Oxford University-led group of prominent Church members were two of the major threats to the Church of England in the nineteenth century, alongside the obvious threat of a growing acceptance in society of **atheism**, which developed as a respectable intellectual position from the 1850s with the publication of Charles Darwin's *On the Origin of Species*. As such, far from being a bastion of society, as is often believed, the Church of England was very much in decline throughout the nineteenth century as people's beliefs evolved with their changing lifestyles, and they began to look elsewhere for religious organisations that reflected a modernising society.

Faithful adherence to the traditional family values, moral frameworks and gender roles propounded by the Church of England was largely a middle-class phenomenon, and it was the middle classes that remained the most numerous amongst churchgoers throughout the nineteenth century. It is important to consider that our perception of the Victorians as a deeply religious society comes from novels, magazines, art and other cultural ephemera, alongside the proliferation of churches built during the era, and all of these were created by the middle classes for the middle classes. As such, we must be careful not to generalise from these remnants of a small section of society. While undoubtedly Victorian Britain was more religiously minded than twenty-first-century Britain, strict adherence to religious beliefs was not as widespread across all spectrums of society as may be stereotypically believed.

Something to look out for in texts of the mid-century, or later texts that hark back to the mid-century, is snide references to Roman Catholicism. Cardinal Newman, an Anglican priest and academic at the University of Oxford, founded the **'Oxford Movement', otherwise known as 'Tractarianism'**, with other prominent members of the Church of England in the 1840s. At this time there was already a split in the Church between those who had 'High Church' and 'Low Church' leanings – High Church being Anglican clergy who wore vestments, used incense and followed liturgy and rituals that aligned their services more closely with the Catholic Church, and Low Church being those who were more evangelical in their approach and wished to simplify services, focusing on a more personal relationship with God rather than following prescribed rituals, and looking to the Bible as the sole source of authority. Members of the Oxford Movement argued that the Roman Catholic Church was the true Church, and wrote a number of publications, called tracts (hence the name Tractarianism) on the topic. This caused a great deal of fuss in the Church and also in the press, as at the time there was considerable fear that these 'Popish' beliefs could undermine the sanctity of the Church of England. There was a hefty anti-Catholic bias at the heart of British society and many articles and cartoons in the popular press were highly critical and disparaging of Newman and other members of the Movement. As it was, only a very small number of Anglican clergy did end up converting to Catholicism, and the movement had all but fizzled out by the 1850s. However, its resonances can be seen in many negative references to Roman Catholicism in novels and other texts throughout the century.

From the 1850s onwards will be found more prominent references to **religious doubt** and the struggle of aligning religious faith with scientific knowledge that disproved Biblical teachings. Society had been gradually adapting to a reality that not everyone was a member of the Church of England from the 1820s onwards, when the law was changed to allow people who were not members of the Church of England to take public office, though it should be noted that until 1854, only Church of England members were allowed to study at the University of Oxford. However, it was the publication of Charles Darwin's *On the Origin of Species* that really brought atheism to the fore as a legitimate standpoint, and it sent enormous tremors throughout intellectual society. Matthew Arnold's marvellous poem 'Dover Beach' (1851) is probably the finest example of a literary work about the loss of religious faith from the period, though Gerard Manley Hopkins' poems are also well worth exploring for his attempts to demonstrate how religion, science and technology can co-exist.

Religious literature

Anthony Trollope's *Barchester Towers* (1857) is about the conflict between High and Low Church factions in the Church of England when a new appointment is made to the Bishopric of the fictitious cathedral city of Barchester – far more interesting than it sounds!

Kilvert's Diary is a lovely slice of country and clergy life, and as a non-fiction text can offer a nice change for students when doing unseen practice. It is the real diary of the rather tragic Reverend Francis Kilvert and covers the 1870s.

Margaret Oliphant's *Chronicles of Carlingford* (1861–75) series is similar to Trollope's Barchester series in looking at the conflict between High and Low Church in a small community; it is well worth a read.

Science and technology

There are so many areas of specific scientific and technological advancement across the nineteenth century to be explored that it would be impossible to list them all here. As such, we are focusing on the major scientific and technological changes that had the biggest effect on day-to-day life for the average Victorian, and these are the **railway**, **the telegraph** and **Darwin**.

The passenger railway in Britain began in 1830, with the opening of the Liverpool and Manchester railway, which linked two of the busiest industrial cities of the age. The potential of the railway was realised immediately, and the 1840s in particular saw a 'railway boom', with railway companies forming and creating railway lines all over the country. Railways were considered to be safe and lucrative investments, with many families investing their money in railway bonds. There was a slowdown in production after a bust in the 1850s, but by the 1860s confidence was restored. Hardly any area of the country, from the Highlands to the home counties, was left untouched by the railway by the end of the century, and in 1863, the London Underground, the world's first underground railway, was opened, transforming the city and leading to the development of the first suburbs.

The railway changed the country in several ways. Firstly, it allowed for the rapid movement of people and goods from one end of the country to the other, making it possible for people to commute for work purposes and to grow domestic trade. This led to increased **tourism** due to the ease of travel, the development of **suburban communities**, more possibilities for nationwide rather than just local business and a **disconnect between individual and community** for the first time, as a person's home town or village was no longer the limit of their universe, which was very much the reality in the pre-railway era. Secondly, the railway **standardised time and increased speed and efficiency**. Before the railway, the time was set locally, and reliant on manual means that meant that some parts of the country differed by up to twenty minutes from the time in London. Obviously with a nationwide railway that was utterly reliant on time being standardised across the system for both safety and punctuality, this system could not continue, and so Greenwich Mean Time was introduced in 1847. Information on accurate timings could be sent to local stationmasters by telegraph, which ran alongside the railway lines, rapidly sending signalling information up and down the line. This standardisation of time arguably developed the concept of Britain becoming a modernised, efficient, unified nation with a collective identity rather than the parochial country it had been before the railway.

The **speed and motion** of the railway also came to be seen very much as emblematic of modernity – being able to move at speeds beyond those capable of any living being was an entirely novel concept, and removed the previous boundaries of space and time set by the horse-drawn vehicles available beforehand. Suddenly Britain was a much smaller, much more easily accessible place, opening up whole new ways of living. The railway, as much as it was seen as a benefit, was also viewed with fear for several reasons. The speed and power of the train terrified many; accidents were common and were reported with much relish in the newspapers, causing panic and fear in travellers. 'Railway spine' was reported as a genuine affliction, with some doctors convinced that the movement of the railway jarred the bones and internal organs, with unknown dangers to human health. The closed environment of the railway carriage was also a cause for concern; unlike today, original railway carriages had no facility to move between cars and no central aisle. The only entrance or exit to a carriage was when the train stopped at a station, and as such there was nothing to stop someone entering a carriage, attacking someone, and then leaving at the next station without being noticed. Several railway murders did occur in the latter half of the century, and many women complained of being assaulted when travelling alone; this element of danger, however, seemed to have very little impact on the numbers of railway travellers and was more fuel for the increasingly sensational plots of novels produced from the 1860s onwards. It is interesting to note that from the 1860s, the railway becomes a central feature of novel plots, and altered the possibilities of stories by allowing for the rapid movement of characters. This was a particularly useful device for sensation and detective novelists, who needed their characters to be able to move around quickly to chase suspects and gather evidence. Rather than spending days on a coach to reach their destination, characters could now legitimately make it as far as Yorkshire and back in a day. Railways also led to an increase in the amount of fiction being produced; yellow-backed novels – inexpensive paperbacks that were often sensation or detective novels – were sold cheaply at stands in railway stations to meet the demands of a travelling public. This cheap publication form democratised literature and enabled many more people to access novels, though they were certainly not all of the highest literary quality!

The **telegraph** was invented in the early part of the nineteenth century, and was initially used by railway companies as a way of communicating signalling information up and down the railway lines; as such, telegraph lines were mainly built alongside railway tracks. The telegraph transformed communication; by the 1860s there was a transatlantic cable connecting Britain and America, with eventually the whole globe becoming connected by a variety of cables laid both over and underground. News could now be transmitted instantly from all corners of the world, and the days of waiting weeks or months for news from abroad were over. The telegram fuelled the boom in the press industry, with newspapers now able to position foreign correspondents and compete to be the first to hear about scoops. In many ways, the telegram allowed the world to become a much smaller and more accessible place, and the communication channels it opened paved the way for the modern global age. The telegram did not supersede the post, of course; it was expensive and limited in the length of messages it could send, and the average Victorian would not have used the telegram system in its early days except to send messages in an emergency. While it was certainly not a day-to-day method of communication for individuals, the information that was shared over the telegram by governments and press organisations allowed for Victorians to become much more aware and involved in the affairs of other nations, and be kept up to date on British interests abroad. The telegram, like the railway, features as a plot device in later nineteenth-century fiction, with many sensation and detective novelists having their characters use the telegram to transmit information quickly in order to catch criminals or impart tragic news at opportune moments. The more global nature of the world and the ease with which information, culture and fashion could be shared between nations is also something to be keenly aware of as the century develops; fiction does reflect this in the behaviours and surroundings of the characters and the nature of plots. The very parochial, small town- and village-based novels of the early half of the century are increasingly superseded by fiction that becomes much more dynamic in its setting and in the movement of its characters.

Darwin's *On the Origin of Species* of 1859 is probably the defining publication of the Victorian era. However, it is important to note that Darwin's theory of evolution was not operating in a vacuum and he was certainly not the first to come up with the concept that human life had developed from more primitive forms. There is a stereotype that Darwin's ideas were an enormous surprise and had the effect of a lightning bolt on society, but this isn't strictly true. Certainly among the scientific and intellectual communities across the western world, debate had existed on the issue of the origins of human life for some time. The discovery of 'deep time' through the realisation that geological formations revealed the true age of the Earth as being far beyond anything claimed in the Bible had caused significant tremors in intellectual communities from the late eighteenth century, and prominent geologist Charles Lyell's *Principles of Geology* influenced Darwin when he read it during his voyage on the HMS Beagle. The discovery of prehistoric fossils seemed to confirm the findings of late eighteenth-century and early nineteenth-century European men of science, who had hypothesised some sort of system of evolution of life on Earth from primitive to sophisticated forms of existence, but were unable to find any categorical proof or causation.

Darwin, who came from an intellectual family, and whose grandfather Erasmus was prominent in scientific communities, had been surrounded by these theories from a young age. What made *On the Origin of Species* so special was his ability to articulate in a reasoned way how evolution had taken place over time, based on the evidence of the flora and fauna he witnessed during his journey on the HMS Beagle. Though Darwin's findings have now been largely recognised as flawed, he managed to put forward in accessible prose a workable and evidenced theory that for the first time positioned life as an entirely random, competitive and brutal process, ordered not by a divine hand, but merely by chance. This vision of a chaotic, cruel world with no benevolent father figure designing and creating life and able to intervene where necessary was a terrifying concept, and though Darwin's theories were widely mocked in the press, particularly his later claims in *The Descent of Man* (1871) that humans were descended from apes (human life was not mentioned at all in *On the Origin of Species*), many people, particularly intellectuals, saw Darwin's ideas as a reason to give up their childhood faith in God. Darwin is therefore incredibly culturally important to the nineteenth century as being the first prominent figure to put forward an alternative to a God-ordained world, and his legacy can be seen as the century developed with a much greater openness to discussing a godless world as a reality in the popular press and literature. Many novelists, particularly those describing the 'abyss' of the increasingly overcrowded cities with their foul slums, used Darwinian metaphors to describe these working-class slum communities in terms of their residents existing in a brutal fight for survival. Others positioned the working classes as the 'weakest' members of society, who deserved to be destroyed by their richer neighbours. Particularly towards the end of the century, social Darwinism, or what we would call eugenics, became a theme in novels that explored the issue of an increasing underclass of the desperate poor, swelling populations in cities and the necessity of managing this population growth. References to science, evolution and Darwinian ideas are prevalent throughout nineteenth-century fiction and it is possible to link many narratives to these concepts; even if a text doesn't explicitly mention Darwin, there may well still be clues to Darwinian ideas beneath the surface.

Scientific literature

Darwin's *On the Origin of Species* (there are many editions of this as Darwin made considerable edits over time – most modern reprints are of the 1859 edition, but do check if you want a specific date) is actually very readable and no scientific knowledge is needed to understand it. Sections from this could make interesting contextual reading for students.

Mary Elizabeth Braddon's *Lady Audley's Secret* (1862) is a wonderful sensation novel where the railway is essential to the plot; this really shows how modern inventions allowed for the transformation of plotting and pace in novels.

Charles Dickens' short story *The Signalman* (1866) shows nineteenth-century anxieties about the railway perfectly. Sections of his novel *Dombey and Son* (1846–8) also provide some of the very few examples in fiction of the chaos caused by railway construction in London; the destruction of Staggs's Gardens in Camden Town to build the London–Birmingham line provides a fascinating glimpse into how the railway transformed the urban landscape.

Industry and urbanisation

Probably the most defining feature of the nineteenth century was the transformation of Britain from a largely rural to a predominantly urban society. The development of the cotton industry in the north of England and the growth of London led to the mass migration of working-class labourers who were promised work in the cities. The reality of this work was often backbreaking, with shifts typically lasting around twelve hours, and involving hot, airless and dangerous conditions. The health of many workers broke down, and there were few support networks to fall back upon if you were unable to continue working. To make matters worse, finding somewhere decent to live for these factory workers was nigh-on impossible. The infrastructure of the cities was not ready for the massive and rapid population growth and housing was in short supply. Terrible slums developed, with families living on top of one another in cramped rooms in boarding houses with minimal sanitation. Disease and hunger were rife and the contrast between Britain's presentation of itself as a powerful Empire and the state of its cities became an increasing embarrassment.

As much as the cities hid terrible slums and provided an awful quality of life for many working-class people, they were also showcases for all that was progressive in Britain. London had become the first modern city to reach a population of 1 million and was the largest and most advanced city in the world. Its use of electric lighting and plethora of theatres, music halls, shops and restaurants made it a cultural centre for the rest of the world, and it boasted excellent connections to the rest of the country through its extensive railway system, as well as the world's first underground railway. Bazalgette's sewer system cleaned up the city considerably from the 1860s and the demolishing of much of the medieval heart of London allowed wide new streets to be built, enabling easier movement across the metropolis. The new, expensive suburban areas of Mayfair, Belgravia and Kensington provided spacious and beautiful homes for the middle and upper classes, and plenty of public parks and museums were created for everyone to enjoy. The city became very much a symbol of modernity, and Britain prided itself on having the most progressive of cities as its capital, which was the beating heart of an increasingly impressive Empire.

Industry and urbanisation literature

Henry Mayhew's *London Labour and the London Poor* (1840s), a series of reports from his interviews of the poor on London's streets, is a key publication from the period that gives a powerful (if perhaps slightly exaggerated) view of the lives of those who dwelled in London's slums.

Charles Booth's poverty maps of London, which are held by the London School of Economics and available to view online, colour coded the city to show the population distribution by wealth across the city. One of the most interesting findings from the maps is how close rich, middle-class and poor lived to one another, and it is fascinating to consider how little they knew of one another's lives despite this proximity.

The best novels that show industrial Britain are those of Elizabeth Gaskell, whose *North and South* (1855) and *Mary Barton* (1848) are classics of the genre. These show clearly the conflict between business owners and employees, and the consequences of the boom and bust economy of the nineteenth century that led to long periods of unemployment and strikes for factory workers.

Charles Kingsley's *The Water Babies* (1863) looks at the plight of child workers in Britain's industries. It is also a very Darwinian narrative that would fit nicely under the category of scientific literature.

George Gissing's *The Nether World* (1889) and Arthur Morrison's *A Child of the Jago* (1896) are bleakly realistic portraits of working-class life in the London slums.

Gender

The mid-Victorian period very much fetishised the nuclear family, with the role of the mother and wife being considered woman's highest calling, and the role of the husband and father, the protector and provider, the depiction of the ideal man. This was an embodiment of the prevalence of conservative middle-class, Christian values, and reflected a growing focus on the home as being a place of sanctuary and the moral heart of the nation. Queen Victoria and Prince Albert provided the perfect model of the Victorian family, with their ever-expanding nursery that would eventually contain nine children, and paintings of the Queen focused on her role as a mother and wife much more than they did on her role as sovereign.

Women were categorised as **'the angel in the house'**, as depicted in the incredibly popular Coventry Patmore poem (1854) of the same name: 'Man must be pleased; but him to please / Is woman's pleasure' are just two lines that cannot fail to raise a wry smile on the face of a twenty-first-century reader. The fact that this was met with enthusiasm by the middle classes says much about nineteenth-century society. The man was seen as leaving the comfort of the domestic interior to go and do battle in the commercial world; the wife remained at home in the safe surroundings provided for her by her husband, administering love, affection and order to her family. The woman's role was to comfort, the man's to protect; this suited the concept of the 'separate spheres' of male and female experience that had been in popular parlance since the early part of the century and was supported in the Church of England's teaching.

This focus on the family necessarily relegated women to the domestic realm, and men to the world of commerce. However, as always, it must be remembered that this was not the reality for the majority: this was very much a middle-class state of affairs, and as they dominated the production of culture, it is their view of gender in the nineteenth century that prevails. The majority of **working-class women** would have worked, either outside the home or from home, in order to feed their families, and lived incredibly hard lives. They would certainly not have recognised the stereotypical twenty-first-century depiction of the leisured, domesticated Victorian woman.

For **middle- and upper-class women**, though, the nineteenth century offered a restricted ability to interact with the world outside of the home. There were rare women who were pioneers and managed to study at university and forge successful careers, but these were very much the exception. It is certainly not true to say that all Victorian women were trapped in lives of quiet desperation, as for many the world of home and family kept them amply occupied and fulfilled, particularly those with large households to manage. However, the reality for many women was that they were brought up to believe their sole purpose in life was to become wives and mothers, and were only educated sufficiently for this purpose. Upon marrying and having children, many found themselves living lives of tedium that did not satisfy them, and many female novelists of the period explore this sensitively.

A key female figure of the century is that of the **'fallen woman'**; women who bore children outside of marriage, losing their virtue as a result, were emblems of both shame and pity in the Victorian imagination. At a time when marriage was the only respectable framework in which women could have a sex life (men's extramarital antics had a blind eye turned to them, of course), the concept of women having and enjoying sex outside of marriage was anathema, and women who transgressed in this way were shunned from good society. The reality for many women in this situation, however, was that they had been forced into prostitution out of desperation, unable to earn money in any other way, or had been seduced by a man who promised marriage and then abandoned them. Many people in intellectual society were sympathetic towards the plight of the fallen woman, and she features regularly as a pitiable figure in fiction, though in middle-class society there was in reality little pity for women who were seen to have sinned and brought shame upon their sex. Elizabeth Gaskell's *Ruth* (1853) is probably the finest example of fallen woman fiction; a sympathetic and deeply moving story, it had a powerful effect on contemporary readers. Interestingly, Charles Dickens set up a refuge for fallen women, called Urania Cottage, in 1847, with the aim of reforming such women and then sending them out to the colonies to start afresh. However, this compassion for fallen women didn't prevent him from taking an unmarried young woman as a mistress himself ten years later!

The notion of the **'surplus' woman** gained an enormous amount of press attention in the 1850s, after the 1851 census revealed that Britain had 1 million more women of marriageable age than men. Evidently this meant that there were huge swathes of women who would never marry, and as no provision was made for this in the upbringing of middle- and upper-class women, the question was raised of what these women were expected to do with their lives. There were a great number of debates in the newspapers between women such as prominent feminist Frances Power Cobbe, whose article 'What Shall We Do with Our Old Maids?' eloquently argued for better education and opportunities for women outside of the home, so that they could achieve their full potential both within and outside of marriage. Gradually as the century progressed, more and more women began to push their way into the workforce, with secretarial work and journalism becoming increasingly acceptable professions alongside the more traditional governess and teaching roles that were previously the only respectable work a woman could do to support herself. The **'New Woman'** was a feminist ideal of womanhood that became popular from the 1890s, depicting women who were working in formerly masculine professions, studying at universities and generally resisting marriage in favour of pursuing personal academic or career success. They were largely derided in the popular press, with them being mocked as a cover for society's genuine fear of women starting to move outside of the domestic sphere and so male control. However, in fiction they were depicted with sensitivity by supportive male novelists such as Henry James and H.G. Wells, and many female novelists also wrote of the struggles of the 'New Woman' to make her way in the world. Henrik Ibsen's plays depict the 'New Woman' in a more European setting, demonstrating how these more revolutionary gender ideas at the end of the century – known in academic parlance as the 'fin de siècle' – were certainly not unique to Britain and represented women across the western world starting to push against the restrictions of the mid-Victorian attitudes that prevented them from living independent lives.

See the section on politics for more information about women's roles in political reform in the nineteenth century.

Gender literature

Elizabeth Gaskell's *Ruth* (1853) is a wonderful example of fallen woman fiction. An extract from this novel could make a very interesting comparison with Christina Rossetti's poem 'Cousin Kate' about another, much more bitter, fallen woman confronting the woman she was replaced by.

H.G. Wells' *Ann Veronica* (1909) is an excellent example of New Woman fiction, as is Henry James' *Daisy Miller* (1878).

George Gissing's *The Odd Women* (1893) is a novel about 'surplus women' and a very interesting read to understand Victorian perceptions of women who didn't marry.

Edith Wharton's novel *The House of Mirth* (1905) looks at the Victorian marriage market and the consequences of not finding a partner – though this is set in America, the social context is not sufficiently different to make it irrelevant to students of British literature. A British equivalent is Rachel Ferguson's *Alas, Poor Lady*, which, though written in 1937, looks back to Ferguson's Victorian youth and is a realistic and heart-breaking look at the limited lives of middle-class women in Victorian England.

No study of women in Victorian England would be complete without the Brontë sisters, and all of their novels show in different ways the roles and limitations of women in the nineteenth century, from the governess and the middle-class husband hunter to the underemployed upper-class lady of leisure and the working-class servant.

The press

The development of the press, from a handful of formal daily newspapers at the beginning of the century to the proliferation of magazines, periodicals and newspapers to suit every taste and interest by the end of the century, had a huge effect on how people read, consumed and shared information. The average Victorian had access to thousands of cheap newspapers and magazines in circulation on a daily, weekly and monthly basis, many of them incredibly specific, covering every conceivable topic from cycling to botany, religion to archaeology, geology to home decoration. Workplaces and industries had their own magazines and newspapers, with the *Police News* proving especially popular with the general public, who loved reading the sensational descriptions of crimes, often accompanied with lurid, graphic illustrations. The majority of major Victorian novelists had their novels originally published in magazines, with Charles Dickens' own magazines, *Household Words* and *All the Year Round*, publishing his novels in instalments. Arthur Conan Doyle's Sherlock Holmes also first appeared in magazine form, in *The Strand*. This affected the way in which nineteenth-century novels were written; to entice the reader to buy the next edition of the magazine, cliff-hangers were employed at the end of every chapter, and strict word counts had to be adhered to in order for the formatting of the pages to fit within the columns allocated to the story. Some novelists were paid by the word or sentence, which certainly added to the floridity of their prose, and plots and characters were often amended as they went along to reflect reader reactions.

Looking at Victorian magazines is a wonderful way to enter the cultural milieu of the average middle-class Victorian. A mixture of articles on all sorts of topics, from science and industry, to book and theatre reviews, can be found in the same publication, often even on the same page. This shows how widely read and polymathic Victorians were; branches of knowledge were not separated in the same way they are now, and people were expected to take a wide interest in all manner of topics and disciplines.

The rise of the press during the nineteenth century had a direct impact on literature, particularly the 'new journalism' brought in by famous newspaper proprietor W.T. Stead, who pioneered investigative journalism in the 1880s and paved the way for the tabloid press. He was the first prominent journalist to see how the press could be used to manipulate public opinion, and his fake exposé of child trafficking in Britain, in a fascinating series of articles entitled 'The Maiden Tribute of Babylon', made him notorious. (Befitting his love of sensation, Stead died in the sinking of the Titanic.) The figure of the investigative journalist was the inspiration for the sensation and detective fiction that became so popular at the end of the century.

Victorian audiences therefore had access to fiction in many more formats than just the traditional one-, two- or three-volume novel, and this plethora of textual material should be considered when thinking about Victorian cultural influences, as well as when considering what texts should be used in the classroom. Fiction printed in novel form is not necessarily the most authentic version of Victorian literary culture available, and there are plenty of websites online, such as the British Library, where digitised copies of Victorian magazines and newspapers can be accessed if you would like to use these in the classroom (see Chapter 6 for more ideas on this).

The press literature

George Gissing's *New Grub Street* (1891) is a wonderful exposé of the realities of life as a Victorian journalist.

Ella Hepworth Dixon's *The Story of a Modern Woman* (1894), a New Woman novel, tells the story of a female journalist in London.

Class

The nineteenth century very much saw the invention and rise of the modern-day **middle class**. With increasing urbanisation and a modernising, commerce-based workforce, the opportunities for people to work their way up from humble beginnings to earning good salaries that could support a family and servants were considerable. With the cult of the family and the designation of the home as an almost sacred space of retreat and comfort, a protection from the stresses and strains of the outside world – the Englishman's home was, after all, his castle – the middle classes, with their very domestically focused lives, became the most predominant sector of society. Their values – conservative, Christian, patriotic – became stereotypical British values, and it is their voices that we associate with Victorian Britain. Our suburbs, filled with neat Victorian terraces and semi-detached houses, were their pleasure grounds, and the figure of the commuting father coming home to his loving wife and children was a Victorian invention that features prominently in fiction.

However, as much as many people were experiencing a degree of comfort and leisure that previous generations could never have imagined, there was an enormous underclass that was the victim of the rise of the middle classes. Working in factories and other manual, poorly paid jobs that robbed them of their health and often provided insecure employment, living cheek-by-jowl with other families in terrible conditions, and the victim of a middle-class 'self-help' mentality that blamed the poor for their own situation, the poor of Victorian Britain lived a miserable existence. **The 1834 Poor Law** was the nail in the coffin for many Victorian poor; the former system of parish relief for those who found themselves out of work and without means to pay rent or buy food was scrapped, and **workhouses** were created instead. The workhouse was founded on the principle that poor people were poor because they were lazy; there was no acceptance from those in power that there genuinely were not enough jobs to go around for those who wanted them. As such, the workhouse was created as very much a place of last resort, designed as a deterrent rather than an aid. In reality, many poor people said they would rather die than go into the workhouse, and many did; many also died within the workhouse's walls, overworked and underfed, and separated from their families. This barbaric and inhuman treatment was widely criticised by liberals, most notably by Charles Dickens in his infamous *Oliver Twist* (1839).

The **upper class and aristocracy** were the ruling power of Britain throughout the nineteenth century. Most prime ministers and politicians during the century were aristocrats, and their resistance to reform stemmed from a fear of losing their position as many a middle-class man was making his fortune in industry and outstripping the falling incomes of traditional landowning families. In the rigid class-based society of Victorian Britain, the right of the aristocracy to rule over the rest of the nation went largely unchallenged, and support for royalty and aristocracy was strong. As the century drew to a close, working- and middle-class voices did begin to make their way into parliament, but the real loosening of political control amongst the aristocracy did not begin to happen until after the First World War.

Class literature

Anything by Trollope and Dickens will give an insight into class boundaries in Victorian society.

George Eliot's *Daniel Deronda* (1876) looks at how class dictated life choices in nineteenth-century society.

Arthur Morrison's *A Child of the Jago* (1896) is an excellent portrayal of London working-class life.

Education

Education was an area in which an enormous revolution happened over the course of the nineteenth century. From only two universities, a handful of boarding schools for boys, limited elementary education and no provision for female education at the beginning of the century to a nationwide system of free elementary schools, several universities, and schools and universities for women by the turn of the century, there was opportunity for everyone to gain at least a basic level of education free of charge by 1900.

Education was provided in a joint venture by the state and the Church, and by 1880 it had become compulsory for all children to be at school between the ages of five and ten. Depending on where you were in the country and what was provided in your local area, you could be attending a state-run **Board school**, or a school run by the local church. Either way, the focus was on reading, writing and arithmetic, and increased state involvement in education led to a very rigid educational regime of the type mocked by Dickens in *Hard Times* (1854).

The **public school system** went through a system of reform from the 1840s, with Thomas Arnold, father of poet Matthew, leading Rugby School and introducing a concept of 'muscular Christianity' to the educating of boys, which focused on sportsmanship, physical strength and activity, and the modelling of good Christian values. These became the founding tenets of British public school education and this instilling of duty and honour in young men had its legacy in so many public school boys being killed during the First World War.

Education for women beyond elementary level became much more widespread throughout the nineteenth century, with several secondary schools being set up in the cities as well as universities for women, such as Bedford College and Royal Holloway College at the University of London, and Girton and Somerville colleges at Cambridge and Oxford. While only women of middle- and upper-class families could realistically look forward to such an education due to the expense involved, this did start to open up more professional opportunities for women beyond teaching. Even so, women were not allowed to take a degree from Oxford or Cambridge until the mid-twentieth century, and there was much lambasting in the press of these 'bluestocking' women who should have been at home with husband and children rather than attempting to educate themselves out of their rightful sphere.

The focus on **free elementary education** for all in the period meant that the standard of literacy became much improved and even the poorest of children would have been able to read and write basic English. This led to a much more literate public in terms of engagement with literature, with many penny publications, often of a trashy nature, being produced for the poor, who had just as ravenous a hunger for stories as their middle-class neighbours. What must be remembered by modern-day readers of Victorian fiction is the heavily Biblical nature of education in the Victorian period; it was through the Bible that most were taught their letters, and as such, Biblical references abound in nineteenth-century fiction. Everyone would have recognised Biblical stories, parables and figures, and references to these are embedded in the novels of the era. These allusions can often have quite significant meanings, and our twenty-first-century ignorance of the Bible means that we can lose out on subtle messages if we don't recognise these allusions in texts. We always encourage our students, particularly at sixth-form level, to read a basic children's Bible that tells the major stories so that they can familiarise themselves with the people and events Victorians would have known inside out if they are lacking in knowledge in this area.

Education literature

Charles Dickens' *Hard Times* (1854) is an entertaining satire of the Victorian education system.

Tom Brown's School Days (1857) by Thomas Hughes is a wonderful, entertaining account of life at Rugby School under the helm of Thomas Arnold.

Vera Brittain's *Testament of Youth* (1933) is a much later text, but her account of university life in 1918 has many parallels to what a Victorian woman would have experienced.

BIBLIOGRAPHY OF SOME USEFUL TEXTS FOR ENGLISH TEACHERS

Barker, Juliet, *The Brontës* (London: Weidenfeld and Nicolson, 1994)
Cannadine, David, *Victorious Century* (London: Allen Lane, 2017)
Desmond, Adrian and James Moore, *Darwin* (London: Penguin, 1992)
Flanders, Judith, *The Victorian House* (London: Harper Perennial, 2004)
Freeman, Michael, *Railways and the Victorian Imagination* (London and New Haven, CT: Yale University Press, 1999)

Harvey, Christopher and H.C.G. Matthew, *Nineteenth Century Britain: A Very Short Introduction* (Oxford: Oxford University Press, 2000)

MacKenzie, John M., *The Victorian Vision: Inventing New Britain* (London: V&A Publications, 2001)

Picard, Liza, *Victorian London: The Life of a City 1840–1870* (London: Weidenfeld and Nicolson, 2006)

Sweet, Matthew, *Inventing the Victorians* (London: Faber and Faber, 2002)

Tomalin, Claire, *Charles Dickens: A Life* (London: Viking, 2011)

Wilson, A.N., *The Victorians* (London: Hutchinson, 2002)

Wise, Sarah, *The Blackest Streets: The Life and Death of a Victorian Slum* (London: Vintage, 2009)

2 Teaching nineteenth-century fiction at KS4 and KS5

Should teaching a nineteenth-century novel be any different from teaching a contemporary one? We don't think so. Teaching nineteenth-century fiction is a wonderful opportunity to acquaint students with many of the most canonical authors in English literature. While there may be some initial trepidation about engaging students in what can often be long and densely written novels, the reality is that the Victorians knew how to spin a good yarn, and once the difficulties of language are dealt with, all the elements of a gripping story, with fantastic characters, a pacey plot and a vivid setting, are still contained within their novels, and are fully capable of engaging students just as much as contemporary fiction. Making these novels come alive may take a little more creative thinking than if you were teaching something more obviously appealing to today's teenagers, but it is most certainly not impossible, and we hope this chapter will provide you with plenty of ideas to help you ignite your own enthusiasm for nineteenth-century fiction, as well as your students'.

We will start by giving an overview of common features specific to nineteenth-century novels, with ideas on how you can use these devices to help students understand their significance to the stories they are reading. We then follow with advice on selecting a text and planning out a scheme of work, before some general ideas on how to bring nineteenth-century novels alive in the classroom. You may also find it useful to read Chapter 5, on teaching long novels, where there are a number of novel-teaching strategies that are still perfectly relevant to the teaching of average-length novels. If you are teaching a long novel, we would recommend going to Chapter 5 first, as the planning of teaching long novels is, in our opinion, significantly different to that of shorter ones.

Features of the nineteenth-century novel

Diaries and reportage

So many nineteenth-century novels contain an element of diaries or reportage, and an awareness of this narrative structure and the way it impacts on the reading experience is vital for students to be able to explain if they are to meet the requirements of AO2. Make them aware that as the novel emerged in the early 1700s with the works of Defoe, Fielding and Richardson, a convention of this new form was to pretend that it was a 'real' memoir or diary recounting a person's genuine experiences. Challenge them to think about why this was – what does it add to the reading experience if you're not sure if what you're reading is truth or fiction?

WHY NOT CONSIDER . . .?

■ Showing students some examples of nineteenth-century diaries – both real or fictional – George and Weedon Grossmith's very funny *Diary of a Nobody* (1892) is a great place to start!

■ Exploring the difference between diaries and memoirs, both fictional and factual. Look at the difference between, for instance, the diary portion of *The Tenant of Wildfell Hall* by Anne Brontë and *Jane Eyre* by Charlotte Brontë, the whole of which is a memoir, and consider how this subtle difference in narrative technique affects the reader's response.

■ For students who are slightly less familiar with the concepts of diaries, epistles and memoirs, asking them to research the difference between the forms and produce a definition, so they are able to refer back to these when needed. This will also be useful for the English Language exam papers.

Ask students to think about why the diary form is so inherent to the novel they are studying. What does it bring to the narrative and to the reader's understanding that a third-person narrative might not? Think about novels where a diary entry is used within the rest of the narrative. Why is this being done? More confident students will be able to discern that this gives the reader the advantage of a completely one-sided viewpoint, an immediacy to the action that would not otherwise be available. Considering the formality of nineteenth-century social conventions, this insight into a character's thoughts could not necessarily be provided through speech, so using a diary entry to express themselves neatly sidesteps this problem. Diary entries also give a sense of immediacy to the narration of events, with a minimal time gap between the events being narrated and the diary being written, very much creating a sense of the events unfolding right before the reader, and without the intrusion of an over-arching narrative point of view.

Epistolary format

As ever, context here is of fundamental importance, and it is key to stress to students just how important letters were in the lives of people during the nineteenth century. Ask them to consider when they last received a letter, versus how often they communicate with those around them by text message. For those in the nineteenth century, of course, letters were simply the only way to communicate with anyone they did not live near to. Allow students to explore the idea of this, and how letters were woven into the fabric of life for those living at the time, and so it should come as no surprise that they are such a huge feature of novels. To contextualise this further for students, show them examples of nineteenth-century letters – there are plenty of images online – so that they can see how mundane and gossipy many of them are. You can also talk about the frequency of the post in the nineteenth century, with the biggest cities having up to ten deliveries a day. This meant that you could send a letter to a friend at 8am asking if they fancied going out to lunch, and receive a reply by 11am. It is important that students understand that the postal system was certainly not a once-per-day institution as it is now, and that letters were not a solely formal way of communication as they may be viewed now, but were simply like today's text messages. Students should also be made aware that the plot device of the forgotten, mislaid or misdirected letter is very common in nineteenth-century fiction – as reliable as the postal service was, mistakes did happen, and many novelists, such as Hardy and Austen, have plots that rely on letters carrying important news going awry. Angel Clare's letter disappearing under Tess' doormat in *Tess of the D'Urbervilles* is a classic example that shifts the entire path of the main characters' lives. A misdirected letter that many people miss in *Pride and Prejudice* is Jane's to Lizzy while she is on holiday in Derbyshire, telling her about Lydia's elopement. The letter is not sent to the right address, and so arrives three days late; had it arrived on time, Lizzy and the Gardiners would never have gone to Pemberley, and as we know, without that, there would be no marriage between Lizzy and Mr Darcy!

Once students understand the importance of letters in nineteenth-century society, ask them to think about the impact they have on the reader. Why have they been chosen, especially where they are featured within a novel, which is generally not epistolary in format? They often come at moments of high drama, replicating for the reader the impact of the letter arriving to the person who has received it. How does this help to raise tension or to move the plot forward, and what was the intention of the author likely to have been? Ensure that you consider with your class who is writing the letter and who is receiving it. It is often not the protagonist writing the letter, particularly if the novel has a first-person narrator. In *Jane Eyre*, the letter that Jane reads revealing her uncle would have adopted her is short, but is a moment of huge drama, revealing the depths of Aunt Reed's hatred for her niece. It also shows the reader the huge impact that letters can have long after they've been sent, suggesting the great power of the letter in the world of the nineteenth century.

It isn't only first-person narratives that can feel the impact of the epistolary form, as they can be hugely important in those novels with an omniscient narrator. *Dr Jekyll and Mr Hyde*, another novel which makes significant use of the epistolary format, is also a useful example of why letters can be used to reveal information that otherwise would not be possible. In chapter 9, 'Dr Lanyon's Narrative', Stevenson uses a letter seemingly just to extract himself from a tricky narrative hole: without some first-person account, Utterson would be missing some vital evidence to solve the mystery of Mr Hyde, yet Dr Lanyon is so affected by what has happened, he dies and is unable to provide this evidence. By using a letter, there is a neat way around this. However, the use of the letter could arguably be more significant than a neat solution to a narrative conundrum.

The letter provides a shocking climax (if we all suspend our disbelief and try to approach the novel like a first-time reader who doesn't know that Hyde is Jekyll), as Lanyon observes the transformation. We get his immediate emotional reaction to what happens, but it is significant that he admits that during the episode he was 'affecting a coolness that I was far from truly possessing' (p. 108), making the reader appreciate that his recollections in letter form allow him to remain the rational man of science he prides himself on being. We are allowed to see his visceral reaction, but it remains coherent precisely because he has had time for reflection before writing the letter, and so his place as the antithesis of Jekyll's approach to science and discovery remains.

Also significant is that his account in the letter does not give Utterson a chance to question him. This is a hugely important point for students to grasp, and spending some discussion time on why this is so important would be valuable. Push them to examine his account of the transformation again. Actually how much detail does Lanyon provide about it? His letter states that

> as I looked there came, I thought, a change – he seemed to swell – his face became suddenly black and the features seemed to melt and alter – and the next moment, I had sprung to my feet and leaped back against the wall, my arm raised to shield me from that prodigy, my mind submerged in terror.
>
> (pp. 108–109)

There really isn't more than these few words about the face changing to explain exactly *what* has happened. We see Lanyon's horror and understand that he has been ruined by what he has seen, but as a reader, we are still in the dark about what the potion is, and exactly how it works. Naturally, if Utterson had been told by Lanyon in a conversation, it is hard to imagine him not pushing for more details! Yet the epistolary format makes this impossible, and Stevenson is able to restrict the narrative, allow Lanyon to remain the rational voice of science and give just as much detail as is needed before the end of the novel. The letter format is incredibly useful for this, as Lanyon declares that although he now knows all the secrets of Dr Jekyll, he 'cannot bring my mind to set on paper' (p. 109) what he has found out. This way, he continues to be like Utterson and Enfield, and remain quiet about unpalatable truths. Structurally, too, the letter allows Jekyll at the very end of the novel to tell his story himself, which would have been something of an anti-climax if Lanyon had related most of these details in conversation with Utterson at this point in the novel.

In Austen's *Pride and Prejudice*, letters are used in a similar way to ensure that information for the reader becomes accessible just at the right moment, without huge chunks of expositional dialogue or the omniscient narrator moving from narrating the current events to providing large swathes of background information. Again, the arrival of letters in the novel allows characters to move from ignorance to gaining insight, which you will be pointing out to your students as a huge motif in the novel. As well as this, the arrival of letters can mimic the sense of discovery receiving a letter could provide in real life to a reader.

Stylistically, the epistolary format is hugely important in *Pride and Prejudice*, and this is an element to explore with more confident students in particular. The arrival of letters with crucial information allows a novel that depends on the brevity of many characters' speech (the odious Mr Collins and scatty Lydia excepted) to keep the story's pace and sparkle. It relies on some characters remaining fairly taciturn to keep their characteristics consistent, but we as readers need to hear more about their past experiences. Mr Darcy is a man known for his lack of speech, and 'his manners gave a disgust' (p. 12) from his very first appearance in Meryton. By nature, he does not chatter or speak much at any time, particularly in the earlier stages of the novel, to anyone apart from his proposal to Lizzy at Hunsford, and even then the narrator takes over his speech and merely reports what was in it. He is stylistically not disposed to talk at length, and Austen maintains this formality of his manner by only allowing him to reveal his 'dealings' with Mr Wickham through his extensive letter to Lizzy in chapter 35. It would be impossible for his character to remain aloof and unapproachable if he were delivering long monologues to Lizzy about his former childhood companion running off with his little sister, and even harder to imagine that Lizzy would not have reacted favourably to Mr Darcy on hearing this intelligence. Receiving the letter gives Lizzy time to reflect, too, and this allows Austen to carefully dissect the behaviour of Wickham through the thoughts of Lizzy, something else that could not have been achieved if this information had not been given in epistolary form. By having the letter before her, Lizzy is able to 'examine the meaning of every sentence' (p. 174) and reflect on what this reveals about her own character, giving the reader an opportunity to agree with her own assessment that she has been 'wretchedly blind' (p. 177), and very much giving the sense that she has been prejudiced, in spite of priding herself on her discernment.

Furthermore, the misdirected letter Lizzy receives from Jane in chapter 46 detailing Lydia's flight with Wickham is lengthy and, at moments, highly charged with emotion, while retaining clarity about the events and a rational assessment of Jane's hopes and fears. However, there seem to be two stylistic reasons for reliance on the epistolary format here, which you can explore with your students. Firstly, although the action of the novel normally remains with Lizzy, there is no real reason that the omniscient narrator could not have expounded upon the scene when the news of Lydia's disappearance broke. However, relying on Jane's letter means that as a reader, we get the initial shock of the news, then immediately with Jane's follow-up letter, more insight into the situation. Moving the plot along this quickly would have been far more challenging if events were being directly narrated. And secondly, ask your students to again consider the character of Jane: she is the model of prudence and consideration. Although she and Lizzy have a delightfully close sibling relationship, it is hard to imagine Jane being this loquacious in person; by writing down her thoughts, she can be much more expressive than she would in conversation.

WHY NOT CONSIDER . . .?

▨ Setting students contextual research on how letters were conveyed and how this changed throughout the nineteenth century.

▨ Ensuring all students are fully aware of exactly how important letters were during the time their novel is set by providing some contextual information.

▨ Pushing students to think about *why* the author has made the decision to include letters in their narrative. Is it to further the plot, restrict the narrative access, ensure characterisation remains consistent or for some other reason entirely?

▨ Looking at contemporary letters for this period, so as to reinforce the idea that letters of the length seen in nineteenth-century novels is realistic, and that breaking significant news was common by letter. This is also excellent preparation for the GCSE English Language examination. The letters of famous writers and aristocrats from the period are freely available online or in published collections.

Difference in narrative styles and voices

With diaries, reportage and the frequent use of letters, narrative voice is often varied in the novels of the nineteenth century, and this can be a highly significant area to consider with your class. To begin with, ensure that all your students are happy with concepts such as first-person/third-person narrator, omniscient narrator and objective narrator. Next stress that narration isn't simply *who* tells the story, but also encompasses *how* that story is told. Ensure that they understand that when we talk about 'narrative point of view', we are referring to the perspective through which the story is told (Is it first person or third? Is the narrator omniscient or not?) and that narrative voice or type is examining how the story is being told (Are there diaries? Or letters? Or is the story simply being 'told' to us?). By equipping your students with the correct terms and the required concepts, examining narrative styles and voices becomes far easier for them.

One of the most complex examples of a varied narrative structure available as a text to study at Key Stages 4 and 5 is Mary Shelley's *Frankenstein*. In *Frankenstein*, the epistolary format is far more intricate than in *Pride and Prejudice* or *Dr Jekyll and Mr Hyde*, with the story being revealed through an embedded narrative that relies on the framing narrative of Walton writing to his sister, and then goes on to have Victor's story as the main narrative, with the narrative of the Monster then contained within this. This means that *Frankenstein* has a total of three narrators, all in non-chronological order; this gives you a great opportunity to talk to your students about why Mary Shelley has made these decisions.

Ask them to consider why the Monster is the narrative voice we encounter after the first two. What might be the effect if we as readers had heard from him first? By having him as the third narrative voice, are we being invited to trust him more than if we had simply heard the story from his point of view at the start? Would we have been too incredulous if the story had begun with him, without the narration of Frankenstein within the story of Walton? Challenge your students to consider if any of the narrators are to be trusted, or whether Shelley has created a scenario when the layers of the story told through these different voices are being used to shift and confuse the reader so that they never stop to examine what they are being told too closely. Initially, it seems rational to trust Walton, and the delayed introduction of 'so strange an accident' until letter four, when as readers we have been led to believe that Walton is calm, educated and reliable, seems to have been designed to support this. We naturally see the tale he is telling his sister as being reasonable, however unlikely it seems to have plucked a man on a sledge off a fragment of ice, because we feel we already know him. Yet how reliable is he really? He's a devoted brother to his sister in terms of being an excellent correspondent, but it could be argued he is a reckless adventurer, potentially endangering his own life and the lives of all those on board with him as he sails ever further north. Should we trust his view of events?

Ask students to consider the account of Frankenstein, which we see through the prism of Walton. Should we believe all he recounts? He is a man tortured by his past, and the horrific nature of what he has unleashed should suggest that his narrative voice is to be trusted, yet should it be? Does he have an ulterior motive to what he is telling us, and is his regret genuine? It can be illuminating to ask your students if they feel he is a narrator to be trusted, or whether they would feel Walton or the Monster are more likely to be reliable. In our experience, some students find they trust the narrator they're reading at that moment the most! But this can be a really interesting starting point too. Encourage students to look at the language used by their narrators, and consider what impact this is having. For example, for all that the Monster is described as being so horrific to look at, and is acknowledged as a murderer, his elegant syntax makes us as readers find him a sympathetic narrator that we can form a relationship with. In volume 2, chapter 5, the Monster declares that

> Of my creation and creator I was absolutely ignorant, but I knew that I possessed no money, no friends, no kind of property. I was, besides, endued with a figure hideously deformed and loathsome; I was not even of the same nature as man.
>
> (p. 119)

His use of triadic structure, and the complex sentences using semi-colons, gives his speech an air of educated veracity, which then helps to inveigle the reader to trust his declarations of wrong being done against him. Evidence like this, which also spans AO2, is a great way for students to connect with what the author is achieving with different narrative voices.

On the surface, the narration of Arthur Conan Doyle's *The Sign of Four* seems far less convoluted, sticking with the usual device of using Watson as the narrator. However, ask students to push their ideas a little further: at crucial moments is Watson actually the character providing the narration? Is the novel really as simple as that in terms of narrative voice? The novel opens with Watson watching Holmes, as he has done for many weeks past, using cocaine and longing for something to occupy him. Introduce your students to the term 'viewpoint character' (a character that is involved in the action, narrating the story, and may or may not present a biased point of view) so they have the correct way to refer to Watson's part in the narrative, but then ask them at the end of reading the novel if they are sure he is the only narrator. Students will soon reflect upon (or can be pushed to reflect upon!) crucial moments in the novel such as during chapter 4 when Thaddeus Sholto recounts the events surrounding the disappearance of Captain Morstan, and the finding of the treasure. Here, Watson is clearly not the narrator in any but the strictest of terms that it is his words we read: the narrative is being pushed forwards through dialogue dominated by others and simply reported by him. Again, when Sholto is murdered, it is Holmes and not Watson who gives the hypothesis of what has occurred in a lengthy speech during chapter 7, 'The Incident of the Barrel', speaking at great length and narrating what has occurred, like a story within the story. Even at the climax of the novel, with the confession of Jonathan Small, Watson seems to be silenced as a narrator, with dialogue confirming the earlier hypothesis of Sherlock Holmes. So, why might Arthur Conan Doyle have made this decision? Perceptive students will be able to make the link between who the hero, the main protagonist, is and why Watson, in spite of being a viewpoint character, is not seen as nearly as important or perceptive as Holmes. We need Watson as the narrator providing a limited view of what is happening, so that Holmes' brilliance and perception when he takes over the story through his speech are clear to everyone. Conan Doyle needs Watson to participate and narrate so that at the denouement, Holmes can startle everyone, including Watson.

WHY NOT CONSIDER . . .?

■ Equipping your students with the vocabulary they need when discussing narrators, particularly those in the third person. Are they a third-person subjective/third-person limited, where they convey their thoughts and feelings throughout their narration? Or perhaps a third-person objective, not allowing those emotions or opinions to intrude?

■ Making it clear to students what the third-person omniscient narrator is, and looking at extracts from the novel you are studying to consider, if there is one, why this works so well. Is there a reason Pip narrates *Great Expectations*, while Dickens uses an omniscient narrator in A *Christmas Carol*?

■ Prompting students to make clear links to AO2 when writing about narration and narrators. Remind them that they need to link what the style of narration reveals and how this is achieved through the craft of the writer, in order to make perceptive points in their essays.

The importance of context

When looking at the nineteenth-century novel, it is so important to stress to your students just how crucial a firm understanding of context is. Context should not simply be seen as something to add on after reading and studying a nineteenth-century novel, nor should contextual details simply be crowbarred into an essay as an afterthought. Fully understanding the context of a novel informs students' interpretations and provides an increased subtlety of analysis that produces much better-quality written responses. Most of your students will be familiar with series like *Harry Potter* or *The Hunger Games* trilogy, set outside the realistic world. Ask your students to consider the action in these series, or the decisions that characters make. Without understanding the magical world Harry

Potter is in, or the futuristic dystopia of Katniss Everdeen, these would seem nonsensical. Trying to understand *Great Expectations* or *Silas Marner* without any knowledge of the world these books are set in is just as confusing and is likely to produce similarly baffled responses even if the plot is enjoyed or, at the bare minimum, followed.

Preparation before you begin to teach is key. While we recommend setting contextual research as homework for students, particularly when you are teaching with very tight timescales, make sure that when you do your first read of the novel before teaching, you have built in time to batten down any antiquated vocabulary or social mores that you're unsure of. It is important that you are able to quickly provide this information to students when you are reading with the class, so to prevent needing to go to Google mid-lesson, do your homework in advance. The historical information given in Chapter 1 will help you with this.

Consider giving students a helping hand by providing resources they can keep and refer back to. If, when you are reading the novel in preparation for teaching, you keep a list of terms or references that you either had to check or know you would have had to check when you were fourteen or fifteen, this can be a great starting point for creating a table with terms and definitions already provided as an aid for students when reading in class. This can be especially helpful if you include the page and chapter reference where the term appears, and students can add to this as they read, adapting and editing their table to reflect their growing knowledge and understanding as they progress through the novel.

Categories in nineteenth-century fiction

Nineteenth-century fiction is a huge umbrella term for a wide variety of work. From the turn of the century's historical swashbucklers of Sir Walter Scott and the genteel romance of Jane Austen, to the densely populated sentimental realism of Dickens and the sensation of Wilkie Collins, the contents and styles of fiction changed enormously over the course of the century. The nineteenth century encompasses the giants of English literature such as Dickens, Austen and Eliot, and is seen as one of the most innovative and significant periods for the English-language novel. Of course, with such a wide variety of novels from the century, there is definite worth in defining how some works relate to each other, and how they are categorised within particular trends. Clearly you will want to concentrate on the type of novel your class is studying, but if you are looking to challenge more able students, it can be a great exercise to look at other categories and challenge them to detect, for instance, a Gothic element in a social-purpose novel.

■ **Social-purpose novels** – these were written to bring social issues such as poverty or the impact of industrialisation to the notice of the general public. Both Dickens and Elizabeth Gaskell are renowned for their social-purpose or 'condition-of-England' novels. Tending to focus on the lives of the working classes, these novels bring the plight of hidden or unsavoury issues to a wider audience, such as child labour, fallen women or working conditions in factories. Although *Great Expectations* does not fall directly into this category, if you are teaching this to your students, it might be worth exploring the social-purpose elements that reveal Dickens' desire to advocate for change. His difficult childhood due to his father's imprisonment for debt and his subsequent need to work in a factory had a huge impact on him, which reverberates through so many of his works. There is clearly poverty in Pip's family at the beginning of the novel, and then the lurking shadow of the prison hulks suggests that Dickens saw incarceration and the treatment of prisoners as a real social problem. Moreover, the gulf between wealth and poverty is shown to be vast in the novel, with Dickens suggesting that neither 'station' in life is the result of the character nor the actions of the individual, and that social mobility is not something available to many – unless it is downwards. Looking at *Great Expectations* within the context of this category can be a fantastic challenge for more confident students.

George Eliot's *Silas Marner*, of course, is a fantastic example of the genre, with its slum-setting opening, and the alienation that the poor can suffer, and this contextual detail will be central to your exploration of the novel with your students. Less confident students might be more comfortable with a simple mention of the genre, and how this relates to *Silas Marner*, but there is definitely scope for you to challenge more confident learners to explore the social impact of the novel, and why George Eliot's work here, and also in *Mill on the Floss* and to some extent *Middlemarch*, explores the social structure of the country and how this limits and sometimes subsumes her characters.

■ **The bildungsroman** – although not a nineteenth-century invention, the bildungsroman is hugely significant as a definition of many of the nineteenth-century novels set for exam boards at both Key Stages 4 and 5. Defined in English literature as a coming-of-age novel, concerned with education and spiritual development, this was a very popular narrative in Victorian fiction, particularly from the mid-century. Brontë's *Jane Eyre*, Shelley's *Frankenstein* and Dickens' *Great Expectations* are all very fine examples of the bildungsroman. Contextually, ask students to think about how children and childhood were viewed in the nineteenth century, particularly in the early years, and push them to consider the role of children during the Industrial Revolution where they were merely seen as mini-adults and perfectly capable of working twelve-hour days in back-breaking conditions from the age of five. By writing about childhood and emphasising the emotional impact that events in childhood can have, these novels reveal the growing awareness of the importance of childhood and protecting children from the harsh realities of the adult world that developed alongside the cult of the family and domestic life in the middle years of the century, leading to the Factory Act which banned child labour and the eventual establishment of free elementary education. The prevalence of the bildungsroman around the mid-century is definitely a reflection of this interest in the sanctity of childhood, but it can also be reflective of the notion of 'self-help', which was a middle-class obsession around this time. Samuel Smiles, a cult Victorian figure, wrote his first book, *Self-Help*, in 1859, which advocated personal responsibility in improving one's own lot in life. This was a publishing sensation and the idea of the self-made man pulling himself up by his own bootstraps feeds into the notion of the bildungsroman in showing how people could grow from terrible poverty in childhood to a successful adulthood through pluck, determination and access to education.

- **The Gothic novel** – with bleak, remote locations, highly charged romance and an emphasis on the supernatural, the Gothic novel was hugely popular during the nineteenth century, and morphed into the category of sensation fiction by the century's end. It is definitely worth exploring with your students why a fascination for the Gothic took hold at this time, considering ideas such as rapid scientific discovery and social change, and thinking about why and how the Gothic novel provides a safe environment for expressing these fears. A pervasive sense of unease, as well as seeing rational explanations for more and more phenomena, can be seen in many texts with Gothic elements set for examination boards at GCSE and A Level. This is a great chance to explore concepts such as the sublime, and consider why at this time of unprecedented upheaval, novels that explored the supernatural, but in a safe environment where anything frightening is often rationalised and all returns to normality at the end, were so popular.

It isn't hard to see the threat of irrational scientific behaviour and pushing the boundaries of discovery permeating both *Frankenstein* and *Dr Jekyll and Mr Hyde*. For those teaching *A Christmas Carol*, it can be helpful to think about why Dickens used such an emphasis on the supernatural to make a point about the behaviour of one man with social responsibilities and why he chose to set *Great Expectations* with such a Gothic feel in both the marshes and Satis House. His flair for theatricality combines with his modern concept of social justice to create something both compelling and – when read contemporaneously – utterly original.

- **The romantic novel** – stories imbued with love, particularly with lovers who were mismatched in terms of social status, were hugely popular during the nineteenth century. Traditionally, romance novels during this time focused on the relationship between two people, and ended with a fulfilling and optimistic ending. Both *Pride and Prejudice* and *Jane Eyre* are classic examples of the genre, and both do encompass a relationship between a female protagonist and a male who is her social superior. Importantly, when teaching these novels, you should be asking your class to start considering *why* novels of this type were so popular. Get students to think about the importance of social status in these novels, and why at a time of huge social change, reading about a lower-class heroine ending the story rich and in love might be so appealing.

- **Sensation and detective fiction** – novels to do with mystery and crime became enormously popular at the end of the nineteenth century. They were in some ways a modernisation of the Gothic novel, but also reflected a growing interest in true crime and detection with the increase in scientific methods of tracking down criminals and the reportage of crimes in the media. The creation of a new type of investigative journalism and the proliferation of news available to the public fed an insatiable diet for sensation, and detective fiction developed out of the sensation fiction of the 1860s to reflect this more modern approach to solving crimes. In an uncertain world, with the Empire starting to collapse, cities swelling to contain uncountable populations of people from all over the world who lived in close proximity without ever really knowing each other and rumblings of discontent amongst the lower classes, sensation and detective fiction offered escapism and a safe environment to express the fears latent in society while offering a neat and tidy conclusion that allowed the reader to feel comforted by seeing that justice and common sense always prevail. Students studying *The Sign of Four* or *Dr Jekyll and Mr Hyde* need to understand this context in order to appreciate contemporary reactions to the novel, and to be able to comprehend why they were so popular on their original publication.

Selecting a text

If you are lucky enough to have some autonomy in the choices of texts you teach, make sure you choose wisely. Just because you have always loved a book does not mean it will necessarily be the best fit for your class. In fact, often, the more you love a novel, the harder it can be to teach, because you're not always able to analyse it objectively! Conversely, even if you are not given a choice and the novel you have to teach is not one you have much affection or enthusiasm for, this does not mean you won't be able to teach it well. Sometimes a more dispassionate approach can produce a fantastic scheme of work, or being forced to look at a text you're unfamiliar with can spark a myriad of new ideas about how you approach your classes.

If you do have some element of choice, why not look outside of your department and see if there is any cross-over with other subjects, either at A Level, GCSE or from Key Stage 3, that will make contextual details easier to follow for your class? For example, if you know that your school has a Year 9 History unit on the Industrial Revolution, then *Silas Marner* might be an obvious choice if it is on the syllabus offered by your exam board. Consider the class you are teaching the novel to: what might suit their needs best? If you have a class that struggles to remember a lot of details about plot and character, consider a shorter novel with a story that is already part of our cultural consciousness, such as *Dr Jekyll and Mr Hyde* or *A Christmas Carol*. There is some argument about gender preferences, although there is no reason to believe that male students will love *Frankenstein* and loathe *Pride and Prejudice*. However, you do need to, where possible, work to the interests of your crowd; if you have a classroom of ardent feminists, for example, will *Jane Eyre* invoke more passionate debate than *The Sign of Four*?

There really isn't an 'easy' or 'difficult' choice from most exam boards, although most do have one novel that is often a little shorter if you are worried about covering the curriculum in the time available. However, this consideration should not be the only criterion you use, as we do not recommend teaching a novel you hate simply because it has a hundred fewer pages than any of the other options. Moreover, just because a novel is short, it doesn't mean that it's easy! Ultimately, how a class will react to the text and how they perform in their exam is down to whether you teach the novel effectively and convey your enthusiasm for a text. If you can find an enthusiasm for the novel, the chances are that you will be able to instil a passion for it and grip your class with the narrative's twists and turns. This engagement will, in turn, help your students to approach their study of it with enthusiasm.

Timescales

This is where to get organized! Look at your text pragmatically and think about how long it is, and how much you will be able to read in class during the lessons. (If you have chosen a particularly long novel, see Chapter 5 for specific advice and strategies on teaching these more unwieldy texts.) Calculate the number of lessons you have and how many pages you can realistically read aloud in that time. If you're teaching *Dr Jekyll and Mr Hyde* or *A Christmas Carol* then this shouldn't be an issue, as the entire novel can be read within a few lessons; however, if you're tackling something chunkier like *Jane Eyre*, *Pride and Prejudice* or *Great Expectations*, for example, then you'll need to be a little bit more strategic. Don't shy away from setting reading for homework, particularly during holidays or over weekends, but do think about what stage you need to be at with the novel before this, as asking a student who has no attachment to Pip or interest in his life to plough through the first five or six chapters of *Great Expectations* might be an alienating beginning. We have found when teaching any nineteenth-century novel that as students have become more engaged with the characters and gripped by the plot, independent reading works very well, particularly at moments of 'What happens next?' such as the elopement in *Pride and Prejudice* or Jane fleeing from Mr Rochester's house after the failed wedding in *Jane Eyre*. Students actively *want* to know what is going to happen next to characters they have built a strong relationship with, and so are happy to read to scratch that itch. However, this is a very different thing to expecting a fourteen-year-old to begin *Silas Marner*, understand the Calvinist society in which he lives and be captivated by the opening scene of weavers. Asking a student to start the novel on their own, or even to read the entire thing over the long summer break, can be a recipe for disaster if you haven't given them any preparatory material beforehand. Without doing so, you risk creating misunderstanding or total incomprehension about some of the highly important contextual details as well as the plot. And worse than this, the novel, by being so difficult to understand, becomes a real annoyance to read. So, if you want your students to read the novel first without you, make sure you give them the support they will need to do so. However, in most cases, unless your novel is incredibly long, reading at home can usually wait until you have started reading together, and students know and understand the characters, plot and context well enough to be able to read productively without your support.

See the term you're teaching the novel in as a process which will inevitably speed up the further into the book you get. The first few lessons reading aloud, while you pause to explain contextual details and establish character background, can seem to make very slow progress, but do remember that as familiarisation happens, you and your class will speed up. Don't panic if the first few chapters take a while or if your class don't immediately seem to connect with the text: it will happen. These novels are enduring classics for a reason, with interesting plots, universal themes and fascinating characters. Your attitude here is also key. By ensuring your students see reading the novel as a great experience you are sharing with them, you are far less likely to create the sense that this is a chore to be slogged through.

You will also need to build in plenty of time for analysis, essay preparation and writing, and timed examination techniques. Tempting though it may be to rush through the text and begin on this work, do remember that a strong textual knowledge to build on is fundamentally important. Factor in time for a thorough reading before you embark on this, and think about the proportion of time you need to spend on each. Differentiation is key here, with some classes able to spend far less time on ensuring a good grasp of the events of the novel, and so then being able to really be pushed when working on exam preparation to ensure their answers can reach the highest marks on the mark scheme. Conversely, you cannot expect a class of lower attainers to begin to analyse a text, through themes or ideas such as foreshadowing, unless they are fully secure in their knowledge of its plot. With the inclusion of the extract question on the GCSE Literature paper, it is especially important that those who do not find English particularly easy are not rattled by seeing an extract they don't remember ever having read or which they are unable to place in the chronology of the novel's events.

Begin the term with a realistic expectation of how long the novel will take to read, and then plan backwards from here, including the time you know it will take to perfect examination-style answers. Build in time for recaps, acting on feedback from practice essays and time to revise the application of assessment objectives. If this is the first text you are studying with your class, bear in mind that learning how to structure an essay or analyse an extract will take significantly longer than if you have already studied the poetry anthology, a modern text or play. Allow yourself some flexibility in your timings, rather than planning to fill every single lesson. To make the process enjoyable, you need to have the flexibility for a discussion about whether Frankenstein should have destroyed his second monster, or whether Charlotte Lucas was right to marry Mr Collins. Make space for engagement with the text, but ensure this happens within the realistic timeframe you have set.

If time is running short, keep a note of moments that particularly engaged your class and make sure you return to them later, or set students a homework task such as writing a comment piece of a newspaper or diary entry for the character to explore the incident if you didn't have enough time to discuss it fully in the lesson. Embedding creative writing or transactional tasks into your teaching can add nice variety to reading-dominated lessons. Getting students to immediately record their response to a particular moment in the novel in a letter, diary or newspaper report format keeps their English Language skills ticking over and ensures that they retain the ability to write for purpose and audience alongside developing their analytical writing skills. This type of writing activity can work very well as a quick fifteen-minute plenary to wrap up the day's reading and solidify students' understanding of that section of the text.

SUGGESTED TIMING PLAN

This approach can easily be adapted for any nineteenth-century novel or class taking into account their ability level, and gives some guidance on how to approach the timing of teaching the novel. The example here is for *Pride and Prejudice* and based on approximately four hours of teaching plus two of homework each week.

- Number of teaching weeks between the start of the summer term and the holiday: seventeen.

- Exam-style assessment preparation: one week. (NB: This could be shorter or longer depending on whether your class has prepared for exam-style questions for any other texts and so is familiar with the demands of your mark scheme.)

- Feedback and improvements: two lessons plus one homework.

- Number of weeks to explore themes, revise events, study character arcs: one week.

- **Number of weeks to read: 14.5.**

- **Number of chapters: sixty-one.** Therefore, the average number of chapters per week is between four and five.

Weeks 1–5

In the first week, you will want to ensure that you have read aloud the first six chapters, with time to discuss characters and begin a quotation page or table for each of the main protagonists, plus details such as the difference between an assembly and a private ball, what St James is, etc.

Suggested homework – research of contextual information about the social mores of the time and class, plus brief research on the life of Austen.

By the end of week 2, make sure you have read as a class up until the end of chapter 14, again with time for students to make summary notes and add to their quotation pages, and be secure in character relationships. With the arrival of Mr Collins the introduction of ideas such as the clergy having a 'living' will need to be explored.

Suggested homework – re-reading the first six chapters so that these remain fresh.

Week 3 will follow a similar pattern, with the class reading to the end of chapter 19, keeping both their summaries and quotation pages up to date. The Netherfield ball and proposal of Mr Collins to Lizzy are hugely important moments, and half your lesson time this week should be devoted to reading and analysis of these moments.

Suggested homework – again, re-reading of the previous week's reading will ensure that students become more and more familiar with the characters and plot.

For weeks 4 and 5, you would follow a similar pattern with the emphasis on reading aloud in class and ensuring contextual details are made clear, and using homework time to re-read the previous week's chapters, so you are confident that all these sections are fully understood by your students. Aim to be at the end of chapter 23 by the end of week 4, and to have finished chapter 27 by the end of week 5, reading aloud with your class.

Weeks 6–10

By week 6, you can begin to change the approach you are taking slightly. Reading can be set for homework, although we would recommend never asking students to read more than two or three chapters independently, and this needs to be done in a structured and planned way, rather than just announcing as the class leave, 'Oh and read the next chapter for homework!' Instead, make sure reading homework is structured and has clear aims. For example, 'Read chapter 29, and note the power-play between Elizabeth and Lady Catherine de Burgh. At which points do you feel each has the advantage, and how is this achieved?' will achieve familiarity with this moment in the plot, allow students to consider the relationship between the two characters and also ensure that language analysis is taking place. They will also all have something concrete to say about what they have read when they return to class, thanks to having a specific topic to think about, allowing class discussion to be much more fruitful and prevent the usual tumbleweed moment whenever you ask what everyone thought of the chapters they read at home!

With reading happening at home, class time can be used to start tying the novel together and practising analytical writing skills. This is the stage to introduce the assessment objectives, and begin to form discussions and brief written answers around these. Always remember to emphasise the need to weave in the contextual details within answers. Build time in your lessons for peer marking of these written answers, plus written feedback from you to help build towards a full exam-style answer at the end of the term. Don't forget to also allow some time for more creative activities, such as students producing their own dramatisations of scenes, or creative or transactional writing tasks in response to key moments. These provide much-needed variety to your lessons as well as allowing students to keep their English Language skills fresh.

By the end of week 10, you should be at around chapter 50, with students continuing to keep summaries and quotation records.

Weeks 10–15

The final five weeks can be used in a combination of reading aloud in class and for homework in short bursts. Hugely pivotal scenes such as chapter 56 are ideal for reading in class, with character analysis and written answers. With fewer chapters to read by this stage, you will have time in class to build towards a full practice exam-style essay with use of varied extracts as examples, done together as a class, then set for homework. Ensure you allow time for feedback to be given and then acted upon. Continue to emphasise the importance of context, so that it becomes second nature for this to be covered in written work.

Weeks 16 and 17

Week 16 is the time to prepare for a timed exam-style question. As a class, do a 'walk-through' of a timed essay, looking at an extract together as a class and then planning the rest of the essay looking at the entire novel, emphasising the need for a focus on context (AO3). At the end of this week, set the timed essay in class.

Homework can include learning some of the quotations which have been recorded through the novel's reading, and improving sections of previous essays to target areas of weakness.

Week 17 will be used to hand back the marked essays, with corrections and areas for improvements, including peer marking of the improvements. By the end of this week, your students will have a model answer for the novel. Why not try to spend your last lesson on a quiz about the novel, pushing your students to work in teams to produce a 'round' of questions that will hopefully challenge the rest of the class?

Engaging your students with nineteenth-century novels

When teaching a novel for an exam, it can be easy to fall into a pattern of only focusing on essay writing skills and memorisation of quotations, and not allowing time for the more creative activities that actually do the most to engage students with the text. With nineteenth-century fiction, students are more likely than with contemporary novels to feel a reluctance to read and/or be disengaged with the text, and so it is even more important to make the time to go beyond exam preparation activities and allow students to have some fun with their novel. The more they enjoy working with it, the more they will learn, and while it may initially appear to be a waste of time to give students an hour to put on their own reduced version of *Pride and Prejudice* or stage a re-enactment of Dr Lanyon's murder, what these activities do is cement those key moments in students' minds and allow them to use higher-order thinking skills to recreate and interpret the texts.

Don't think that just because you're teaching A Level, students won't enjoy these types of activities at their advanced age – you'd be surprised at how much they love getting dressed up, sometimes even more so than Year 7! These last years of school are often so stressful for students, and giving them some time to relax and have fun is vital for their wellbeing. Not everything you do has to relate directly back to the exam; we should be preparing students for a lifelong love of literature, after all, not just how to write the perfect essay.

Ideas to try in the classroom when teaching nineteenth-century literature

Using film/theatre

All students love a DVD lesson and there are a myriad of ways to use film to bring novels alive (see Chapter 5 for more on this). Helping students to envisage the world they are reading about is vital to enabling them to engage with the action, and film adaptations provide a perfect way to do this. You don't necessarily have to show the whole film in one go; showing clips of key scenes after reading them works well to cement them in students' minds, and thinking about the director's decisions and the actor's interpretations can foster plenty of interesting discussion. Getting students to produce their own short films or stage versions of novels, or writing and performing their own prequel/sequel, can be a fantastic way to get them thinking about the events and how and why characters behave the way they do. If time in the classroom is running short, set these tasks for homework and then set aside a Friday afternoon lesson to show them to the class.

Using original sources and images

Understanding the world the characters of your novel live in helps students to appreciate so much more of the text. You can bring this alive for them by showing them images of objects, interiors, clothing, etc., and copies of letters, newspaper articles, reviews and so on that give contextual life to the debates and issues within the novel. See Chapter 6 on teaching non-fiction for more advice on this. If possible, arranging a visit to an appropriate museum to allow students to see objects up close can be fantastic; author's house museums are brilliant for this, and Dickens, Austen and Brontë all have very atmospheric house museums that offer great educational programmes. If a visit isn't possible, see whether you can source some original objects to bring in. If you can find an example of a Victorian corset, bringing that in and allowing students to try it on can reveal so much about women's lives in the nineteenth century. Likewise, bringing in a top hat or bonnet and having students experience what it was like to walk around wearing clothing like this can tell them a lot about social status while also helping them to get into a nineteenth-century mindset.

Encouraging students to speak like nineteenth-century people

Create a glossary of commonly used words and phrases in the text you're studying, as well as in nineteenth-century fiction in general, and encourage students to start using these in their everyday speech. You could even have lessons where students have to express themselves only in nineteenth-century vocabulary and syntax. This is challenging but good fun, as everyone can laugh at each other, and they will be familiarising themselves with the language without even realising they are learning anything!

Encouraging links to contemporary society

Wherever possible, make connections to the modern day through the events and situations in your novel. Giving analogies helps students to understand why characters are responding to events in the way they do, and also prevents them from misunderstandings and attaching too much or too little significance to situations such as elopements, illegitimate pregnancies and so on.

Encouraging students to research their family history and make connections to real Victorians

A fun project for students can be researching their own family history back to the nineteenth century and making real connections with faces and stories from the time. With some help from parents and grandparents – and great-grandparents, if they are still alive – they should be able to reconstruct their family tree and find out about the lives of their ancestors, reducing the feeling of distance between now and then. If you have time, students could present their findings as a speaking and listening task, and you could encourage them to see if they can make any connections between the events of their novel and the lives of their Victorian family members. Some students who have done this in the past have found out some fascinating stories that are actually stranger than fiction!

Making it visual

Most nineteenth-century novels have quite convoluted plots and a wide cast of characters, which can make it hard for students to remember who is doing what and when. Having a visual timeline of key events on the wall can really help with this, as can a dynamic display of the setting of the book with character cut-outs and quotations to remind students of who lives where, who goes where and who says what. For more on this, go to Chapter 5.

Summarising the novel in five key words

The length and complexity of nineteenth-century novels can be daunting for students, and make it difficult for them to tie everything together. We recommend choosing up to five key words – these would ordinarily be themes – that summarise your novel, and then keep referring back to these throughout to keep reminding students what events and which characters are linked to which theme.

For example, if teaching *Jane Eyre*, your key words might be rejection, loneliness, independence, love and morality, and by linking everything back to these, you can keep students on track and understanding how everything relates to everything else. Obviously novels are much more complex than just five words, but by choosing these carefully, you can provide students, especially those who struggle, with a set of clear narrative threads to keep returning to.

Summary

We hope that this chapter has given you a solid background in categories of nineteenth-century fiction, and helped you to be able to locate the texts you teach within a wider historical timeframe. We also hope that the ideas we have suggested as ways of approaching the novels from the period have inspired and encouraged you, and made you feel enthusiastic about getting to grips with whatever exam text you have chosen. Nineteenth-century fiction is so rich and varied, and offers a myriad of wonderful opportunities to widen students' understanding of literary and social history as well as to engage them in moral debates that still have significance to their lives today. Rather than being the daunting challenge it is often viewed as by students and teachers alike, nineteenth-century fiction is not really very different to contemporary texts in its plots and themes. We hope that we've shown that a little contextual knowledge and creativity can go a long way towards bridging the gap between then and now and make students feel a real connection with the characters and events in whatever novel they study.

3 Teaching nineteenth-century poetry

A fantastic way into nineteenth-century literature for younger students can be through poetry. Major historical, cultural and literary ideas and traditions can be introduced through exploring a much more manageable amount of text, and as students are familiarised with poetical devices from the latter years of primary school, even if the language is initially unfamiliar, they will be able to gain confidence through spotting devices such as simile and metaphor. One of the major joys of teaching Key Stage 3 is the flexibility of the curriculum; without needing to cover particular texts to satisfy the requirements of examination boards, you can be free to pick and choose literature that you enjoy and that you think will most appeal to your particular student body. As such, building a nineteenth-century poetry scheme of work at Key Stage 3 can be a wonderful opportunity to gently introduce the period's literature through a variety of different thematic strands while also delving deeper into the skills of poetic analysis. If building an entire scheme of work around nineteenth-century poetry is not possible or desirable, there will be a nineteenth-century poem to fit any thematic poetry scheme of work you have already designed, such as poetry from other cultures, war poetry, women's poetry, nature poetry, etc.

When it comes to older year groups, the poetry you study with them is usually outside of your choice and may not be something you feel particularly passionate about. For many students the poetry element of a literature syllabus is the one they feel least engaged in and find the most difficult to write about. We wonder whether this is because poetry is genuinely more challenging or whether it's because we as teachers tend to spend more time on novels and plays and so students feel less comfortable around poetry due to lack of exposure over time. Poetry can often be taught as an 'add-on' or in a panicked rush after the longer texts have been studied in depth, and this can lead to students feeling underprepared, unenthused and unengaged. Poetry should not be seen as a chore, but many students have this negative attitude towards it; careful choice of poems at Key Stage 3 can help to combat this, but for many, by Key Stage 4, the damage has been done. This is not irreversible, however! While this chapter will obviously focus on how to approach nineteenth-century poetry in particular, we hope that some of the techniques and ideas we discuss will be of use to you in the general teaching of poetry and give you some fresh approaches to make it something you and your students feel excited about studying.

General notes on poetry teaching

Every teacher has their own methodology for approaching poetry, and there are an abundance of available acronyms, tables and tricks that are available online that purport to provide a failsafe method for students to record language and themes to ensure examination success. There is very much a place for this approach, especially when it comes to revision for exams, as most students feel reassured when they can reduce poems to a clearly defined formula that fits neatly into a table they can memorise. However, if students are only ever taught to read and understand poetry from this 'tick-box' approach, they will struggle to learn to love and appreciate the words as a whole, and poetry will continue to be a dull and often impenetrable puzzle to be solved and categorised rather than a wonderful insight into the writer's soul. Therefore, while it might seem sensible to approach poems stanza by stanza, or in sections, looking at all the elements that an examination board would expect to be covered before moving on, this is not the approach that we suggest. The beauty of poems is that they are (mostly) short enough to be looked at as a whole, and we find that studying them by idea or concept enhances student understanding, and often gives a better 'way in' to the text than treating it as a series of fragments, or as a list of techniques or devices to be decoded.

Teaching nineteenth-century poetry, then, shouldn't be too different from teaching modern poetry. Yes, the use of language may be more antiquated, but the emotions it expresses and the ideas it explores shouldn't be too far away from students' own experiences, and drawing them into making comparisons between the lives and attitudes of the personas of the poems you are studying and their own will help to make these seemingly distant texts come alive for them. Contextual factors will need to be taken into account, too, of course, and careful teaching of historical and cultural context alongside the poem should allow students to consider how and why contemporary debates may have influenced the poet and add richness to their interpretation. Christina Rossetti's 'Goblin Market' (1862) may seem like a rather odd piece of childish fantasy without an appreciation of Victorian debates around female sexuality and the fallen woman, and William Wordsworth's 'Composed Upon Westminster Bridge' (1802) may just seem a simple love letter to the beauty of London without a consideration of how Wordsworth was part of the

Romantic movement. The more you can enable students to understand the world in which the poem was written, the more meaning they will be able to draw from it, and our examples of poetry analysis and accompanying lesson activities for all Key Stages in this chapter will demonstrate to you just how our methods really can bring nineteenth-century poetry alive in the classroom.

Nineteenth-century poetic traditions

Understanding general trends in poetry across the nineteenth century can help you to build a curriculum that allows students to gain a solid grasp of the progression of ideas and trends over the course of the period. Structuring a scheme of work where poems are studied by movement, idea or form rather than by theme can enable students to think more holistically and make more successful links to context than a thematic approach. Thematic teaching obviously has its place and there can be much of interest to discuss in the different attitudes towards, for example, love, or nature, over the course of one hundred years. However, to really give students a meaningful, transferable understanding of nineteenth-century literature and culture, thematic teaching also needs to allow space for discussion of how these themes fit into wider literary movements and traditions.

The most well-known poetry of the early nineteenth century belongs to the **Romantic** movement, with the most famous Romantics being Wordsworth, Keats, Shelley, Taylor Coleridge and Blake. The Romantic tradition came out of late eighteenth-century attitudes towards personal liberty and the renunciation of the order and rationality imposed on society during the Enlightenment. Romantics believed passionately in the importance of the rights of the individual and wanted to use their poetry to express authentic emotional experiences and bring about social change by highlighting the suffering of the poor and marginalised. The concept of the sublime – the feelings experienced when looking at something awe-inspiring, particularly in nature – is also a key feature in Romantic poetry, as is the notion of the child and looking at the world from an innocent perspective. Nature is at the heart of Romantic poetry, appreciating its beauty and magnificence and acknowledging its power over mankind; students should be encouraged to think here about how the Industrial Revolution was making many people uncomfortable right from the earliest years of the nineteenth century in its destruction of the natural environment and rural life. Romantic poetry was written in a very different world to that experienced by those writing in the latter half of the nineteenth century, and so sounds and feels very dissimilar to the work of someone like Tennyson or Rossetti. Helping students to understand these different perspectives should make for some very interesting comparisons if you are able to teach a wide range of poetry from across the hundred years of the century.

The **ballad** held a fascination for Victorians, and many poets chose to write in ballad form. A ballad is a narrative poem that always tells a story. They are often in the form of quatrains with an ABCB rhyme structure, but this is by no means a strict rule. Ballads were traditionally written as songs as part of an oral culture, but with the rise of print, they were increasingly designed to be read and frequently composed on topical issues. Ballads do not enter into personal emotions, and the **dramatic monologue**, a very Victorian invention (and one Robert Browning was a particular master of), is an interpretation of the ballad form in its storytelling technique, but an adaption of it in allowing the persona to speak of their experiences. The Victorians read poetry for pleasure much more than we do today and the ballad, in being action-focused and of a good length to enable being read aloud over the course of an evening, reflects this taste for poetry reading. The Victorians were also very interested in preserving cultural traditions and reviving forgotten histories and the ballad form fed into this predilection for the past.

Harking back to the past can also be seen in the Victorian interest in medieval **Arthurian legends** triggered by the republishing of the *Morte d'Arthur*, telling the stories of the Arthurian knights, in the early nineteenth century. The Pre-Raphaelites, particularly Edward Burne-Jones, embodied this in their paintings of Arthurian figures, and Alfred, Lord Tennyson became especially known for his Arthurian poems, with 'The Lady of Shalott' (1833/1842 – there are two versions) probably the most famous example. References to Arthurian legends abound in nineteenth-century literature and it is worth encouraging students to consider the reasons why Victorians may have been interested in the past and particularly in the medieval past. What might have attracted them to this time in history? Did they perhaps view it to be a simpler time, devoid of the cares and existential crises of their own century? Did they see themselves reflected in the fact that it was a time of great innovation and change as society emerged from the 'Dark Ages' towards the Enlightenment? Did they admire the religious certainty of medieval society amidst the uncertainty of their own times? There are many ways of thinking about the Victorian psyche here and helping students to appreciate that many nineteenth-century poems do hark back to a distant past can enable some interesting discussions as well as more thoughtful analysis.

The latter half of the nineteenth century sees many poets start to tackle the topics of **faith and doubt** in response to the debates generated by scientific advances such as Darwin's publication of *On the Origin of Species* in 1859. The emotional possibilities of poetry allowed many poets to explore their feelings about their religious doubts and loss of faith in a way that spoke to many people who were feeling the same sense of religious unease. Other poets, conversely, used poetry as a way to affirm their faith in God, with nature resurfacing as a prominent theme as poets looked to the wonders of the natural world as proof of God's existence. Matthew Arnold's 'Dover Beach' (1851) is a wonderful, heart-rending poem exploring the poet's loss of faith, Gerard Manley Hopkins' poems look at how nature confirms God's existence and Christina Rossetti's poems explore her Christian faith. Students should be encouraged to think about how religion and religious doubt played a key role in intellectual life in the nineteenth century and be alert to spotting references to this in poetry, particularly in work produced after 1850.

In the latter half of the nineteenth century, **patriotic poetry** that celebrated British achievements on the world stage in the context of the growing Empire began to emerge. The popularity of Tennyson's 'The Charge of the Light Brigade' (1854), about a battle that took place during the Crimean War, is evidence of how much the public enjoyed these rousing, militaristic and even jingoistic depictions of British pluck and bravery.

Poetry by and about **women** is something worth thinking about when ensuring that any curriculum built around nineteenth-century poetry is suitably diverse. Most of the famous Victorian poets are men, but there are plenty of female voices that are worthy of study, as well as poems by men that offer an intriguing glimpse of male attitudes towards women. Christina Rossetti is a wonderful poet whose poetry defies expectations of suitable fictional topics for women and explores a variety of different themes, from her religious faith to the fate of fallen women. The Brontë sisters' poetry is rarely studied in comparison to the popularity of their fiction, but much of their poetry is just as challenging and unconventional as their novels, and can be a wonderful companion to the study of these, as well as standing alone. Elizabeth Barrett Browning and Charlotte Mew are frequently found on exam syllabi, and their treatment of women's lives and emotional experiences can provide much discussion for students. Looking at how women are presented in poetry written by men also offers some intriguing insights into Victorian gender roles and stereotypes, and more traditional poets can be contrasted with the likes of Robert Browning, whose subversive dramatic monologues paint men's treatment of women in a very unattractive light.

Approaches to teaching poetry at Key Stage 3

Before starting to read a poem with students, we think it is worth emphasising to them that poetry isn't about having to solve a really difficult puzzle or find a list of devices. It is about them finding an emotional connection to the poet's words and coming to their own interpretation of what they mean to them. They are supposed to enjoy the sound of the words and the rhythm and rhymes they create, and the experience of seeing images conjured up in their minds as the words create pictures and form associations in their brains, and to take pleasure in the process of interpreting meaning from what can often be ambiguous combinations of words. Debating potential interpretations, drawing pictures or modelling things out of playdoh of what they see when they listen to the poem, creating freeze frames or drama pieces to portray the events of the poem, producing their own version of the poem or writing a short story in response to the poem can all help students to feel more engaged in the poetry you study and feel less intimidated by it. All of the creative and imaginative activities you use with novels and plays can also be done with poetry; poems are stories, too, and yet too often they are taught in a dry and formulaic way that focuses too heavily on spotting features and explaining effects. Students are much more likely to understand a poem and be able to talk about the effects of its language if they are allowed to immerse themselves in the story it tells and have fun interpreting it in a variety of different ways. The end goal of teaching a poem should not be a nicely highlighted and annotated sheet of paper and a neat paragraph explaining its meaning. It should be having students who are engaged and enthused, able to think about a variety of ways in which the poem might be received and able to articulate what that poem means to them. Taking time to allow students to have fun with poetry reaps so many rewards later on, so don't be afraid to take it slowly and place the emphasis on interpretation rather than analysis until you feel students are really ready for this. Nothing kills poetry more than forcing students to shoehorn their responses into PEE paragraphs.

We are going to begin with some of Blake's poetry for Key Stage 3, with the caveat that actually they are slightly pre-nineteenth century, having been published during the 1790s. His poetry is often a fantastic place to start for younger students who may have recited 'The Tiger' at primary school, and who may well already be familiar with his work, while being ready to be stretched in terms of context.

'A Poison Tree' by William Blake (1794)

WHY NOT CONSIDER . . .?

- What is the poem actually about? Does Blake have a message or is he purposely trying to be ambiguous?

- How can you bring in the terminology that you would like your students to be familiar with?

- Is the form of the poem important in interpreting meanings, and if so, how do they relate to each other?

One of the real beauties of teaching Blake is that he is such a visual poet, and we would urge you to at the very least display the image that accompanies the poem when you teach it, and if you have time, explore more of his art to ask students to consider what sort of poet he might have been. You may need to guide some students towards Blake's use of religious imagery in these visuals, but it can be an incredibly useful starting point for students to think about the fundamental importance of Christianity to many writers of the period.

The poem itself is, on the surface, very simple and extremely accessible. When reading the first stanza aloud to a class, most students will immediately understand what the poem is about, although it might be helpful to clarify vocabulary such as 'wrath' and 'foe'. By asking students what they think the poem is about, most will be able to explain that the poet is suggesting that by articulating and expressing our anger, it will lessen, but by keeping anger pent up, the emotion will continue to fester away and grow. The poet spoke to his friend about what was bothering him, and his 'wrath did end', while he kept his anger with his enemy contained and as a consequence his 'wrath did grow'. Take a moment at this point to discuss with your students whether they agree with this – that the expression of emotion, particularly anger, is important. Really getting them to engage with the ideas in the poem through exploration of their own experiences helps to connect fully with a text written over two hundred years before they were born. Think about the use of questioning here. You'll be using this poem as a way to explore context later, so probing them to think about their own reactions to expression or repression of emotion is incredibly useful, but you need to move them beyond 'how' questions ('How does this relate to your experiences?', 'How do you deal with anger when you feel it?') to the importance of *why*. As a highly religious poet, the contextual detail of Blake's faith influencing the narrative of this poem is hugely important, and by covering their personal reactions like this now, you are preparing the ground for exploring this element later.

Before reading the rest of the poem, it is a good time to remind your class about what a metaphor is, and how this concept can be stretched into an extended metaphor. As the remainder of the poem is essentially an extended metaphor, it is essential that you equip them with the vocabulary to express what they recognise as the poet's technique. While solidifying terminology, the introduction of antithesis could also be considered for more confident students. After reading it, you could initiate a discussion about whether or not the poet intends us to approach the narrative as though it is 'fact'. Is it realistic? Hopefully the drama of the poem's end should allow students to see that Blake's dramatic ending is not supposed to be taken literally, and being able to articulate that the poem is an extended metaphor will help them to highlight that this is an artistic construction rather than a recounting of real events.

Once you have read through the poem and made sure everyone understands the thread of the narrative, ask your students to think about what themes are evident in the poem. Nearly all will identify anger and deception without too many problems, and most students will be able to identify quotations that demonstrate these ideas. Now is the time to introduce the context of Blake's writing. Unless you're a very keen historian, it is probably best to prepare this in advance! It can be helpful to show students a timeline of events which happened during Blake's lifetime, particularly events such as the American War of Independence and the

French Revolution, and ask them to think about how this might have impacted on a man like Blake, born into a family of fairly moderate means, and how it might have caused him and those like him to view the authority of the state and the Church. Did it encourage him to see himself as having the potential to change the lives around him? Blake was a deeply and fervently religious man, and we need to consider the upheaval of the times he had lived through as well as the importance of his religious faith when we teach his poetry. (As an aside, it is worth checking that all students have a solid understanding of the basic concepts of Christianity, as this is certainly not a given in some school communities.)

Ask students where we can identify ideas about religion in 'A Poison Tree'. Link it back to their initial reactions to Blake's ideas about expressing anger, reinforcing the point that we cannot read the poem without the context of knowing about Blake. Explore the poem in terms of religious imagery. Those with a good awareness of the story of Adam and Eve will instinctively seize upon the imagery of the apple and consider the significance of it. As before, when using questioning, consider the importance of pushing beyond 'how' questioning to the all-important 'why' questions. Asking them 'why is it so important that Blake suggests forgiveness has such an impact and what is the link to the social and religious context of the time?' is far more useful than 'How is the poet's religious faith shown?'.

You will also want to ensure that students are thinking about the fact that the poem's form can tell us a lot about Blake's message. Written in quatrains, with four stanzas and a very clear scheme of rhyming couplets, 'A Poison Tree' has a very straightforward structure – what might students have to say about this? Is the simplicity of the poem's form deliberate? Why? The rhythm is so simple and the majority of the vocabulary is too, but the poem's meaning is complex. With the repeated use of the preposition 'and' there is a child-like, singsong feel to the poem, and perceptive students will be quick to recognise that over half the lines in the poem begin with 'and'. Challenge them to consider why this is and its effect. Does it create momentum? Is there a menacing quality to the build-up of the poem in the way the narrator's anger grows?

It is also worth considering the first stanza in terms of this kind of analysis, looking at it again in greater detail. What patterns can they discern? The obvious point, that each line begins with the pronoun 'I', will be spotted by most students and this is a great opportunity for you to challenge them about why they think this is. The idea that this is a highly personalised story and that the role of the narrator in it needs to be acknowledged is one way to view this, but do allow your students to come up with their own interpretations. There is also the need to consider the symmetry of this first stanza, as the poet writes:

I was angry with my friend;
I told my wrath, my wrath did end.
I was angry with my foe:
I told it not, my wrath did grow.

How does this set out the tone for the rest of the poem? Ask them to explore any other ideas that mirror throughout the poem.

To conclude your exploration of the poem with your class, consider setting up a judge and jury to 'try' the narrator for murder. This can be a great way to stretch more confident students as they incorporate the concept of metaphor ('He didn't really die! It's just imagery!') and social and historical context into their defence, while those who are less secure in their interpretation have the chance as the jury to reconsider the poem, hearing ideas again and having another opportunity to think about the ideas it evokes.

Other ways you could explore the poem more creatively are through drama; what about encouraging students to work in groups to write a short play script with a moral message about the importance of forgiveness, and then perform it to the class? If your students enjoy art, why not ask them to draw, paint or use collage to create their own 'poison trees'? What might these look like? If you'd like your students to practise writing their own poetry, maybe they could think about a time when they were angry, and write a poem about it, or they could write a poem with a moral message, one using a Biblical metaphor, or a poem about anything they like as long as it connects with the title 'A Poison Tree'. You could add challenge here by asking students to echo the structure and form of Blake's poem in their own work.

'The Pied Piper of Hamelin' by Robert Browning (1842)

There can seem something a little daunting about tackling such a long poem with Key Stage 3 classes, but in fact Browning's ballad is brilliantly accessible while still having plenty of fantastic language features to get stuck into. It may have a whopping fifteen stanzas, but it is a great place to start looking at Browning, who is perennially popular as a GCSE text; covering some historical context and background on the poet at Key Stage 3 will therefore be time well spent.

WHY NOT CONSIDER . . .?

■ Using 'The Pied Piper' as an opportunity to expand into looking at other popular ballads, such as 'The Lady of Shalott' by Tennyson or 'Flannan Isle' by Wilfred Wilson Gibson.

■ Incorporating the context of oral traditions in poetry and the fact that the Victorians enjoyed using historical forms and stories in their writing.

■ Using the ballad as a way for students to consider the impact of rhyme and rhythm in poetry.

As the poem has a story that most students will at least have a passing familiarity with, it can be worth asking them before reading it exactly what they think they already know. Inevitably, some will be more familiar than others with the tale, but working together they might be able to tease out more information from each other, and it can be very worthwhile to ask them to consider exactly from where they have gained their knowledge. The context of the poem in coming from an oral tradition is important to understanding its structure, and so allowing students to explore the idea that there is a shared oral culture for poetic works even today can be incredibly powerful.

As the poem is so driven by narrative, it makes sense to read the entire poem out loud first, and move to interpretation and analysis afterwards. With the lively language and the characterisation of the people of Hamelin, it really is meant to be enjoyed as a shared listening experience. Once this has been done, it is time to have your students consider the separate elements that make up the poem.

Rhythm and rhyme are vital. Ask your students to look through the poem and decide what sort of rhyme scheme Browning uses and why. Does the regular rhyme scheme seem to push the action on to the inevitable climax? And what about the rhythm? Does the sense of regularity make it mimic the relentless noise of the rats' feet in the village or suggest the music the Pied Piper plays? It can be really helpful to encourage students to see these elements of the poem's form as not just the outside trappings of the poem, but also contributing to the meaning and narrative within it.

WHY NOT CONSIDER . . .?

- Rhyme scheme is so important in the poem. As well as aiding the oral tradition of narrative poems, ask your students to consider where it has other purposes.

- Internal rhyme is used in places, such as 'Small feet were pattering, wooden shoes clattering'; what is the impact of this, and why might Browning have made these choices?

- How is characterisation achieved in the poem? Challenge your students to pick out quotations that help form a view of the people of Hamelin and the Pied Piper.

When the form of the poem has been explored, we find it is really interesting to ask students what sort of people they think the Mayor and Corporation and the townspeople are. They are likely to have formed very strong opinions about this, and can give detailed descriptions of what they are like. Push them further to make comparisons with famous characters from books, television and films. If they were a famous person, who would they be? How would they behave in certain situations? What do we think they might look like? Now direct them back to the text. Using the poem itself, ask them to find quotations to support their view of the characters. They might be surprised to find that even in a poem of such length, there's actually not much detail about the appearance of the characters, apart from the Pied Piper himself. Challenge them to think about how Browning cleverly creates such a strong impression. Looking at the Mayor, we know the people of Hamelin call him a 'noddy' (a nobody) but we also gain the impression from how he speaks and behaves as he addresses the Pied Piper, and his reaction to the disappearance of the rats. What vocabulary can they pick out that supports their view of the Mayor? And why do they think Browning has chosen such a morally corrupt character as the leader of Hamelin? What might he be suggesting about authority?

The use of the word 'Corporation' to describe Hamelin's ruling system is incredibly interesting, and it is worth asking students to consider the implications of this word. The poem is based on possible events from the fourteenth century, and this world feels very contemporary, even for Browning having written it in the 1840s. It gives us a very strong suggestion that the town is run as a business rather than as a democracy. This is a perfect moment to bring in a small amount of context, as the world Browning was writing in was one where revolutionary waves were sweeping across Europe, so the idea of an end to the traditional forms of governance was a pertinent one. Push your students to consider what the idea of a 'Corporation' might suggest. There's very much a sense that the town is being run on economic considerations, rather than moral ones, and that the people in the town are complicit in this, as they complain that 'we buy gowns lined with ermine / For dolts that can't or won't determine / What's best to rid us of our vermin!' The use of the pronoun 'we' gives us a very strong impression that the people of Hamelin are part of this pomp and only object when the members of the Corporation are not holding up their part of the bargain – getting rid of the rats. It seems to be a system of governance entirely based on economic exchange, and this is typified in the actions of the Mayor. Students can be asked to consider if he acts as the people of the town would like him to when he cheats the Pied Piper, or is merely doing what the Corporation approves of. Perceptive students might notice that when he tells the Pied Piper that 'But as for the guilders, what we spoke / Of them, as you very well know, was in joke. / Beside, our losses have made us thrifty', the pronouns he uses are all plurals. Who are the 'we' and the 'us'? Was it him and the Corporation, or the Mayor and the people of Hamelin? More confident students will also be able to draw out what Browning is saying about mercenary behaviour, and pick out the vocabulary which is demonstrating this, for instance the slyness of the Mayor's 'knowing wink'.

This leads to a consideration of what morals Browning is expecting the reader to take from the poem. It ends, very obviously, on the moral that 'If we've promised them aught, let us keep our promise'. It gives a really clear opportunity to explore some more contextual ideas, such as sin and dishonesty, and how these were viewed in the Christian society Browning was living in. The other clear moral is the idea of excessive wealth preventing true holiness, as the poem mentions 'A text which says that heaven's gate / Opens to the rich at an easy rate / As the needle's eye takes a camel in!' There are echoes here of the Biblical reference of the gospel of Matthew that 'It is easier for a camel to go through the eye of a needle than for a rich man to enter the kingdom of God'. This is again a good link to look at with your students. Ultimately, financial greed has led to a town which is 'so solemn' and in which the 'children were stolen away', and Browning is making a clear moral point here, having highlighted to the reader that those in power were too concerned with the trappings of riches, such as their 'ermine' clothes. Greed and dishonesty have resulted in the downfall of the town.

Finally, move your students away from the literal sense of the story and ask them to begin to think about it more symbolically. You could begin your discussion by getting them to consider whether or not we are supposed to read it as a fairy story, or fact, or something else. What do they think the symbolism or the significance of the rats could be? Does it link to the 'morals' Browning seems to have included in his ballad? The actions of the Pied Piper are also morally fascinating. Does he act proportionately to not being paid, or are his actions in taking the children wrong?

'The Pied Piper of Hamelin' is such a fascinating poem to study with Key Stage 3, and can be rewarding particularly for students who are not the most confident, due to the accessibility of the subject and language, while retaining opportunities to challenge the most able. It also, importantly, allows for the weaving in of the contextual ideas that will become so important as students start to study nineteenth-century literature for GCSE. The story itself also allows for plenty of interesting and creative interpretative activities. You could source and show students a wide variety of illustrations of the Pied Piper of Hamelin story and have them choose which depictions they think are most accurate, before creating their own. Students could perform the poem as a class, each group taking a separate section so that everyone has a role to play. If producing the poem as a performance, encourage students to think about inventive ways in which they could portray the characters or deliver the dialogue – could they incorporate choral techniques, soundscape, physical theatre? What costumes could they make for the characters, or props, and how could these represent their symbolic role in the poem? For the most confident students, what about getting them to rewrite the Pied Piper of Hamelin for our contemporary times? What institutions and individuals could be referenced to make Browning's message relevant to our society?

Suggested Key Stage 3 Lesson Plan

Equipment needed:
Copies of the poem, cut up
Copies of the poem, complete
Romantic Poets' 'Manifesto'
L/O: To link language and form to the context of 'Composed Upon Westminster Bridge'

This lesson has been designed to ensure that students are able to link ideas such as a poem's form and language to the importance of context. By taking apart the poem and then working to reform it, students will have a chance to consider each line and to wring the meaning out of it, before considering who wrote it and how it can be put back together. You will need to do some preparation, especially for the 'manifesto', but the ideas for that can be taken directly from this book, and then the rest of the lesson is quite 'hands off' at times. As this is a lesson for Key Stage 3, the Romantic poetry ideas have purposely been kept relatively simple, but do extend these or add more detail for particularly able students.

Romantic Poets' 'Manifesto' ideas:

- Wordsworth liked to link together the power of nature and the ordinary people living and working on the land

- Emotions and feelings are the most important elements, and these are invoked from interacting with the world around us

- Creativity and a less prescriptive approach to writing are essential to produce meaningful literature

- Romantic poets sometimes rejected the confines of pre-determined structure where they felt it hampered their creativity

Arrange your classroom so students are sitting in groups of four, if possible.

Starter (ten minutes)

Give each pair within the group of four seven separate and random lines of the poem (for example, student A and B will have lines 2, 5, 6, 9, 10, 11 and 14, while students C and D will have the rest).

Let them know that they will need to work out the L/O throughout the lesson, but to start with, they need to find anything within the lines they have which they can comment on, underlining it on their copy or annotating in whatever way they find most helpful.

Do consider having a bank of suggested terminology on the board as prompts if you feel this would be helpful, such as:

Personification

Consonance

Hyperbole

Pathetic fallacy

Sonnet

Give them time to explore, to annotate and discuss within their pair. Then allow the students in each group to feed back to each other on their lines of poetry. What mood and atmosphere did they discern? What could we conclude from the fact that there are fourteen lines? It is important here that everyone in the group feels comfortable and familiar with all the lines of the poem, and for less confident students, articulating their reaction to their lines can be a great way to push their progress.

Main (thirty to forty minutes)

This is where to really challenge students to explore language and form, ensuring that they are also becoming aware of how this links to the context of the poem.

Share a copy of the manifesto with each group and give them a chance to read this aloud. Ensure that everyone is comfortable with all the language and concepts before moving on – this is a great opportunity to stretch and challenge very able students, and easy to give additional support to those who might need it. Depending on your lesson time, a discussion about their views and beliefs can be very useful, particularly thinking about how they differ from ideas often held about the nineteenth century. Is it surprising that there is such an emphasis on the importance of emotions, considering the stereotype of the nineteenth century as being repressed?

Next, move back to the poetry fragments. Challenge each group to put the poem back together and consider what order they would consider correct. Ask them to use the manifesto as a guide: how can they create a meaning that fits with these ideas? Prompt your students to use their analytical skills on language and poetic techniques, and how this might help them to make sense of the poem. Although it can be tempting to rush in and give students the first line or the final two lines to speed up the process, let them think through the poem and as long as they remain on task and are usefully discussing aspects like the rhyme scheme or the syntax or the use of enjambment and end-stopped lines, then allow the discussion to unfold.

When students feel they have 'created' a version of the poem they are happy with, ask them to come up with a number of reasons why they have decided upon the order, which can be done informally through jotting down some bullet-points or recorded in a more formal way. This is a great opportunity for group feedback and a discussion about the choices made, before revealing the actual poem. Take the time for this to be read aloud, and give students a moment to see how close they got. This is the time to add in any references to the sonnet form that the students have not covered, and ensure that they are thinking about why Wordsworth has decided upon a form most usually associated with love to express his feelings here. How does the poem's language contribute to the idea of it still being a 'love poem'?

Now is the time to bring the different elements together – the final poem, the context about the views of the Romantic poets and the terminology you teased out in the starter activity. During this consolidation phase, set an essay-style question such as 'How typically Romantic is "Composed Upon Westminster Bridge?"' and get your students to plan and write a response. We always find it is useful to remind a class about their assessment objectives here, stressing that although they need to show an understanding of the text and its meaning, they need to give equal weight to the writer's craft and remember to include context as well. By ticking off each of these areas in their answer, they are likely to produce work that is of a far higher standard. If you don't feel your class are ready for an essay-style response (this is probably more suitable for Year 9 as opposed to Years 7 and 8), then you could do this part of the lesson as a Socratic discussion, either led by you or by the students, or allow students to work in pairs or groups to come up with a 'Romantic' and 'Not Romantic' list of ideas to share.

Plenary (five to ten minutes)

As the joint focus in the lesson objective is both language and context, it can be great to use the plenary as a time to really solidify how the two work together by looking back at the lesson's activities.

Ask students to return to their original interpretations of the poem, looking at both the annotated lines from the starter and the poem they put together before seeing the original. Get them to now consider if seeing the poem as a sonnet and written as Wordsworth intended has any impact upon how they have interpreted language. Does the sonnet form create emphasis in mood where there was none before? How does understanding the viewpoint of the Romantics inform Wordsworth waiting to name the subject of his praise in line 4?

A brief class discussion on the topics or more formal recording of ideas can be used as appropriate under time constraints.

Differentiation

For more confident students, consider adding the concept of the sublime to the Romantic Poets' Manifesto. You can also really stretch them by getting them to consider the importance of form: why has Wordsworth chosen the sonnet form, most commonly used to write about love, to express his feelings about landscape?

How does this fit into the ideas and ideals of the Romantic poets? Push them to think about how strictly Wordsworth has adhered to the sonnet form (and ask them to identify whether this is Petrarchan or Shakespearean for extra credit!) and why he might have made the choices he has.

Less confident students may need the L/O given to them at the start of the lesson so that they approach the tasks with the idea already in their minds that at some point they will need to think about how context has influenced the writing of the poem. It could also be useful for them to have prompts or questions under each line of the poem they are exploring for the starter activity, to guide them.

When putting the poem back together, it might be worth having a template for students who struggle, with a few of the lines already in place to assist them, as well as considering providing a model answer to the essay-style question, or sentence starters for those who find writing a challenge.

Key Stage 4

At Key Stage 4, the poem choices you make as a teacher will be dictated to you by the texts of the exam board. These may well not be poems you particularly rate, have read or studied before, or feel that your students will have much connection to. You will certainly not be the first teacher to feel dread at looking at the list of poems set by the exam board and wondering why on earth this or that one was chosen, and how you're going to begin to teach it! However, by being able to place the poems you teach within their relevant historical and literary contexts, and bringing the subject matter alive with snippets from other appropriate texts, we hope that you'll be able to push the teaching of poems for GCSE to a more exciting and engaging level. While of course the focus is on ensuring your students can meet the assessment objectives when they come to write about the poems, there is much to be said for students achieving at a greater level when they are excited by what they are learning. Even though you will be under time pressure, don't feel that you can't spend fifteen minutes or so looking at some wider context and doing some creative activities. Try to break free of the monotony of filling in charts and tables of features and effects; you wouldn't teach a novel in this way, so why approach poetry as if it were some foreign literary land that needs to be carved up and categorised in order to be navigated?

This section will look at two common poems from the anthologies, as well as a lesson plan on Thomas Hardy's 'Neutral Tones' (1898).

'When We Two Parted' by Lord Byron (1816)

The poem is about the end of a secret relationship and the devastation of the poet as he feels heartbreak but knows the other party seems unaffected by it. Before starting to read the poem, think about your audience – in this case, it is a class of teenagers. Teenage years are fraught with first fallings in and out of love, so harness this to think about the poem's themes before tackling the text. Ask your students if they've ever been in love, or thought they were in love, and how they felt when this ended. What did it feel like? Was it almost like a bereavement? By having this discussion, you will be directing them to the theme of the poem, so this can be their first focus, and only when this has been explored should you move to the task of thinking about *how* Byron is describing his loss, giving students a chance to explore the poem's language in detail. We find that using a series of questions to begin the process can help, and so can utilising short, accessible snippets of the poem in the question so that students become familiar with the text quickly and can start to piece meaning together. For example, asking if anyone who has had a boyfriend or girlfriend split up with them felt that the 'silence and tears' was the worst part of it, or whether they felt that the emotions were felt 'too deeply to tell', starts a useful discussion while providing early familiarisation with the text (and is likely to provide some useful quotations to learn for the all-important closed-book examination at the end of Key Stage 4). Asking them how they would like to act if they saw someone who broke their heart, whether with 'tears' or they would prefer to keep their emotions to themselves and 'in silence I grieve', helps students think about why Byron has written the poem, and whether or not his approach of writing about how secret the affair was and how the person he loved must not know his feelings now, having published a poem about it, suggests more than they might initially think.

Drawing an outline of the relationship covered in the poem first can also be a great way to unlock the poem's meaning for students who are less confident, so that they can concentrate on how the poem is creating an effect, rather than simply what is happening. For example, explain that person A has had an affair with person B, but the affair has now ended, and person A is heartbroken. Person B, meanwhile, is notorious and is being discussed everywhere, including in front of person A, as no-one knows they were together. Once the premise of the poem is clear, resist the temptation to immediately read the poem as a class. Your aim is not only to familiarise your students with the text, but also to encourage them to feel confident about selecting quotations and working with the poems independently. Bearing this in mind, have a discussion about how you think each person feels. If you were person A, what would your reaction be? What emotions might you be experiencing? Remind them to jot down the main points of their discussion, as this will be a useful bank of emotions that they can look for in the poem. Once this discussion has been fully explored, only then is it time to reach for the text.

Ask them to look back at their notes and now turn into detectives and try to find evidence that Byron felt some of these emotions by searching for supporting quotations in the text. If they believed that person A would have felt sad, then vocabulary like 'broken-hearted' and 'sorrow' are easily accessible in the first stanza, increasing the confidence of students that they can tackle a poem from the nineteenth century without too much difficulty. When they are then confident about the content, and being able to link the emotions felt during the end of a relationship with the vocabulary, it is then time to explore some of the poem's more complex ideas.

By asking students to start examining the language and the deeper meanings in the poem only once they've reached this stage, where they are comfortable with the main events and with the emotional tone of the poem, you'll be allowing them to see that Byron, in spite of when he was writing, is a hugely accessible poet, who will still provide them with complex ideas through language which will allow them to fulfil the demands of the GCSE examination assessment objectives. As students begin to interrogate the language more fully, they should now be directed to linking the language they are encountering with the emotions of the narrator, and by asking them to consider vocabulary which stands out most to them, it is a great way to explore ideas such as the motif of language associated with death, dying or funeral language (tears, colder, sorrow, chill, knell, etc.) and what this tells us about how the narrator feels about the end of the relationship. We find it helpful to ask students to consider themes beyond simply the end of a relationship, and look at ideas such as silence and sound, exploring quotations where these concepts feature.

From here, the introduction of ideas about form and structure, as well as poetic techniques, seems like an easy step for most students. These are terms and concepts with which they should already be familiar, and having spent time working on the meaning of the poem, and the language used, students will then feel a level of comfort with the text that allows them to consider the eight-line stanzas, the regular rhyme scheme and how this contributes to our understanding of the poem. You might suggest to them that they consider that the control the narrator shows in public, keeping his emotions hidden, is reflected in the form of the poem, while the structure, which moves from the past, to the present and then on to an imagined future meeting, suggests to us that the heartbreak he feels is never-ending and all-encompassing.

Once you feel students have a strong grasp of the poem's message and how this is expressed though language, form and structure, you might like to solidify some of these ideas further though looking at some contemporary sources. The poem has an intriguing publication history as Byron sought to cover his tracks regarding the true identity of his lover, Lady Frances Wedderburn Webster, a married woman who had also been a lover of the Duke of Wellington. Giving students some background on this should pique their interest, and help them to remember the themes of the poem more effectively. You could also give your students some sources on attitudes towards marriage, gender and appropriate behaviour for women at the time (see Chapter 7 for some help with this). If your students don't know much about Byron, some sources, such as nineteenth-century newspaper articles about him, his lifestyle and his death, his obituaries, etc., can help students to understand just what a cult, celebrity figure he was during his lifetime. How might an appreciation of how Byron challenged conventions during his life help us to understand why he might have written this poem? What point is he making? Is he expressing the reality of his emotions, or is he just shamelessly attention seeking to further his reputation as a dandy who was 'mad, bad and dangerous to know'?

WHY NOT CONSIDER . . .?

■ How is the concept of emotion in the poem still modern to a reader in spite of being written in the nineteenth century?

■ What is the significance of so much language connected to death? How does this contribute to understanding the meaning of the poem?

■ The form of the poem is incredibly regular. How does this further our understanding of how the poet is feeling?

Sonnet 29, 'I think of thee' by Elizabeth Barrett Browning (1845–6)

This Barrett Browning poem is a perennial favourite of exam boards and appears in many GCSE anthologies. On first reading, students can feel perhaps a sense of ennui about both the sonnet form and the subject of the poem, so it can be worth approaching the poem from a different angle than a traditional read-meaning-analysis system, and similarly to the Bryon poem above, to think about the themes and the emotions before applying these to the poem's form and structure.

As context is so important to understand here, it can be a good starting point. Before even putting the poem in front of your students, ask them what the stereotype of the Victorian lady is. How do they see her, particularly if she is a writer? The chances are that words such as repressed, buttoned-up, emotionless and contained will all come to mind. It can be hard to see beyond the stereotype of the 'pure' Victorian woman, hands in gloves and wearing a bustle, repressing her emotions and living quietly within a patriarchal society. Now contrast this idea with that of the story of Elizabeth Barrett Browning, who carried out a secret courtship with a man who was six years younger than herself, eventually leaving her father's house to marry him and run away to Europe. The context is important here, because of the expression of passionate love in the sonnet, so it is crucial that students start with the idea that this is an unusual woman, one who subverts our accepted notions of Victorian womanhood, and that it is a poem expressing a huge depth of love.

From here, move on to the poem itself. Although the form of the poem is hugely important, try not to immediately get embroiled in looking at it as though it is only a collection of fourteen lines with a regular rhyme scheme. Consider reading it aloud before the class sees the poem so that the naturalness of the syntax and the rhythm can be detected by ear, unclouded by how the poem looks. What is their initial reaction to it? Often, the unfamiliarity of the use of 'thee' can sound jarring to the modern ear, and some students can find it hard to get past this and delve into the poem's meaning.

To counteract this, lead a discussion about why Barrett Browning has chosen this form of address. Point out to your students that even though the nineteenth century can feel a long time ago, people certainly weren't routinely addressing each other with 'thee' in their conversation. So why is Barrett Browning doing it? It can be helpful to think about what Sonnet 29 is actually *for* when considering this. If the poet had just used 'you' it might well have interfered with the rhyme scheme, but more importantly, we have to remind students that the function of the sonnet is to express love. Barrett Browning is writing as part of a great literary tradition which, even as she moves beyond purely imitating the form of the Shakespearian sonnet, shows she is holding onto the spirit of it through addressing her lover as 'thee', evoking a timelessness and intimacy to the sonnet through the choice of pronoun. Does this reflect the timeless nature of her love, too?

With the emphasis now thoroughly on textual analysis, ask your students to consider the first and second lines ('my thoughts do twine and bud / About thee, as wild vines, about a tree'). They may well also want to look back to previous work on the Romantics, and bring in the context of the importance of nature to these poets, and see Barrett Browning as a later disciple of this, but they might also be led to consider the natural imagery as something more, so that as well as the metaphor of the narrator's thought clinging to the loved one, you can push them to think about this further. What is the image that the 'bud' connotes? There is the obvious answer of it symbolising the couple's love 'flowering' or 'blossoming', but you could ask your students to look back at the ideas they had about the stereotypes of Victorian womanhood and to think about how Barrett Browning subverts this. What part of her anatomy might the poet be alluding to? Get them to consider whether in fact there is a far more sexual reference here, and an allusion to what she desires.

And this love and desire has soon obliterated everything else as 'soon there's nought to see' but her love. The use of the adjective 'straggling' might be further useful contextual information, as it could be suggesting Barrett Browning's physical weakness, while the plant that 'hides the wood' could be showing us that this love has dominated everything, even her ability to write. You could even point your students towards the rhyme scheme here, where the ABBA scheme is slightly disrupted by the half-rhyme of 'wood' and 'bud', echoing the idea that her great love is interfering with her craft. Yet Barrett Browning moves from this declaration to another idea, which pulls students back to the importance of context and background. Barrett Browning was deeply religious, as was not unusual for the time, and here she mixes religious imagery with her love, writing of the 'palm tree' which suggests Christian faith and devotion, perhaps even creating a link between the act of laying down palm fronds on Palm Sunday for Jesus to ride over and the act of the poet laying down her devotion in front of her husband, almost in a religious fervour.

The following section of the poem can be the perfect opportunity to remind your students about the sonnet form. Prompt them to think about the rhyme scheme in both a Shakespearean and Petrarchan sonnet. Which do they think this is and why? With the rhyme scheme, this sonnet is very clearly Petrarchan in form, but as discussed above, there is a lingering legacy of the Shakespearean sonnet in the language choices, an inheritance we can assume Barrett Browning was well aware of. This is a great time to revise terms like 'volta' and discuss where it appears in *Sonnet 29*. Does it come as early as the 'Yet' at line 5, or as late as 'Because' in line 12? Is it in the middle of line 7 at 'Rather'? Where does Barrett Browning seem to offer a 'solution' to the 'problem' of her overwhelming love? This sort of discussion, particularly if there are opposing views, can be incredibly helpful in allowing students to explore a text.

Context and meaning are intrinsically linked in the poem, and it is good for students to try to unravel this. The lines 'I will not have my thoughts instead of thee / Who art dearer, better' push the discussion back to the figure of Barrett Browning as a nineteenth-century woman, a person who would have had to battle the casual assumption from many that females were not the artistic and intellectual equal of men, and yet here, the poet is almost abandoning the critical success she has achieved in being viewed as an intellectual by admitting that her 'thoughts', the very reason for her success, are not worth as much as the 'dearer, better' figure of the husband. That she longs for his presence, not her own thoughts, allows us to almost intrude on a poem of aching intimacy.

And finally, push your students to look at how the poet continues the metaphor of the tree, through the passion and abandon of Barrett Browning exhorting her lover to 'let these bands of greenery which insphere thee / Drop heavily down – burst, shatter, everywhere', imploring him to turn her thoughts away and for her to simply revel in his presence, in the 'deep joy' that she has 'to see and hear' him. Give your class time to really appreciate the depth of the emotion that the poet is expressing, and how when she writes that 'I do not think of thee – I am too near thee', we see a woman consumed by love in the parallel opening and closing lines. Reiterate that this is a sonnet, a traditional form of a love poem, but that Barrett

Browning has moved far away from the concept of courtly love the sonnet had previously expressed, to create a poem of almost visceral and intimate longing.

To widen students' understanding of Barrett Browning and expectations of women's roles within romantic relationships in the nineteenth century, consider spending some time looking at some contemporary sources. There are paintings and photographs of Barrett Browning on the National Portrait Gallery website; why not show these to students and ask them to consider how these present her to the public compared to how she presented herself through her poems? Show students some selections from Coventry Patmore's poem 'The Angel in the House' and some images of the perfect domestic woman in nineteenth-century society: looking at Franz Winterhalter's portraits of Queen Victoria with her family is a good place to start, as are nineteenth-century Christmas card images. What do these tell us about women's expected role in Victorian society? How are the very domesticated images of Victorian women in many ways exclusive of any recognition of women as individuals with individual passions? Some fun – if you have time – can also be had in looking at Virginia Woolf's novel *Flush: An Autobiography*, which pretends to be in the voice of Elizabeth Barrett Browning's dog. This offers an intriguing insight into early twentieth-century attitudes to the Victorians, from whom many of our incorrect assumptions about them come.

WHY NOT CONSIDER . . .?

- How does the poem subvert our expectations of a nineteenth-century woman?

- Why is the sonnet form so important in doing this?

- How does Barrett Browning use the extended natural metaphor of the tree to create meaning, and how can we link this to the Romantics' obsession with the natural world and the concept of the sublime?

Suggested Key Stage 4 Lesson Plan

Equipment needed:
Copies of the poem
Paper
Copies of the mark scheme/marking criteria
Comparison tables (optional)
Information about Thomas Hardy (this could be printed out or displayed on the board)

In preparation for the GCSE examination, this lesson has been designed to explore the poem's meaning through theme and language, with an emphasis on producing an understanding of how to tailor an essay response to best exploit the mark scheme. There is a lot of emphasis on the use of assessment objectives, so that after considering a poem on its own, students are then able to transfer the skills that they have to a comparative essay, ensuring that they do not neglect AO2 and AO3. Students can be inclined to write only about the meaning of a poem, and placing this emphasis on the importance of exploring the writer's craft, plus how this links to context, is an invaluable skill. The lesson can be adapted to give further support to students who are less confident or scaled back in order to push students who are more able. Group work is definitely needed during the exploratory parts of the lesson, but the writing tasks can be tackled either as an individual project or in a group for less secure learners. This lesson has been planned for Hardy's 'Neutral Tones' but could easily be adapted for any of the poems from an anthology.

L/O: To explore how language and theme work together to produce meaning in Hardy's 'Neutral Tones'

WHY NOT CONSIDER . . .?

- The poem is told from only one perspective. To increase your students' familiarity with the poem, why not encourage students to rewrite it from the position of the other half of the relationship?

- Encourage students to pick out quotations such as 'Your eyes on me were as eyes that rove / Over tedious riddles of years ago' and see it from the point of view of that person. What were they thinking?

- Why were they smiling a 'grin of bitterness'? Is that how they intended to look?

Starter (five to ten minutes)

In groups, get students to read the poem aloud and decide upon the mood and atmosphere. Ask them to pick out vocabulary and phrases they feel would support this view of the poem. When they've done this, ask them to look at the mark scheme or the marking criteria you have adapted from the exam board, and think about which assessment objectives this activity would refer to. (It is worth noting here, as an aside, that we find it invaluable to spend time with students on ensuring they actually understand exactly what each of the assessment objectives is asking them to do in practice. Showing them a marked essay with each AO highlighted in a different colour, or telling them as you talk about a text which comments you're making fit which AO, really helps them to understand what they need to include in their written responses. Though it may appear obvious to us, it isn't always to students!) Give time for verbal class feedback, and to ensure that the whole group is aware of the assessment objective, and they have tackled it through extrapolating mood and atmosphere during their reading, finding quotations to support their ideas. Now get them to look at the weighting of the mark scheme and ask them what their exploration is missing.

Main task (thirty minutes)

As your students are able to see the importance of using further skills than simply showing their understanding of the poem's meaning, they will be ready to ensure that they are now looking at the poem from the point of view of AO2 and AO3 too. This can often be best tackled in stages, with the writer's craft and terminology explored, before seeing how social and historical context are also influential.

Again working in groups, point your students back to the poem, where they will identify at least four themes, motifs or ideas and look at them across all assessment objectives. For example, they might want to think about the motif of nature, loss of love or use of location. They can record their ideas and quotations in a grid like the one below, which some students find really useful for ease of revision later, or they could record their ideas as annotations on their copy of the poem or as bullet-points in their notebooks. However they record their ideas, they will need to have one large A3-sized copy as well as individual copies of their notes.

Plenary (fifteen minutes)

Students should stick their A3 paper up on the wall with Blu Tack. Spread the work around the room so that there is plenty of space for students to read what other groups have done. Everyone should then walk around the room, pen in hand, reading the comments made by other groups and annotating their work. They can ask questions or write that they agree or disagree, though obviously this needs to be a constructive rather than destructive exercise. Once everyone has had a chance to read everything, the groups should look at the comments on their work and see whether they have gained any new insights from the experience, before having a shared class discussion on the findings from the lesson. Make sure you give students a little bit of time at

Table 3.1 Poetry analysis table

Theme/idea/motif	AO1	AO2	AO3

the end to amend their own notes should they want to add any ideas from the other groups or change their mind about their previous interpretations.

Differentiation

For students who are less confident, read the poem aloud to them at the start of the lesson, getting them to follow along. You could provide cards of 'mood' and quotations and encourage them to match them together as a starter activity, rather than exploring the poem independently. For more confident students, during the starter, ask them to produce a brief paragraph on mood and atmosphere, asking them to ensure that they use quotations to support all their ideas. Some students, or those who have been studying poetry in preparation for the exam for some time, will automatically begin to use AO2 skills, or even AO3 skills, in their answer. When they look back at their work during the starter activity, ensure that they are clearly able to identify where these skills have been used.

During the main task, students who have slower processing or find producing tables a challenge will benefit from having a table pre-produced for them, especially if you are short on lesson time. Those who find English more of a challenge might find the task easier if their pre-prepared table has some of the information already provided, such as theme and context. Labelling the table with additional information might also be helpful (see below).

Table 3.2 Differentiated poetry analysis table

Theme/idea/ motif	AO1 Quotation/ what is happening	AO2 Using terminology/ looking at the writer's craft	AO3 Adding in context/what we know about the writer or time the poem is written in that might have been influential

---

WHY NOT CONSIDER . . .?

- Which other poems can 'Neutral Tones' be easily compared with?

- Suggest to your students that they draw up a list of possible themes that exam questions could cover, and then link these to poems that might be appropriate.

- Draw out from each poem a number of useful quotations that can cover AO1, AO2 and AO3.

Teaching poetry at Key Stage 5

The teaching of poetry at Key Stage 5 should not be very different from the methods we have described at Key Stage 4, though there will be the time, space and ability to push students further in their interpretations and incorporate some literary theory to help develop their ideas and add complexity to their written work. Perhaps a key differential at Key Stage 5, however, is how much more independence you can give them. Students should be doing plenty of research into their texts in their own time, and encouraging them to look at contextual and critical material and bring their ideas to class before you study a poem can allow for much richer discussion and debate between students as well as between you and them.

Some poems studied at Key Stage 5 are very challenging, and starting the study of these with a 'see, think, wonder' activity can be helpful to give students a 'way in'. After an initial reading, students can write down what they literally see – it's got four stanzas, it's got a rhyme scheme, it's written by a woman, etc. – what they think – I think it might be about unrequited love, I think it might be a sonnet but I'm not sure, I think the poet might be criticising the government, etc. – and then what they wonder – I wonder if the poem is autobiographical, I wonder if this is based on true events, I wonder if the image of the apple in stanza 3 has got anything to do with the story of Adam and Eve, etc. Students can then share these with each other and see what common insights, observations and questions people have come up with. Creating a master list of questions to try and answer by the end of the first lesson can be good fun, and each student can be given a list of unanswered questions to go home and research, coming back to the next lesson with answers to share. This type of questioning activity allows students to be much more open-minded than when they are just looking for a list of devices, features or one definitive interpretation, and opens them up to looking at the poem from a range of different perspectives.

The activity described in the Key Stage 4 lesson plan, where students complete an analysis in groups on poster paper and stick it up on the wall, allowing other students to read and comment on their work, can also work well when analysing very complex poems. Allowing students to assess each other's ideas and provide advice on how to improve them gets them thinking far more deeply than if you had just commented on their work, and provides a lively foundation for debate in the classroom.

Key Stage 5 students should also be much more open to being challenged by reading contemporary reviews of the nineteenth-century poetry they are studying. See if you can find what the literary critics thought of their poet or the specific poem they are reading when it was first published; what insights did they have, and how could this help them to interpret the poem? The British Library

Discovering Literature website is a great source for this kind of material. Use visual stimuli, too; if you're looking at Keats' 'Eve of St Agnes' or Barrett Browning's 'Aurora Leigh', for example, see what Victorian book illustrations or paintings you can find of these poems and think about what these images can tell us about what nineteenth-century audiences perceived to be important or meaningful in the texts. Your aim with teaching nineteenth-century poetry at this level should be to expose students to as much material as possible, to enable them to decide what is and isn't important to factor into their own reading, and what they do and don't agree with when it comes to their own interpretations. Don't feel pressured to rush through, and allow students plenty of time to talk and debate and go back to poems, too – once a few weeks have elapsed, and more literary experience has been gained, perhaps go back and look again at a poem you've already annotated, and see whether any knowledge they have picked up in the interim can be useful in adding to their existing interpretation. Encourage students to not look at a poem as 'finished' – they should be re-reading and rethinking, making new connections and transferring knowledge between texts as their course of study progresses. Allowing time for this periodic revisiting of poems can reap enormous rewards as students' critical faculties mature.

Summary

We hope that this chapter has shown you how richly rewarding the teaching and learning of nineteenth-century poetry can be to all age groups. Looking at the poems from the point of view of their historical, cultural and literary context allows for a much more holistic understanding of what these poems meant to contemporary readers, and making the effort to teach them in a more creative and less prescriptive way can help to foster a lifelong love of poetry in students rather than dread and boredom. Make use of contemporary reviews, newspaper articles and images to bring the world of your poems to life, and allow students to retell the narratives in a variety of ways to help them feel connected to and excited about the world the poem creates. Nineteenth-century poetry is an incredibly varied canon with something for everyone; we really hope that you have been inspired to revisit your poetry teaching with the help of some Victorian poets!

4 Teaching nineteenth-century texts to younger students

It can seem a big step to teach nineteenth-century texts to Key Stage 3 students, with lurking ideas about the complicated syntax and vocabulary putting off all but the keenest readers, and the length of some texts seeming an impossible undertaking in any non-GCSE group. However, it is, in our opinion, a mistake to wait until Key Stage 4 to introduce nineteenth-century literature. Students in Years 7, 8 and 9 can often be incredibly receptive to new and challenging ideas, and there are plenty of ways to introduce them to the richness of the literature of the period without intimidating them. These years can offer a great opportunity to introduce vocabulary, style, syntax, contextual ideas and common themes within nineteenth-century texts in a variety of creative and interesting ways that do not necessarily require you to actually teach a whole nineteenth-century novel if you don't feel that your class would cope with one.

Picking your material carefully is half the battle in getting a class excited about a new project, and while many nineteenth-century texts are great reads for many ages, no-one is suggesting you should leap in with your Year 7 class and read *Daniel Deronda* from start to finish! Rather than immediately plunging in with a classic and risking alienating students with something too challenging, a much more accessible introduction can be made through teaching neo-Victorian fiction, which is a great way to explore context and some nineteenth-century social mores without the dense prose and unfamiliar vocabulary that may put some students off in authentic texts.

Of course, non-fiction texts can also be explored in an equally gentle way. Sensational newspaper articles or travel diaries can be really entertaining and stimulating for students, and are easily accessible when carefully glossed for trickier terms. Many students have a keen interest in events of the nineteenth century, and so finding contemporaneous non-fiction writing can really play up to their curiosity and make students keen to explore further. Throughout this chapter, there are lengthy excerpts from nineteenth-century texts that we think are helpful to explore alongside suggested neo-Victorian novels. All of these nineteenth-century texts are out of copyright, and the full texts are readily available online, making them an easily accessible resource for lessons.

Using neo-Victorian novels

Neo-Victorian novels have long been popular with younger readers, and you might be surprised by how familiar your students already are with the nineteenth century through books they've read at home or at primary school. Many students, for instance, will be very familiar with Jacqueline Wilson's neo-Victorian novels *Hetty Feather* and *Clover Moon*, or *Street Child* by Berlie Doherty, and all students coming from UK primary schools will have covered the nineteenth century in some detail during primary school. Starting a unit on nineteenth-century literature by asking students what contextual knowledge they have about life in the period, such as workhouses, transport and social class, can be a great way to build their confidence and make them realise how much knowledge they already have to draw upon. Also, don't discount the fact that many students will be familiar with classic stories like *The Secret Garden* or *The Railway Children*, and some will be familiar with the plots of novels such as *Oliver Twist* or *A Christmas Carol*, even if they haven't read the actual books, and can have details about setting or attitudes teased out. For the introduction of specific themes or ideas, the texts below can be an excellent starting point.

Cogheart

Cogheart by Peter Bunzl (London: Usborne, 2016) is a fascinating steam-punk adventure that provides a fantastic level of context about life in the nineteenth century as well as a fast-paced and easy-to-follow narrative. The addition of 'mechanicals' (life-like wind-up robotic servants) and 'mechanimals' (robotic animals) does not detract from the realism of the Victorian setting. As a great starting point to build on for more complex texts, there is a thoughtful exploration of what it means to be human and what it is to have a soul, which are themes covered in more depth at GCSE, such as through looking at the nature of man in *The Strange Case of Dr Jekyll and Mr Hyde*.

WHY NOT CONSIDER . . .?

- Exploration of the changes that occurred to the belief systems of much of society as Darwin's *On the Origin of Species* (1859) was widely discussed and disseminated.

- Discussing the nineteenth-century class system following a wider acceptance of evolution and the doubt it placed in society. If God did not 'place' people in a certain situation in life, how fair was it that some had so much more than others?

(continued)

(continued)

- ■ Making links to nineteenth-century fiction texts such as *Frankenstein* by Mary Shelley (1818) or *The Strange Case of Dr Jekyll and Mr Hyde* by Robert Louis Stevenson (1886). There's no need to tackle the entire text with students at this early stage – they are very much for Key Stages 5 and 4 respectively – but the narratives are so well known that excerpts can be studied, or even just a few key quotations. This way, both texts will feel less daunting when embarked on in future years.

- ■ Moving away from expecting written responses. Instead, consider a press conference, a newspaper report or even ask your students to make a short film.

In chapter 1 of *Cogheart*, when the protagonist Lily stands up for the mechanical servant, Molly, she is caught in a confrontation with some of the other pupils at her school, as she believes that the servant has feelings and should be treated with dignity.

> Lucretia folded her arms across her chest and gave a disdainful laugh. "It's not alive, Lily. Mechs aren't living."
>
> "Besides," Alice scuttled closer to Lucretia, "everyone knows mechs and humans can't be friends. Mechs have no feelings." Lily sighed. It was exhausting dealing with such idiots.
>
> "Don't be ridiculous," she told them. "Of course they have feelings. They're no different to you or me." Lucretia tutted at her.
>
> "Oh Lily, Lily, how wrong you are. Let me show you." She whipped out a hand and struck Molly round the head. Molly's eyes flared, but she didn't respond. "You see?" Lucretia said. "It didn't even flinch."
>
> (p. 22)

Later on, when clockmaker Thaddeus is attempting to mend the mechanimal fox, Malkin, he muses on these ideas with his young son, Robert:

> "All of John's mechs were so delicately made," Thaddeus continued, "and when they were working, something about them seemed different, more . . . alive."
>
> "How so?"
>
> "They're not like the regular models. They have quirks, can think for themselves. If that doesn't make them living things, I don't know what does."
>
> (p. 88)

It is worth noting here that Thaddeus' name is often believed to translate as Greek for 'heart', giving connotations that he believes the mechanicals have a heart, or something akin to them that gives them life, rather than simply a wind-up mechanism that makes them function.

The text, with so many thrilling chases and narrative twists, would be a perfect class text to read, and would provide an excellent basis for exploration of the changes in belief systems during the nineteenth century. Task your students with examining the widely held beliefs of the nineteenth century, and how with the publication of Charles Darwin's *On the Origin of Species* in 1859, there was the beginning of the widespread belief in evolutionary biology and the growing acceptance of atheism. Discussions about how the idea that God had created the world and everything in it was disrupted, and the impact this had on notions such as a soul, which was previously generally accepted as something that made an individual human, can be easily linked to *Cogheart*. There is a chance here to really push students by getting them to look at Darwin's text below, which is from chapter 4 of *On the Origin of Species*. 'Natural Selection' and the 'whole machinery of life' that Darwin writes of, which examines how man does not have the power that nature does, could provide a fantastic base for discussion as part of a study of the novel's ideas about humanity:

As man can produce and certainly has produced a great result by his methodical and unconscious means of selection, what may not nature effect? Man can act only on external and visible characters: nature cares nothing for appearances, except in so far as they may be useful to any being. She can act on every internal organ, on every shade of constitutional difference, on the whole machinery of life. Man selects only for his own good; Nature only for that of the being which she tends. Every selected character is fully exercised by her; and the being is placed under well-suited conditions of life. Man keeps the natives of many climates in the same country; he seldom exercises each selected character in some peculiar and fitting manner; he feeds a long and a short beaked pigeon on the same food; he does not exercise a long-backed or long-legged quadruped in any peculiar manner; he exposes sheep with long and short wool to the same climate. He does not allow the most vigorous males to struggle for the females. He does not rigidly destroy all inferior animals, but protects during each varying season, as far as lies in his power, all his productions. He often begins his selection by some half-monstrous form; or at least by some modification prominent enough to catch his eye, or to be plainly useful to him. Under nature, the slightest difference of structure or constitution may well turn the nicely-balanced scale in the struggle for life, and so be preserved. How fleeting are the wishes and efforts of man! how short his time! and consequently how poor will his products be, compared with those accumulated by nature during whole geological periods. Can we wonder, then, that nature's productions should be far "truer" in character than man's productions; that they should be infinitely better adapted to the most complex conditions of life, and should plainly bear the stamp of far higher workmanship?

(2009, pp. 602–603)

If you're worried that this extract from *The Origin of Species* would be too challenging, try providing a glossary and bullet-pointed summary by the side of the text, summing up each sentence so that students who find it challenging can follow the argument that Darwin is setting out. Afterwards, prompt students to consider how Darwin's scientific approach is both similar and different to that of John Hartman and Professor Silverfish in *Cogheart*. Which is the most potentially disruptive to society – the idea that mankind was not created by God but by naturally occurring evolution, or the invention of a perpetual-motion machine that means a human could live forever? Darwin writes of 'the stamp of far higher workmanship': do they agree, or is the perpetual-motion machine something far greater than nature could ever produce?

Don't be afraid of moving past written work for this activity. Could you challenge students to present their ideas as a press conference? You will need to designate some students as the experts making the announcement of Darwin's theory, and then prime the rest of the class to be reporters reacting to their statement, giving them a chance to ask the experts questions and stimulate a lively discussion.

Links to *Frankenstein* by Mary Shelley

Your students will no doubt be familiar with the premise of *Frankenstein* in being about a monster, and it is a good opportunity to undertake the English teacher's favourite pastime of explaining that the monster is *not* called Frankenstein, but instead he is the creator. There are clear links to explore with the themes of *Frankenstein* after or during the reading of *Cogheart*, such as the creation or adaptation of life forms, as well as contextual links through ideas around the advancement of science, with the accompanying moral dilemmas.

The characters of Roach and Mould are both described as having 'lenses sewn into the raw red sockets of his eyes' (p. 64), and the parallels between humans who are being made of different parts can be clearly compared with the construction of the monster in *Frankenstein*. The extract from chapter 4 of *Frankenstein* below can be a good place to begin to make comparisons with *Cogheart*.

Who shall conceive the horrors of my secret toil as I dabbled among the unhallowed damps of the grave or tortured the living animal to animate the lifeless clay? My limbs now tremble, and my eyes swim with the remembrance; but then a resistless and almost frantic impulse urged me forward; I seemed to have lost all soul or sensation but for this one pursuit. It was indeed but a passing trance, that only made me feel with renewed acuteness so soon as, the unnatural stimulus ceasing to operate, I had returned to my old habits. I collected bones from charnel-houses and disturbed, with profane fingers, the tremendous secrets of the human frame.

(2012, pp. 47–48)

Challenge students to look back at the scenes with Mould and Roach throughout *Cogheart*, and ask them to consider how these characters are presented. What does Peter Bunzl seem to suggest the impact of humans like Professor Silverfish have when they try to change the human body, as he has done to the ex-soldiers? How can students find connotations about this in the language choices of the author? What are the parallels with what Shelley is suggesting about trying to 'create' a human in *Frankenstein*?

There is also the frightening sense in both novels that each construction – Frankenstein's monster, Roach and Mould – has a terrifying and super-human strength. During the confrontation at Professor Silverfish's house, Mould is shown as a horrific physical force when he 'bent down and grasped Papa by the neck', and when Robert tries to fend him off: 'He picked up a china plate and threw it at Roach, but Roach batted it away harmlessly with his stick' (p. 275).

We also see hints that Lily's father, Professor Hartman, is created as a contrast with Dr Frankenstein in that he made a huge scientific discovery, yet rather than pushing ahead with it and remaining intent on his original plans, he realised the importance of what he discovered, and thought about the implications for society from his invention of the perpetual-motion machine. Dr Frankenstein, in chapter 4, is able to reflect on his youthful self and his quest for knowledge and innovation above everything else, as he reflects:

Learn from me, if not by my precepts, at least by my example, how danger-ous is the acquirement of knowledge, and how much happier that man is who believes his native town to be his world, than he who aspires to become greater than his nature will allow.

(p. 46)

Consider putting Professor Silverfish, John Hartman and Dr Frankenstein on trial. What are they guilty of? Or are they innocent of any charge? Either give out roles to your students, or draw lots to be the men on trial, the defence and prosecution, the judge and jury. Challenge your most able students to find quotations from the two novels to make up part of their speeches, and encourage them to use arguments from nineteenth-century sources such as *On the Origin of Species* to support their views.

During chapter 18 in *Cogheart*, Professor Silverfish recounts to Robert and Lily the origin of the perpetual-motion machine, and how Professor Hartman refused to allow it to be given to Professor Silverfish. Professor Hartman confides, 'I believe I've discovered a way to keep humans alive forever. And that's not something which should make its way into the world' (pp. 268–269). Ask students to contrast the reactions of Professor Hartman with those of Dr Frankenstein from chapter 4 of the novel:

Remember, I am not recording the vision of a madman. The sun does not more certainly shine in the heavens than that which I now affirm is true. Some miracle might have produced it, yet the stages of the discovery were distinct and probable. After days and nights of incredible labour and fatigue, I succeeded in discovering the cause of generation and life; nay, more, I became myself capable of bestowing animation upon lifeless matter.

The astonishment which I had at first experienced on this discovery soon gave place to delight and rapture. After so much time spent in painful labour, to arrive at once at the summit of my desires was the most gratifying consummation of my toils. But this discovery was so great and overwhelming that all the steps by which I had been progressively led to it were obliterated, and I beheld only the result. What had been the study and desire of the wisest men since the creation of the world was now within my grasp. Not that, like a magic scene, it all opened upon me at once: the information I had obtained was of a nature rather to direct my endeavours so soon as I should point them towards the object of my search than to exhibit that object already accomplished. I was like the Arabian who had been buried with the dead and found a passage to life, aided only by one glimmering and seemingly ineffectual light.

I see by your eagerness and the wonder and hope which your eyes express, my friend, that you expect to be informed of the secret with which I am acquainted; that cannot be; listen patiently until the end of my story, and you will easily perceive why I am reserved upon that subject. I will not lead you on, unguarded and ardent as I then was, to your destruction and infallible misery. Learn from me, if not by my precepts, at least by my example, how dangerous is the acquirement of knowledge and how much happier that man is who believes his native town to be the world, than he who aspires to become greater than his nature will allow.

When I found so astonishing a power placed within my hands, I hesitated a long time concerning the manner in which I should employ it. Although I possessed the capacity of bestowing animation, yet to prepare a frame for the reception of it, with all its intricacies of fibres, muscles, and veins, still remained a work of inconceivable difficulty and labour. I doubted at first whether I should attempt the creation of a being like myself, or one of simpler organization; but my imagination was too much exalted by my first success to permit me to doubt of my ability to give life to an animal as complex and wonderful as man. The materials at present within my command hardly appeared adequate to so arduous an undertaking, but I doubted not that I should ultimately succeed. I prepared myself for a multitude of reverses; my operations might be incessantly baffled, and at last my work be imperfect, yet when I considered the improvement which every day takes place in science and mechanics, I was encouraged to hope my present attempts would at least lay the foundations of future success. Nor could I consider the magnitude and complexity of my plan as any argument of its impracticability. It was with these feelings that I began the creation of a human being. As the minuteness of the parts formed a great hindrance to my speed, I resolved, contrary to my first intention, to make the being of a gigantic stature, that is to say, about eight feet in height, and proportionably large. After having formed this determination and having spent some months in successfully collecting and arranging my materials, I began.

(pp. 45–47)

The nineteenth century was an era of huge leaps forward in scientific understanding, and students could be challenged to think about how this affected those living through the changes. What was the impact on society when ideas such as vaccination or public health were suddenly thrust into the spotlight? Dr Frankenstein and Professor Hartman react in different ways to making monumental scientific breakthroughs. This could be an excellent opportunity to explore the concept of hubris within both novels. Professor Silverman, unlike the more cautious Professor Hartman, is unable to believe that anyone who had made a discovery of perpetual motion would hide it, and can only assume that anyone would try 'to learn more of the secrets of the impossible energy' of the cogheart. He is not dissimilar to Dr Frankenstein, who is so intent on creating his creature that he dismisses the moral objections of how he is gaining the body parts, and whether or not creating a creature is a moral affront. It could be helpful to ask your students to look at Dr Frankenstein's reason for creating his creature in chapter 4, when he believes that:

A new species would bless me as its creator and source; many happy and excellent natures would owe their being to me. No father could claim the gratitude of his child so completely as I should deserve theirs.

(p. 47)

Why not bring in the idea that the full name of the novel is *Frankenstein: or, The Modern Prometheus*, and set students the challenge of finding out who Prometheus was? By making the link between the Titan credited with stealing fire from the Greek gods and making man from clay, and *Frankenstein*, they can then consider how this relates back to the characters in *Cogheart*. Prometheus was punished by the gods by having his liver eaten each day by an eagle, with the liver growing back the next night so the torment could begin again the following day. How does the endless pursuit of John Hartman, the death of his wife and the danger his child is put in because of his actions make him too a 'modern Prometheus'? Professor Silverfish, tortured by his longing for a machine he believes will make him immortal, is also an excellent way to pursue this idea. Perhaps use illustrations or comic strip drawings to bring out the similarities between the two. As always, more confident students will be able to use quotations directly from the texts to illustrate their ideas.

WHY NOT CONSIDER . . .?

- Names are very evocative in *Cogheart*, with Professor Hartman's name being full of connotations of goodness and truth, as well as being a loving father to Lily. Professor Silverfish, named after the verminous insect, with connotations of being unwelcome, slightly creepy in appearance and generally agreed to be a little bit revolting, is also a name which merits exploration.

- Push students further to think about how some nineteenth-century novelists used names as a way of foreshadowing the actions and personalities of their characters. Dickens, for instance, was a master of this, and you could give students a list of famous characters from his novels, such as Uriah Heep and Edward Murdstone in *David Copperfield*, Mr Pumblechook in *Great Expectations* or Wackford Squeers and Arthur Gride in *Nicholas Nickleby*. Challenge them to come up with ideas about the characters based on their names, and share extracts with them in so they can see how accurate their ideas were. Students who find writing more of a struggle could produce a labelled illustration as an alternative. Consider other nineteenth-century texts where names foreshadow the characters' personality such as *Vanity Fair* by Thackeray where Pitt Crawley and the Marquis of Steyne might also be useful studies in nomenclature.

- Can students create some character names of their own in the style of Dickens and Thackeray? By producing a brief character sketch, they can use their imaginations and improve their creative writing.

Links to *The Strange Case of Dr Jekyll and Mr Hyde* by Robert Louis Stevenson

Jekyll and Hyde will, like *Frankenstein*, be a concept that your students are likely to be very familiar with, and this makes the novel an ideal supplementary text to look at with *Cogheart*. Similarly to *Frankenstein*, looking at *Cogheart* with *Dr Jekyll and Mr Hyde* works well for students because again they are looking at the morality of pushing the boundaries of science. In *Cogheart*, the steam-punk setting and the feisty mechanimal, Malkin, give a sense of the wonders that invention and science can create, but there is a lurking sense that with scientific advancement comes moral danger. In both novels, there is an exploration of what it truly means to be human, and how playing with that concept can be catastrophic.

Prompt your students again to look at the 'mechs' such as Mrs Rust and Captain Springer, and decide what makes them human (or not, if they don't believe there is anything human about them). Is it because they can think independently, or because they form human relationships? Mrs Rust, with her unswerving love and loyalty to Lily, seems far more than a machine. Ask students to think about what makes the humans with the mechanical alterations so horrifying. Is it the blank eyes of Rust and Mould, or is it the mechanical heart of Professor Silverfish? Now task them to look at the extract below from *Dr Jekyll and Mr Hyde*, which is the first description of Mr Hyde in the novel:

> He is not easy to describe. There is something wrong with his appearance; something displeasing, something down-right detestable. I never saw a man I so disliked, and yet I scarce know why. He must be deformed somewhere; he gives a strong feeling of deformity, although I couldn't specify the point. He's an extraordinary looking man, and yet I really can name nothing out of the way. No, sir; I can make no hand of it; I can't describe him. And it's not want of memory; for I declare I can see him this moment.
>
> (2012, p. 53)

Now ask them to think back to *Cogheart* and the descriptions of Mould and Roach. Where do they see the crossover? The two ex-army soldiers with their blank, mirrored eyes are deeply disturbing because they seem to lack something human in being devoid of any compassion, but they are also physically abnormal in having inhuman elements grafted to their bodies. This can be a logical place to introduce some creative writing to allow students to create their own nineteenth-century antagonist in the manner of these characters. Using pertinent contextual details like the sort of clothes they'd expect to find on a nineteenth-century character, students can think about creating a character sketch of someone with a horrifying detail, and either write about them, label a drawing or create a mood-board.

Beyond this, both *Cogheart* and *Dr Jekyll and Mr Hyde* play on the fear of the unknown. During the nineteenth century, with rapid changes in science and with vast urbanisation, individuals' sense of belonging to a place and knowing those who lived there was being chipped away. This is a current that runs through many novels of the period, and makes the setting of nineteenth-century novels and contemporarily written novels set in the period so fundamentally important. Indeed, you can make your students aware of the importance of the setting of both novels, and how this creates greater contextual understanding, which will be invaluable when tackling more challenging Key Stage 4 texts. In *Cogheart*, London is originally viewed as a place of refuge where Lily and Robert believe they will be helped by Professor Silverfish, but there is very much a feeling that Bunzl is foreshadowing the threat the youngsters will face. In chapter 17, as they approach London, both children are disappointed that London is 'barely visible' (p. 248) through a pea-souper fog, suggesting that the truth is being hidden from them. Bunzl's language choices in this extract subtly show that London is not a safe haven, and that threat is all around them:

> An endless stream of carts and wagons, trams and double-decker omnibuses, steam-drays and clockwork carriages chugged along, spitting out smoke. Clamour and shouting emerged from every alley, while hawkers with hand-carts wove about the pavements, and the stench of oil, gas and manure filled the air, suffusing everything.
>
> (p. 253)

Using their language analysis skills, ask students to think about what sort of portrayal of London this is. Obviously, there is the influence of the steam-punk inventions, but aside from these, ask them whether London seem to be the answer to Lily and Robert's problems? Ask them to pick out words and phrases that support their viewpoint, directing less able students to vocabulary like the verbs 'spitting' and 'shouting', and the abstract noun 'stench' and concrete noun 'manure', if they are unsure. There is no sense that Lily and Robert have ended up in a friendly environment, even if they believe they've found somewhere with help close at hand. Even the details about Professor Silverfish's house, at the start of chapter 18, with the iron railings and chimney pots 'grabbing' (p. 255) at the sky, compound this impression.

Allow students to compare this to the portrayal of London in *Dr Jekyll and Mr Hyde*. London is again, at times, shown to be a threatening and corrupt place. During chapter 4, 'The Carew Murder Case', Stevenson describes London and his journey through it:

> It was by this time about nine in the morning, and the first fog of the season. A great chocolate-coloured pall lowered over heaven, but the wind was continually charging and routing these embattled vapours; so that as the cab crawled from street to street, Mr. Utterson beheld a marvellous number of degrees and hues of twilight; for here it would be dark like the back-end of evening; and there would be a glow of a rich, lurid brown, like the light

of some strange conflagration; and here, for a moment, the fog would be quite broken up, and a haggard shaft of daylight would glance in between the swirling wreaths. The dismal quarter of Soho seen under these changing glimpses, with its muddy ways, and slatternly passengers, and its lamps, which had never been extinguished or had been kindled afresh to combat this mournful re-invasion of darkness, seemed, in the lawyer's eyes, like a district of some city in a nightmare. The thoughts of his mind, besides, were of the gloomiest dye; and when he glanced at the companion of his drive, he was conscious of some touch of that terror of the law and the law's officers, which may at times assail the most honest.

As the cab drew up before the address indicated, the fog lifted a little and showed him a dingy street, a gin palace, a low French eating-house, a shop for the retail of penny numbers and twopenny salads, many ragged children huddled in the doorways, and many women of different nationalities passing out, key in hand, to have a morning glass; and the next moment the fog settled down again upon that part, as brown as umber, and cut him off from his blackguardly surroundings. This was the home of Henry Jekyll's favourite; of a man who was heir to a quarter of a million sterling.

(pp. 70–71)

Reading through the extract, again ask students to look out for vocabulary that presents London as a threatening and hostile place. Does this seem like the same city that Lily and Robert have landed in? What are the similarities, and what are the differences?

Also take a moment to compare how the façade of houses in both texts is being used to portray the individual inside. Robert and his straightforward father, Thaddeus, live in a building which is 'plain and classic' (p. 42), unlike the forbidding entrance to Professor Silverfish's house. In *Dr Jekyll and Mr Hyde*, students will easily be able to detect the difference in the abodes of Dr Jekyll and Mr Hyde, and consider what this reveals about them as characters. When Utterson visits Dr Jekyll in chapter 2, 'Search for Mr Hyde', his refinement and high class are evident in the portrayal of his house:

Round the corner from the by-street, there was a square of ancient, handsome houses, now for the most part decayed from their high estate and let in flats and chambers to all sorts and conditions of men: map-engravers, architects, shady lawyers, and the agents of obscure enterprises. One house, however, second from the corner, was still occupied entire; and at the door of this, which wore a great air of wealth and comfort, though it was now plunged in darkness except for the fan-light, Mr. Utterson stopped and knocked. A well-dressed, elderly servant opened the door.

(p. 62)

In contrast, Mr Hyde's house has been described above and even the door he is first seen disappearing into during chapter 1 seems disreputable:

> Two doors from one corner, on the left hand going east, the line was broken by the entry of a court; and just at that point, a certain sinister block of building thrust forward its gable on the street. It was two stories high; showed no window, nothing but a door on the lower story and a blind forehead of discoloured wall on the upper; and bore in every feature, the marks of prolonged and sordid negligence. The door, which was equipped with neither bell nor knocker, was blistered and distained. Tramps slouched into the recess and struck matches on the panels; children kept shop upon the steps; the schoolboy had tried his knife on the mouldings; and for close on a generation, no one had appeared to drive away these random visitors or to repair their ravages.
>
> (p. 49)

This is a great opportunity to explore some contextual details about the changes in London during this period, with the huge influx of people due to the industrialisation of society during the nineteenth century. If you are looking to move away from written assessment or work at this stage, consider setting your students a task of filming the setting of any of the scenes above. They can simply storyboard them, drawing the images or using cut-out pictures, or, if you're feeling more ambitious, ask them to create a mini film set in 3D. With the prevalence of smartphones, you might even want to ask them to create a short film using the setting or house fronts as an important detail, using establishing shots which fit the descriptions in the text.

WHY NOT CONSIDER . . .?

■ The city of London as a threatening and potentially dangerous character is a common trope in nineteenth-century literature. After reading the sections of *Cogheart* set in London, why not present your students with some other famous examples from the nineteenth century, and challenge them to assess the sort of city being portrayed? The opening chapter of Dickens' *Bleak House* (1853) is an iconic example, which uses the brilliant image of the fog and rawness of the afternoon as a striking beginning to the novel. Other Dickens novels set in London at the time include *Dombey and Son* (1848), *David Copperfield* (1850), *Our Mutual Friend* (1865) and *Oliver Twist* (1839). All have good film, radio or television adaptations for potential viewing to gain more of an understanding of life in London in the nineteenth century.

- Thackeray's *Vanity Fair* (1848) gives many hints about the corrupt nature of life in the capital, from the aptly named Great Gaunt Street residence of the lecherous Sir Pitt Crawley, to the return of Rawdon Crawley to the house in which he finds out about Becky's betrayal in the chapter 'A Rescue and a Catastrophe' which is surrounded by railings, suggesting the heartless nature of the resident inside.

- *Dracula* (1897) opens in London, with Jonathan Harker mentioning his trip to the British Museum, in which he was able to find out about Transylvania, suggesting to the reader that London is the centre of the civilised world, in contrast to the continent, where he mentions his train was an hour late. This can be a good opportunity to explore ideas about imperialism and colonialism, and the insistence that Britain was at the centre of the Empire and superior because of it.

The Ruby in the Smoke by Philip Pullman

The Ruby in the Smoke is a modern classic melodrama with a Victorian setting, which pursues the mystery of a highly prized jewel through the East End of London to the opium dens of China alongside the feisty female detective Sally Lockhart. The novel has been a firm favourite with Key Stage 3 readers for many years because of the fast-paced plot and complex, gripping narrative, and it is the perfect novel to read as preparation for tackling a more challenging nineteenth-century text at Key Stage 4. Pullman uses vocabulary such as mudlarks, hansom cab and box lock pistols, so the text is dripping with authentic nineteenth-century references, but unfamiliar vocabulary is also explained, making it suitable for less confident students. The setting and narrative make a perfect introduction to reading the Sherlock Holmes novel *The Sign of Four* by Arthur Conan Doyle (1890), and there are opportunities to explore other nineteenth-century detective novels, such as Wilkie Collins' *The Moonstone* (1868). Contextually, you might wish to guide students to consider what happened to young women like Sally Lockhart if they were left without a family and means to support themselves. The whole novel is rich in literary allusions and intertextuality, so aside from the great narrative, this makes it a perfect preparation to reading some of the longer nineteenth-century texts that it evokes.

Links to *The Sign of Four* by Arthur Conan Doyle and *The Moonstone* by Wilkie Collins

Aside from the period setting of both novels, and the fact that they are stories in which a mystery about a precious jewel or jewels are solved, studying the two together is a great way to enrich understanding of both, even if you only tackle them through short extracts. There are parallels in the narratives which are interesting, such as the Indian connection, the jewels and the mysterious death of a female character's father.

The Ruby in the Smoke opens with the arresting statement that Sally Lockhart 'within fifteen minutes . . . was going to kill a man' (p. 3). The manner of the man's death, of a heart attack after the shock of hearing the phrase 'The Seven Blessings', is always gripping to students and makes for a great beginning to the novel. Do we blame Sally? Or does this create even more sympathy for her character? A similar section from *The Sign of Four* can be found in chapter 4, 'The Story of the Bald-Headed Man', where Thaddeus Sholto relates the story of the death of both Captain Morstan and his father, Major John Sholto:

> "Early in 1882 my father received a letter from India which was a great shock to him. He nearly fainted at the breakfast-table when he opened it, and from that day he sickened to his death. What was in the letter we could never discover, but I could see as he held it that it was short and written in a scrawling hand. He had suffered for years from an enlarged spleen, but he now became rapidly worse, and towards the end of April we were informed that he was beyond all hope, and that he wished to make a last communication to us.
>
> "When we entered his room he was propped up with pillows and breathing heavily. He besought us to lock the door and to come upon either side of the bed. Then, grasping our hands, he made a remarkable statement to us, in a voice which was broken as much by emotion as by pain. I shall try and give it to you in his own very words.
>
> "'I have only one thing,' he said, 'which weighs upon my mind at this supreme moment. It is my treatment of poor Morstan's orphan. The cursed greed which has been my besetting sin through life has withheld from her the treasure, half at least of which should have been hers. And yet I have made no use of it myself, – so blind and foolish a thing is avarice. The mere feeling of possession has been so dear to me that I could not bear to share it with another. See that chaplet dipped with pearls beside the quinine-bottle. Even that I could not bear to part with, although I had got it out with the design of sending it to her. You, my sons, will give her a fair share of the Agra treasure. But send her nothing – not even the chaplet – until I am gone. After all, men have been as bad as this and have recovered.
>
> "'I will tell you how Morstan died,' he continued. 'He had suffered for years from a weak heart, but he concealed it from every one. I alone knew it. When in India, he and I, through a remarkable chain of circumstances, came into possession of a considerable treasure. I brought it over to England, and on the night of Morstan's arrival he came straight over here to claim his share.

He walked over from the station, and was admitted by my faithful Lal Chowdar, who is now dead. Morstan and I had a difference of opinion as to the division of the treasure, and we came to heated words. Morstan had sprung out of his chair in a paroxysm of anger, when he suddenly pressed his hand to his side, his face turned a dusky hue, and he fell backwards, cutting his head against the corner of the treasure-chest. When I stooped over him I found, to my horror, that he was dead.

"'For a long time I sat half distracted, wondering what I should do. My first impulse was, of course, to call for assistance; but I could not but recognize that there was every chance that I would be accused of his murder. His death at the moment of a quarrel, and the gash in his head, would be black against me. Again, an official inquiry could not be made without bringing out some facts about the treasure, which I was particularly anxious to keep secret. He had told me that no soul upon earth knew where he had gone. There seemed to be no necessity why any soul ever should know.

"'I was still pondering over the matter, when, looking up, I saw my servant, Lal Chowdar, in the doorway. He stole in and bolted the door behind him. "Do not fear, Sahib," he said. "No one need know that you have killed him. Let us hide him away, and who is the wiser?" "I did not kill him," said I. Lal Chowdar shook his head and smiled. "I heard it all, Sahib," said he. "I heard you quarrel, and I heard the blow. But my lips are sealed. All are asleep in the house. Let us put him away together." That was enough to decide me. If my own servant could not believe my innocence, how could I hope to make it good before twelve foolish tradesmen in a jury-box? Lal Chowdar and I disposed of the body that night, and within a few days the London papers were full of the mysterious disappearance of Captain Morstan. You will see from what I say that I can hardly be blamed in the matter.'"

(1966, pp. 36–38)

This is a great way to explore a number of issues with your students. Challenge them to think about the death of Mr Higgs versus the deaths of both Captain Morstan and Major Sholto. Who is to blame? And with the gradual sickening of Major Sholto after he receives the letter, what does this tell us about death in Victorian melodrama? Do they think that getting bad or worrying news via a letter is enough to cause someone's death, even if they have got the death of another person on their conscience? This is an excellent moment to think about setting either a diary entry for someone who feels responsible for the death of another person, or writing a dramatic monologue. Explore the different reactions to the same scenario now and in the nineteenth century. How important is the assumption of religious belief in the nineteenth century, and how does this impact on the reaction of the character?

WHY NOT CONSIDER . . .?

■ How realistic are the deaths through shock in both *The Ruby in the Smoke* and *The Sign of Four*? Why is melodrama such an important element in the novels?

■ London is so important in novels of this period. What creative visual work can you do around this idea?

■ Don't shy away from looking at other allusions to London mentioned earlier in the chapter as another basis for comparison. Making links between texts is so valuable for students.

■ Allow your students to explore ideas about identity and ethnicity, and how these have changed since the nineteenth century. Re-telling the narrative from the point of view of the minority in the story can be incredibly illuminating about colonial attitudes at the time.

■ Thinking about the roles available to women who had to earn their living can be very instructive, and using Sally Lockhart's situation is a great way to begin to explore the work of the Brontës, for example.

In both novels, London again takes on a starring role, creating a sense of verisimilitude and foreshadowing of the murky moral standards that the protagonists will face. In *The Sign of Four*, Dr Watson describes the scene as he and Holmes head out to begin to unravel the mystery presented by Mary Morstan:

It was a September evening, and not yet seven o'clock, but the day had been a dreary one, and a dense drizzly fog lay low upon the great city. Mud-colored clouds drooped sadly over the muddy streets. Down the Strand the lamps were but misty splotches of diffused light which threw a feeble circular glimmer upon the slimy pavement. The yellow glare from the shop-windows streamed out into the steamy, vaporous air, and threw a murky, shifting radiance across the crowded thoroughfare. There was, to my mind, something eerie and ghost-like in the endless procession of faces which flitted across these narrow bars of light, – sad faces and glad, haggard and merry. Like all human kind, they flitted from the gloom into the light, and so back into the gloom once more. I am not subject to impressions, but the dull, heavy evening, with the strange business upon which we were engaged, combined to make me nervous and depressed.

(p. 28)

As setting is so important in novels, it is definitely worth spending time on this, and there is scope for augmenting your work on *The Ruby in the Smoke* with an exploration of London in both novels. Setting a homework project, for example, on researching and presenting what London was like in the nineteenth century can be a great task to encourage a connection with a range of nineteenth-century texts.

Aside from setting, another area to consider is the representation of different classes and ethnicities of people in both novels. In *The Ruby in the Smoke*, we see Jim, who is ragged and dirty, very differently to the genteel Sally, but how is he presented to the reader? Are we supposed to admire his wiliness and intelligence even more because of his social disadvantage? And what about Lal Chowdar in the extract from chapter 4 of *The Sign of Four*? Task students to consider how he is portrayed in this extract, and what it might reveal to us about nineteenth-century attitudes to those who were not British, and particularly those of a different ethnicity. It is a great chance to build some AO3 awareness of attitudes of British people at the time towards race and explore ideas about colonialism that will provide further illumination later on in the story of *The Ruby in the Smoke*. This can often provide an excellent opportunity for students to do independent research and present their findings as a speaking and listening assessment.

These ideas can be explored further with Wilkie Collins' *The Moonstone*, where another missing jewel is at the centre of a mystery. Collins' story, often seen as the first detective novel, can be a good alternative to study alongside *The Ruby in the Smoke* if you would prefer to leave *The Sign of Four* untouched until GCSE. Again, there is a familiar crossover with the story of the hunt for a jewel, and the origins of the jewel linked to India. The novel's opening, which sees John Herncastle fighting for the British Army in India in the late 1790s, provides an excellent counterpoint to the beginning of Sally's story with the death of her mother in chapter 1, 'The Seven Blessings' during the section beginning, 'Sally's mother had died during the Indian Mutiny':

Let me now take you on to the day of the assault. My cousin and I were separated at the outset. I never saw him when we forded the river; when we planted the English flag in the first breach; when we crossed the ditch beyond; and, fighting every inch of our way, entered the town. It was only at dusk, when the place was ours, and after General Baird himself had found the dead body of Tippoo under a heap of the slain, that Herncastle and I met.

We were each attached to a party sent out by the general's orders to prevent the plunder and confusion which followed our conquest. The camp-followers committed deplorable excesses; and, worse still, the soldiers found their way, by a guarded door, into the treasury of the Palace, and loaded themselves with gold and jewels. It was in the court outside the treasury that my cousin and I met, to enforce the laws of discipline on our own soldiers. Herncastle's fiery temper had been, as I could plainly see, exasperated to a kind of frenzy by the terrible slaughter through which we had passed. He was very unfit, in my opinion, to perform the duty that had been entrusted to him.

There was riot and confusion enough in the treasury, but no violence that I saw. The men (if I may use such an expression) disgraced themselves good-humouredly. All sorts of rough jests and catchwords were bandied about among them; and the story of the Diamond turned up again unexpectedly, in the form of a mischievous joke. "Who's got the Moonstone?" was the rallying cry which perpetually caused the plundering, as soon as it was stopped in one place, to break out in another. While I was still vainly trying to establish order, I heard a frightful yelling on the other side of the courtyard, and at once ran towards the cries, in dread of finding some new outbreak of the pillage in that direction.

I got to an open door, and saw the bodies of two Indians (by their dress, as I guessed, officers of the palace) lying across the entrance, dead.

A cry inside hurried me into a room, which appeared to serve as an armoury. A third Indian, mortally wounded, was sinking at the feet of a man whose back was towards me. The man turned at the instant when I came in, and I saw John Herncastle, with a torch in one hand, and a dagger dripping with blood in the other. A stone, set like a pommel, in the end of the dagger's handle, flashed in the torchlight, as he turned on me, like a gleam of fire. The dying Indian sank to his knees, pointed to the dagger in Herncastle's hand, and said, in his native language – "The Moonstone will have its vengeance yet on you and yours!" He spoke those words, and fell dead on the floor.

Before I could stir in the matter, the men who had followed me across the courtyard crowded in. My cousin rushed to meet them, like a madman. "Clear the room!" he shouted to me, "and set a guard on the door!" The men fell back as he threw himself on them with his torch and his dagger. I put two sentinels of my own company, on whom I could rely, to keep the door. Through the remainder of the night, I saw no more of my cousin.

(1986, p. 36)

What does this extract, and the brief mention of Sally's mother's death, have in common? What do they suggest about India? Is there a difference in the attitude of the authors to the Indians, depending on when the novels are written? Again, push students to consider how these narratives reflect Britain at the heart of the Empire. How might they differ if they were written from the point of view of the Indian characters? This can be an illuminating and challenging exercise to undertake for students, encouraging them to see the Indian characters and settings treated with the same level of validity as the English ones. You could perhaps also get them to consider the narrative provided by the servant, Gabriel Betteredge, and his attitude to the Indians he encounters. How would this scene play out if the narrative were from the point of view of the foreign visitors? Does knowing the plot of the novel, especially the provenance of the jewel, change the emphasis of this scene when the perspective is changed?

Removing the narrator here can be a useful way to tackle the idea of whose perspective the story is being told from and how this affects the reaction to it. Give your students the section from *The Moonstone* below and in groups, challenge them to act out the scene. This can be done either formally, through the production of a script, or improvised with students allocated a character, then deciding amongst themselves how they wish to portray the story. When considering the whole story of *The Moonstone*, does this portrayal from the extract seem fair, or would they prefer to perform the narrative in a more balanced way?

Going round to the terrace, I found three mahogany-coloured Indians, in white linen frocks and trousers, looking up at the house.

The Indians, as I saw on looking closer, had small hand-drums slung in front of them. Behind them stood a little delicate-looking light-haired English boy carrying a bag. I judged the fellows to be strolling conjurors, and the boy with the bag to be carrying the tools of their trade. One of the three, who spoke English and who exhibited, I must own, the most elegant manners, presently informed me that my judgment was right. He requested permission to show his tricks in the presence of the lady of the house.

Now I am not a sour old man. I am generally all for amusement, and the last person in the world to distrust another person because he happens to be a few shades darker than myself. But the best of us have our weaknesses – and my weakness, when I know a family plate-basket to be out on a pantry-table, is to be instantly reminded of that basket by the sight of a strolling stranger whose manners are superior to my own. I accordingly informed the Indian that the lady of the house was out; and I warned him and his party off the premises. He made me a beautiful bow in return; and he and his party went off the premises. On my side, I returned to my beehive chair, and set myself down on the sunny side of the court, and fell (if the truth must be owned), not exactly into a sleep, but into the next best thing to it.

I was roused up by my daughter Penelope running out at me as if the house was on fire. What do you think she wanted? She wanted to have the three Indian jugglers instantly taken up; for this reason, namely, that they knew who was coming from London to visit us, and that they meant some mischief to Mr. Franklin Blake.

Mr. Franklin's name roused me. I opened my eyes, and made my girl explain herself.

It appeared that Penelope had just come from our lodge, where she had been having a gossip with the lodge-keeper's daughter. The two girls had seen the Indians pass out, after I had warned them off, followed by their little boy. Taking it into their heads that the boy was ill-used by the foreigners – for no reason that I could discover, except that he was pretty and delicate-looking – the two girls had stolen along the inner side of the hedge between us and the road, and had watched the proceedings of the foreigners on the outer side. Those proceedings resulted in the performance of the following extraordinary tricks.

They first looked up the road, and down the road, and made sure that they were alone. Then they all three faced about, and stared hard in the direction of our house. Then they jabbered and disputed in their own language, and looked at each other like men in doubt. Then they all turned to their little English boy, as if they expected HIM to help them. And then the chief Indian, who spoke English, said to the boy, "Hold out your hand."

On hearing those dreadful words, my daughter Penelope said she didn't know what prevented her heart from flying straight out of her. I thought privately that it might have been her stays. All I said, however, was, "You make my flesh creep." (NOTA BENE: Women like these little compliments.)

Well, when the Indian said, "Hold out your hand," the boy shrunk back, and shook his head, and said he didn't like it. The Indian, thereupon, asked him (not at all unkindly), whether he would like to be sent back to London, and left where they had found him, sleeping in an empty basket in a market – a hungry, ragged, and forsaken little boy. This, it seems, ended the difficulty. The little chap unwillingly held out his hand. Upon that, the Indian took a bottle from his bosom, and poured out of it some black stuff, like ink, into the palm of the boy's hand. The Indian – first touching the boy's head, and making signs over it in the air – then said, "Look." The boy became quite stiff, and stood like a statue, looking into the ink in the hollow of his hand.

(So far, it seemed to me to be juggling, accompanied by a foolish waste of ink. I was beginning to feel sleepy again, when Penelope's next words stirred me up.)

The Indians looked up the road and down the road once more – and then the chief Indian said these words to the boy; "See the English gentleman from foreign parts."

The boy said, "I see him."

The Indian said, "Is it on the road to this house, and on no other, that the English gentleman will travel to-day?"

The boy said, "It is on the road to this house, and on no other, that the English gentleman will travel to-day." The Indian put a second question – after waiting a little first. He said: "Has the English gentleman got It about him?"

The boy answered – also, after waiting a little first – "Yes."

The Indian put a third and last question: "Will the English gentleman come here, as he has promised to come, at the close of day?"

The boy said, "I can't tell."

The Indian asked why.

The boy said, "I am tired. The mist rises in my head, and puzzles me. I can see no more to-day."

With that the catechism ended. The chief Indian said something in his own language to the other two, pointing to the boy, and pointing towards the town, in which (as we afterwards discovered) they were lodged. He then, after making more signs on the boy's head, blew on his forehead, and so woke him up with a start. After that, they all went on their way towards the town, and the girls saw them no more.

(pp. 48–51)

After the performances, ask your class about why they feel these portrayals were this way, and what this adds to our understanding of attitudes during the nineteenth century. Helping your students address these ideas will allow them to form a much greater understanding of the differences between their lives and the lives of the people they read about in works both written and set in the nineteenth century.

Links to *Jane Eyre* by Charlotte Brontë and *Agnes Grey* by Anne Brontë

Although Sally Lockhart finds her first job as an accountant with Frederick Garland, the spectre of her lack of employment opportunities hangs over the start of *The Ruby in the Smoke* from the first time the reader encounters Mrs Rees, who points out to her in chapter 1 that 'even the modest role of governess is barred to you' (p. 13). Sally herself 'shuddered' at the thought of becoming a governess (p. 74).

Both *Agnes Grey* and *Jane Eyre* deal with young women who, like Sally Lockhart, are forced to seek employment: Agnes because of the poverty of her clergyman father, and Jane because she is an orphan like Sally with an aunt that is unsympathetic and vicious to her ward. Think about beginning your lesson with a challenge for your students to consider: what were the usual options for a young woman of the same class as Sally? Considering the strict gender roles and the class assumptions of the nineteenth century, ask them to list the possible future for a sixteen-year-old female in the nineteenth century.

Now split your class into pairs, with one half of the pair being the careers advisor and the other a sixteen-year-old girl like Sally Lockhart, looking for employment. You could get your students to research what a normal education would be like for girls of different social classes at the time and ask them to write a CV, looking at the subjects they would study, as well as the accomplishments they would be expected to have. This excerpt from chapter 10 of *Jane Eyre* might be a useful place for them to begin, especially if you point out that Jane has been educated in this way to be useful, rather than to ready her for the social whirl of the marriage market or 'coming out':

"I dare say you are clever, though," continued Bessie, by way of solace. "What can you do? Can you play on the piano?"

"A little." There was one in the room; Bessie went and opened it, and then asked me to sit down and give her a tune: I played a waltz or two, and she was charmed.

"The Miss Reeds could not play as well!" said she exultingly. "I always said you would surpass them in learning: and can you draw?" "That is one of my paintings over the chimney-piece." It was a landscape in water colours, of which I had made a present to the superintendent, in acknowledgment of her obliging mediation with the committee on my behalf, and which she had framed and glazed. "Well, that is beautiful, Miss Jane! It is as fine a picture as any Miss Reed's drawing-master could paint, let alone the young ladies themselves, who could not come near it: and have you learnt French?"

"Yes, Bessie, I can both read it and speak it."

"And you can work on muslin and canvas?"

"I can."

"Oh, you are quite a lady, Miss Jane! I knew you would be: you will get on whether your relations notice you or not."

(1949, p. 66)

The careers advisors could research jobs open to girls, as well as the duties expected of them and the pay offered for each role. As an extension, get them to contrast this with the paths open to boys of the same social class, such as a commission in the Army, a living as a clergyman and even more adventurous choices such as the law, an investor in the railways or a journalist. How do they feel about the different roles available to each gender?

And what about life as a governess for girls in the nineteenth century? Ask your students to read the excerpt below from *Agnes Grey* and think about how they would advertise her job, being honest. Task them with producing either a poster or a job advert for a newspaper that sets out the duties and challenges the job presents.

My task of instruction and surveillance, instead of becoming easier as my charges and I got better accustomed to each other, became more arduous as their characters unfolded. The name of governess, I soon found, was a mere mockery as applied to me: my pupils had no more notion of obedience than a wild, unbroken colt. The habitual fear of their father's peevish temper, and the dread of the punishments he was wont to inflict when irritated, kept them generally within bounds in his immediate presence. The girls, too, had some fear of their mother's anger; and the boy might occasionally be bribed to do as she bid him by the hope of reward; but I had no rewards to offer; and as for punishments, I was given to understand, the parents reserved that privilege to themselves; and yet they expected me to keep my pupils in order. Other children might be guided by the fear of anger and the desire of approbation; but neither the one nor the other had any effect upon these.

The task of instruction was as arduous for the body as the mind. I had to run after my pupils to catch them, to carry or drag them to the table, and often forcibly to hold them there till the lesson was done. Tom I frequently put into a corner, seating myself before him in a chair, with a book which contained the little task that must be said or read, before he was released, in my hand. He was not strong enough to push both me and the chair away, so he would stand twisting his body and face into the most grotesque and singular contortions – laughable, no doubt, to an unconcerned spectator, but not to me – and uttering loud yells and doleful outcries, intended to represent weeping but wholly without the accompaniment of tears. I knew this was done solely for the purpose of annoying me; and, therefore, however I might inwardly tremble with impatience and irritation, I manfully strove to suppress all visible signs of molestation, and affected to sit with calm indifference, waiting till it should please him to cease this pastime, and prepare for a run in the garden, by casting his eye on the book and reading or repeating the few words he was required to say. Sometimes he was determined to do his writing badly; and I had to hold his hand to prevent him from purposely blotting or disfiguring the paper. Frequently I threatened that, if he did not do better, he should have another line: then he would stubbornly refuse to write this line; and I, to save my word, had finally to resort to the expedient of holding his fingers upon the pen, and forcibly drawing his hand up and down, till, in spite of his resistance, the line was in some sort completed.

Yet Tom was by no means the most unmanageable of my pupils: sometimes, to my great joy, he would have the sense to see that his wisest policy was to finish his tasks, and go out and amuse himself till I and his sisters came to join him; which frequently was not at all, for Mary Ann seldom followed his example in this particular: she apparently preferred rolling on the floor to any other amusement: down she would drop like a leaden weight; and when I, with great difficulty, had succeeded in rooting her thence, I had still to hold her up with one arm, while with the other I held the book from which she was to read or spell her lesson. As the dead weight of the big girl of six became too heavy for one arm to bear, I transferred it to the other; or, if both were weary of the burden, I carried her into a corner, and told her she might come out when she should find the use of her feet, and stand up: but she generally preferred lying there like a log till dinner or tea-time, when, as I could not deprive her of her meals, she must be liberated, and would come crawling out with a grin of triumph on her round, red face. Often she would stubbornly refuse to pronounce some particular word in her lesson; and now I regret the lost labour I have had in striving to conquer her obstinacy. If I had passed it over as a matter of no consequence, it would have been better for both parties, than vainly striving to overcome it as I did; but I thought it my absolute duty to crush this vicious tendency in the bud: and so it was, if I could have done it;

and had my powers been less limited, I might have enforced obedience; but, as it was, it was a trial of strength between her and me, in which she generally came off victorious; and every victory served to encourage and strengthen her for a future contest. In vain I argued, coaxed, entreated, threatened, scolded; in vain I kept her in from play, or, if obliged to take her out, refused to play with her, or to speak kindly or have anything to do with her; in vain I tried to set before her the advantages of doing as she was bid, and being loved, and kindly treated in consequence, and the disadvantages of persisting in her absurd perversity. Sometimes, when she would ask me to do something for her, I would answer, – 'Yes, I will, Mary Ann, if you will only say that word. Come! you'd better say it at once, and have no more trouble about it.'

'No.'

'Then, of course, I can do nothing for you.'

(1922, pp. 412–415)

Jane Eyre also becomes a governess. Like Sally Lockhart, she is an orphan and although she is very much a heroine of her time in comparison to some of the very modern elements of Pullman's contemporarily written Sally, they share the same sense of indomitability and pluck. After reading Jane's advertisement in the local paper to obtain a position as a governess, ask them to create a similar advert that would advertise their own skills:

"A young lady accustomed to tuition" (had I not been a teacher two years?) "is desirous of meeting with a situation in a private family where the children are under fourteen" (I thought that as I was barely eighteen, it would not do to undertake the guidance of pupils nearer my own age). "She is qualified to teach the usual branches of a good English education, together with French, Drawing, and Music" (in those days, reader, this now narrow catalogue of accomplishments, would have been held tolerably comprehensive). "Address, J.E., Post-office, Lowton, —shire."

(p. 62)

Ask them to annotate how their skills differ from those Jane Eyre has, and which skills are most useful nowadays.

Jane Eyre's experience as a governess contrasts with Agnes Grey's and it could also be worthwhile exploring a small extract such as the one below from chapter 11, which paints a far more relaxed and pleasurable experience of being a governess:

After breakfast, Adèle and I withdrew to the library, which room, it appears, Mr. Rochester had directed should be used as the schoolroom. Most of the books were locked up behind glass doors; but there was one bookcase left open containing everything that could be needed in the way of elementary works, and several volumes of light literature, poetry, biography, travels, a few romances, &c. I suppose he had considered that these were all the governess would require for her private perusal; and, indeed, they contented me amply for the present; compared with the scanty pickings I had now and then been able to glean at Lowood, they seemed to offer an abundant harvest of entertainment and information. In this room, too, there was a cabinet piano, quite new and of superior tone; also an easel for painting and a pair of globes.

I found my pupil sufficiently docile, though disinclined to apply: she had not been used to regular occupation of any kind. I felt it would be injudicious to confine her too much at first; so, when I had talked to her a great deal, and got her to learn a little, and when the morning had advanced to noon, I allowed her to return to her nurse. I then proposed to occupy myself till dinner-time in drawing some little sketches for her use.

(p. 75)

This is a great opportunity for dramatisation, particularly for students who you may wish to push to greater understanding through comparisons. Set a task for students to act out this first morning of Jane Eyre with her pupil, perhaps with another student providing a commentary on her thoughts and feelings. Now contrast this with a dramatisation of the experiences of Agnes Grey. Which do they think would be more usual? You could even set some research homework so that students can look at the lives and experiences of the Brontës, and think about why each wrote about being a governess in the way that they did. They can present their ideas in a speaking and listening format so that the whole class can benefit from the sharing of ideas.

Hopefully, this exploration of how you can use neo-Victorian texts to challenge and stimulate students whilst giving them a gentle introduction to the literature and history of the nineteenth century will have inspired you to give this technique a try. By taking away the fear of both the setting and writing from the nineteenth century, you will be helping your students to approach this aspect of the curriculum with enthusiasm and confidence. Remember, we are definitely not advocating avoiding authentic nineteenth-century texts altogether, so don't shy away from introducing an extract from a nineteenth-century fiction or non-fiction text you feel particular enthusiasm for. However, if you feel the neo-Victorian approach isn't for you, or if you are restricted by having to teach existing text choices that you do not have the authority to change, some more ideas for teaching nineteenth-century texts to younger students are below.

Additional ideas for engaging younger students in nineteenth-century texts

1. Many classic nineteenth-century novels have been adapted into plays. Performing scenes from these can be a wonderful way for students to become familiar with the stories of their source novels, as well as nineteenth-century

vocabulary, without the pressure of having to formally study the original texts. They will be learning vocabulary without even realising it as they memorise lines, and a productive scheme of work could be built around the plot, characters and the context of the original novel once students have worked on the play. Extracts from the source novel can be used to develop understanding, and those students who need more challenge could be encouraged to read the whole book as an enrichment activity. If you want to teach the entire source novel, spending a week or so on allowing students to rehearse and then perform key scenes from a play adaptation before tackling the novel itself can reap rewards in increasing confidence and enthusiasm for a text that may have been too daunting without this gentle introduction. A good place to look for suitable plays is the Collins Drama series, which consists of plays that have been purposely written for schools. Their publications include titles such as *Dr Jekyll and Mr Hyde*, *Dracula* and *The Hound of the Baskervilles*. The Royal Shakespeare Company also has some fantastic adaptations of traditional novels such as *A Christmas Carol*, *Peter Pan* and *A Tale of Two Cities*.

2. Carefully chosen nineteenth-century newspaper articles, speeches, diaries or travelogues are a brilliant resource to engage younger students. They are a rich source of vocabulary and syntax to show them how nineteenth-century language is constructed differently, but their short length and easy-to-understand subject matter make the linguistic challenges much more manageable. Using non-fiction is a fantastic way to incorporate nineteenth-century texts within an existing curriculum without needing to create a specific 'nineteenth-century' unit of work, as thematically chosen texts can be slotted in alongside contemporary ones. Units on travel, adventure or detective writing can be livened up by a Victorian explorer's account of the jungle, or a sensational newspaper article on the Jack the Ripper murders. Over time, frequent exposure to nineteenth-century vocabulary and syntax in this non-threatening and often entertaining way will make the eventual reading of a novel from the period so much less daunting. *See Chapter 7 for resources to help you with this.*

3. Poetry can work very well as a soft introduction to nineteenth-century literature. If you feel your younger students aren't quite ready for a whole nineteenth-century novel, then a unit on carefully chosen nineteenth-century poetry can help to familiarise them with language features and context while keeping their reading material short and accessible. Thinking about key contextual themes from the nineteenth century could help you to structure your poetry choices: Tennyson's 'The Charge of the Light Brigade' could be used alongside newspaper articles about the Crimean War and extracts from Florence Nightingale's letters to look at Victorian attitudes to war, and Matthew Arnold's haunting 'Dover Beach' could be used alongside extracts from Darwin's *On the Origin of Species* and *Kilvert's Diary* to explore science and religion. *See Chapter 3 for more ideas on teaching nineteenth-century poetry.*

4. Don't be afraid to teach nineteenth-century children's books at secondary level. A common approach to nineteenth-century literature at Key Stage 3 is to teach short stories, and while this can work well, the assumption that just because something is shorter will make it easier doesn't always follow. Short stories can be just as dense and complex as novels, and so this approach to introducing nineteenth-century texts to younger students can end up resulting in just as much difficulty as studying a whole book. If you don't want to teach a neo-Victorian novel, and don't feel that your students can manage an adult novel from the period, then going back to childhood favourites that students are already familiar with can prove a fantastic way to introduce the study of nineteenth-century literature in a non-threatening way. The richness of children's literature from the period is often underappreciated, with many fascinating avenues beneath the surface open to be explored once you engage with their context. Reading *The Secret Garden* by Frances Hodgson Burnett through the lens of empire (the novel begins in India) and attitudes towards health, nature, religion and mortality can allow a deceptively simple story to be explored on a deep level, introducing students to key nineteenth-century concerns and vocabulary while allowing them to read a story that is simple and easy to grasp. *A Little Princess*, *Peter Pan*, *Alice's Adventures in Wonderland*, *Moonfleet*, *The Railway Children* (some of these are technically Edwardian but only just!) and *Treasure Island* can also provide much contextual richness while remaining entertaining and easy to follow.

RECOMMENDED NEO-VICTORIAN NOVELS FOR KEY STAGE 3 STUDENTS

Aiken, Joan, *The Wolves of Willoughby Chase* (London: Vintage, 2012)

Bunzl, Peter, *Cogheart* (London: Usborne, 2016)

Carroll, Emma, *Strange Star* (London: Faber and Faber, 2016)

Hill, Susan, *The Woman in Black* (we would not recommend this for below Year 9 as it is scary!) (London: Vintage, 1998)

McCaughrean, Geraldine, *The Middle of Nowhere* (London: Usborne, 2014)

Priestley, Chris, *Uncle Montague's Tales of Terror* (London: Bloomsbury, 2016)

Pullman, Philip, *The Ruby in the Smoke* (London: Scholastic, 2015)

Williams, Eloise, *Gaslight* (London: Firefly Press, 2016)

5 Tackling long novels

REFLECTION ZONE

■ What is your immediate reaction to the idea of teaching long novels?

■ Would you choose to teach a novel you thought was not as interesting/enriching as another choice, merely because it was shorter?

■ What assumptions do you have about the impact of the length of a novel on students' response to it?

■ If you feel reluctance about teaching a long novel, why is this? Is it mainly about your ability to teach long novels, or your students' ability to read them?

■ What would help you to feel more positively about teaching a long novel if you don't feel so already?

Take some time to think about the questions in the reflection zone above before reading this chapter. Many teachers have a strong response to the idea of teaching long novels, and we think it is helpful for you to unpack your feelings about this before considering the ideas for teaching them that we discuss over the next few pages. If your immediate response is a negative one, take a moment to consider why this might be, and assess whether your feelings are related to your perception of your teaching abilities, your anticipation of your students' response or perhaps a mixture of both. Thinking about your preconceptions and prejudices, and where you have got these from, can help to unravel anxieties around an area of teaching that many teachers don't actually have much, if any, experience of, given that we are not often called upon to teach long novels. We find that much fear of teaching longer novels comes from the anticipation of an assumed response from students, or from war stories told by colleagues who warn you off texts before you've had a chance to try them for yourself. If this rings true for you, we really encourage you to come to this chapter with an open mind and be willing to look at teaching longer novels from a different perspective.

At Key Stages 4 and 5, undoubtedly one of the most daunting tasks an English teacher faces is the increased length of the novels on examination syllabi, with no corresponding increase in the amount of time allotted to teach them. The challenge of an unwieldy text with several hundred pages to wade through, a wide cast of characters and multiple narrative threads is often considered beyond the abilities and enthusiasm of many students. With the looming pressure of an exam, it is understandable that many teachers want to choose a novel they perceive will make the process of correctly remembering the sequence of events, memorising quotations or quickly identifying the most pertinent examples to answer an essay question as easy as possible. There is also the undeniable reality that many students, who in a large number of schools are not given a choice about taking English Literature for GCSE, are not enthusiastic readers and would rather clean the school toilets than read *Great Expectations*. We know full well that getting such students to even read the book, let alone feel any connection to the characters or events, can be a real uphill struggle. However, this should not and does not make teaching a long novel an impossible task. Making length or perceived easiness the deciding factor in which texts we teach restricts and narrows the curriculum we offer our students and prevents them from gaining resilience and independence. We believe that the length of a novel should never make it 'unteachable' or inaccessible, and we hope that this chapter will provide you with a range of ideas and approaches to give you the confidence and enthusiasm to broaden the types of novels you are willing to teach.

As with any of the approaches we explore in this book, there will be those that work for some teachers and some students better than others, and you will probably find that you need to go through a process of trial and error before you hit on the right approach for your class. Differentiation is often key in forming your approach. However, we would encourage you not to go into the teaching of long novels with the anticipation that your students will feel negatively towards the book, or that they will notice a difference between the study of longer and shorter novels. If you make an issue of the novel's length, they will too; if you don't, then they won't. It is perfectly natural that as they grow older and progress towards more challenging external exams, they will have to read more complex texts, and the longer length of novels is part and parcel of that complexity. As such, normalising the teaching and studying of long novels is a key factor in their accessibility.

We don't believe there is any particular 'right' way to teach a long novel, and nor do we think there is a particular formula that will guarantee success. However, all of the suggested approaches we explore in this chapter begin with the assumption that you will not be able to read the book in class with your students in a way that you most probably would with a shorter novel. This is the key difference, in our minds, between teaching longer and shorter novels, and the challenge of ensuring students who are reading independently are able to access and interrogate the text in as much detail as they would had you read it with them in class has been our priority when considering how best to go about the teaching process.

Getting started: the planning stage

When teaching a shorter novel, it can often be easier to plan on a more short-term basis, working chapter by chapter, and analysing each one in turn. This allows students to know each chapter well, to sequence the plot effectively and to look at how themes, motifs, events, context and imagery are being built up over the course of the novel. With a longer novel, this chapter-by-chapter approach has to be abandoned due to the obvious time restrictions involved, and as such, we find it best to have a detailed lesson-by-lesson plan of the whole course of study drawn up before we begin teaching. An example of how this plan might look, for the teaching of Jane Austen's *Mansfield Park*, is included in the appendices at the end of the book. This type of detailed planning will allow you to think through the key areas of the novel that need to be addressed, in which order you want to approach them, and to identify major sections of the book to focus on when looking at those areas. This also means that you can direct students towards particular chapters or passages in advance, allowing them to do more focused and purposeful reading at home.

Taking away the chapter-by-chapter approach to teaching a novel can make a lot of teachers feel totally out of their depth and unsure how to structure their scheme of work. The temptation is to maintain a broadly chronological approach to the novel, and simply bunch chapters together rather than doing individual chapters at a time, but we find this leads to a quite limited exploration of a long novel and prevents students from making connections between different sections of the book. Breaking out of the tyranny of a chronological approach is actually a very liberating experience and allows students to develop a more holistic view of the novel, and the ability to range across the text when giving examples rather than sticking to particular sections they may know better than others.

As such, we find the most productive way to teach long novels is to approach them from an overarching perspective rather than trying to analyse chapters in depth. We start with ensuring the students can sequence the plot, identify the characters and understand the major messages of the story, before looking at general context so that they can appreciate the background of the novel and have a loose understanding of major contemporary issues they should be considering when thinking about the events and characters. We then move on to looking at character development, structure and setting, before looking in detail at themes and more specific areas of context relating to these. Interwoven within this structure are opportunities for students to practise close textual analysis and essay writing, as well as pursue individual research on aspects of the novel. Every novel will have different areas of interest to explore, and some may require more time spent on one area than another, but this type of loose novel-teaching structure, coupled with students doing a substantial amount of reading at home, makes it perfectly possible to teach a 500-page novel thoroughly in as little as six weeks. It is a different type of teaching, and does rely on students being disciplined at home, but the rewards of approaching a novel in this more thematic way are considerable, allowing for much more wide-ranging conversation and debate within lessons than a chapter-by-chapter teaching method affords.

Structuring students' reading

Depending on the novel, your students and the time of year when you are teaching the novel (i.e. if students have just had a holiday during which they can read the book, or not), you may want to direct your students to read the whole novel in one go, or you may want to break it down into smaller sections and tackle each one at a time in class before the students read the next section. Personally we prefer the students to have read the whole novel in one go so that all in-class discussions can refer to the entire story, and there is no risk of any keen students ruining the plot for those who haven't yet finished, but you will be best placed to judge which is the most appropriate approach for your students. There is more guidance on this, including timings, in Chapter 2.

Whichever amount of reading you are asking your students to do at home, the fact that they are doing this reading unsupervised and will be expected to come to lessons able to discuss what they have read in a meaningful way will necessitate a certain amount of support from you to ensure their reading is productive and purposeful.

First of all, we would recommend not just letting your students loose on the text by themselves; before asking them to go home and read it, give them some background. Some brief information about the author and when the text was written, an introduction to the main gist of the plot (without revealing anything to spoil it, of course!), and themes and ideas to be looking out for can be invaluable for those students who are likely to get lost. If they have a vague idea of what the novel is about before starting to read, they will be much more likely to be able to follow the plot from the start and so become more engaged in the story. Obviously students have plenty of websites they can use to help them with decoding classic novels, but a little bit of input from you first should prevent them from needing to rely on external sources just to get through the book in the first place. Something you can do is create a bookmark for each student that has a Twitter-style plot summary (without the ending!), a timeline of events, an interesting image related to the text and key quotes etc. that they can use to refer back to while reading – these are very quick to create and students love them!

Once they get started, we find it invaluable to give students a framework to record their reading. A chart for writing chapter summaries, character information and key quotations is easy to draw up, and can be made as detailed as you like, depending on the length of the novel and the purpose for which you wish to use it. For a very long novel, such as *Great Expectations* or *Jane Eyre*, individual chapter summaries are a huge task and not particularly necessary, so you may find asking students to do a summary of groups of chapters more effective. Filling out a summary chart of this nature allows students to record key events and key quotations, and also have a timeline of the plot. Having this overview to hand in lessons for quick reference and for the writing of essays is so useful, and also ensures that students have to really think about what they're reading and assess what is important for them to record and what isn't. In any novel there are always peripheral characters or more insignificant events that take place, and it is vital that students can start to differentiate between what is essential to the plot and what isn't. An example, again from *Mansfield Park*, of what a filled-in chart might look like is included at the end of the book to give you an idea of what students could be asked to record. Obviously some students will find this more of a challenge than others, and this is a task you can differentiate accordingly by filling in some sections for students in advance where necessary.

Giving students a framework for thinking about what they are reading is vital for ensuring they are engaging fully with the text and can come to lessons prepared to take part in discussion. You may wish to take an enquiry-based learning approach and encourage students to devise their own research questions to answer while they read the text, give them a list of questions you have come up with to think about while they are reading, direct them to particular chapters or passages for closer reading work, or ask them to identify a key quotation or moment to share in class. We find that having students read the entire novel and complete the summary sheet before the study of the novel starts in class, followed by re-reading sections with questions to answer in preparation for specific lessons, tends to be the most productive approach in ensuring students know the text well and can think about it independently on a deeper level. However, this is just our preference and is by no means the only way to approach independent reading.

For students who are finding the novel quite challenging, or who struggle to motivate themselves to do their reading, you may find it useful to pair them up with a classmate to form reading partners, or create small reading groups. If you have enough time, this paired or group reading could be done partly in class if you are finding students aren't doing it diligently enough at home. You might find that having some form of 'check-in' process to ensure that students have been reading is useful; a quick 'pop quiz' at the beginning of lessons on the chapter/s covered at home, mini extract analyses from one of the chapters read at home as a starter activity, 'who said that?' quote quizzes, etc., to create an engaged and even competitive class environment where students know they can't get away with not reading.

A method that can really encourage reluctant readers is setting a challenge or puzzle for each section of reading. When you are preparing the novel for teaching, identify an item of interest, such as an intriguing usage of language or structure, the repetition of a particular symbol or motif, a significant detail that might easily be overlooked, etc., and ask students to come to the lesson with what they think the answer to the challenge question is, with a prize for the best answer. For competitive students, this can really propel them to read with more enthusiasm, and also to read more closely, which is the most important aim of independent reading. This works particularly well when you ensure all students have the same edition of the text as you can set questions such as, 'what word on pages 21, 26 and 29 is repeated and what significance does this have?'.

On a practical level, with a longer novel, you will be doing a lot of jumping around between sections of the book during lessons. As such, we find it invaluable to insist that all students, if buying their own copies, buy exactly the same edition. If you are able to facilitate this, it will make your life much easier. We think it is also a good idea to source a reliable scholarly edition with an introduction and notes that will give students support with understanding more obscure contextual references within the text when reading at home. Some nineteenth-century texts also have large sections of foreign-language conversation or quotation, particularly in French and German, and so having an edition that provides a translation for students who are not *au fait* with these languages is important.

Making it visual

We tend to find that students respond much better to texts when they can vividly imagine the setting and the characters. With a long novel, there is a greater likelihood of the novelist having used a wide variety of settings and a large cast of characters, which can be confusing for some students – and teachers! In order to bring the novel to life in a visual way, we like to create wall displays that depict the setting and characters, and feature prominent objects and other visual cues from the text, as well as key quotations. These displays work especially well when they are dynamic, with students adding details and quotations over time to reflect their growing knowledge and understanding. Having a wall of the classroom dedicated to your novel can be a wonderful way to engage students, who can decide amongst themselves which elements of the novel they want to depict, and then unleash their creativity in drawing, painting or using collage to create the world of the novel as they see it. Characters can be added – if there is a film version of the novel, it can be useful to use cut-outs of the actors' faces – and moved around in different lessons to show physical movement or changing alliances between characters, as can objects. Important quotations can be added to the wall, either as speech bubbles if spoken, or on pieces of paper if said in the narrative voice. All of these images and words act as useful prompts for students, and gradually imprint the world of the novel into their minds. Some students even enjoy getting up and moving characters or objects around while sharing their thoughts about the novel, in order to visually represent their thought processes as they speak. If you do not have a dedicated classroom, this display can be created on a roll of lining or poster paper that can be rolled up after each lesson and easily transported between class-rooms as required.

Displaying a timeline of the novel's main events can be another useful tool to aid students who are struggling to remember the plot or place events in their correct order. Agreeing together what those main events are before collectively writing them up on a large piece of poster paper, or creating a washing line with string and pegs and individually writing events on pieces of paper that can then be pegged up and moved around according to students' ideas about what should go where, is a really useful way of securing students' understanding as well as acting as an aide-memoire during lessons. If using a washing line, this can be additionally used in lessons as a tool in debates or when planning essays; the pegged-up events can be reordered by priority within the plot, grouped by theme or character, etc. However you decide to do this activity, the resources are easy to pack up and carry around with you should you not have a permanent classroom base.

Another visual activity students often enjoy is using large rolls of lining paper to create life-size character outlines, which they then fill with quotations and adjectives about that character, before sticking them up on the wall. This can be a wonderful tool to have to hand during lessons when students are stuck for ideas or want to see clearly similarities and differences between characters, and is also an excellent revision activity – students can compete in teams to see who can fill a character outline with quotations first.

Using films

Too often, we feel that films are used as a treat for having slogged through the novel, and by watching them after having studied the book, they are wasted as a teaching tool. We firmly believe that a good film adaptation can be a vital tool in the teaching of long novels, and is certainly something that is integral to our teach-ing. Showing students a film or, if available, a stage adaptation not only brings the novel to life, but also enables them to see a range of different interpretative foci, especially when there is more than one version to draw upon. A director's decision to highlight particular themes, to utilise the setting in a certain way or to cut out specific scenes or characters all provide grounds for debate and shine a light on different areas of the text and their significance (or lack thereof). Many adaptations borrow heavily from the original novel, too, and the choice to retain specific lines of text can also be useful in helping students to identify key moments of dialogue within the novel that they can memorise for use in essays.

An integrative approach to the use of film within a scheme of work does take a fair bit of planning. You will need to watch the film version a couple of times beforehand, and identify key scenes you particularly want to highlight to students. You can then use the film in a number of different ways. A simple approach will be finding scenes that are particularly relevant to a theme, contextual point or character, and taking clips out of the film using a media player or other software and embedding them into a PowerPoint slide. When comparing and contrasting different adaptations, you can easily embed two or more clips into the same PowerPoint slide. These short clips can then form the basis of discussion or be used to illustrate and bring to life particular moments in the novel you wish to explore further. (If you are not sure how to do this, a step-by-step guide is available online here: http://blog.trainerswarehouse.com/wp-content/uploads/2011/05/Movies-in-Powerpoint-March-2010.pdf.)

Taking screenshots of key scenes and building a sequenced contact sheet of images is also an excellent way to use a film adaptation. This gives students a quick at-a-glance guide to key moments in the film, and these contact sheets can be cut up into individual scene cards, which can also be used for a variety of activities. A pack of scene cards can function as a way for students to make all sorts of connections between different elements of the novel. You can ask them to choose the five key scenes in the film, choose the scene(s) that best represent a particular character or theme, choose three random cards and explain the significance of these representative scenes to each other and the novel as a whole, etc. Careful choice of still images is key to the success of these activities, and students very much enjoy using them to consolidate their learning. We tend to mostly use the cards as quick starter or plenary activities, and the more students know the film, the quicker and more creative they become with identifying scenes and discussing their significance. A top tip is to laminate the cards, as then they will be reusable for years to come!

Watching the whole film at the beginning of the teaching process is, we think, incredibly useful for students. We never show the students the film before they have read the whole novel, as we do feel that is counter-intuitive, but once read, we feel strongly that a good film version being shown alongside the study of the novel can only add a richness to the learning experience. One caveat we would give, however, is that the adaptation must be chosen carefully. Some adaptations vary so widely from the novel that their use is actually a hindrance rather than a help, as the altered events confuse students and can lead them to write essays filled with references to things that only take place in the film and not the actual novel. If the novel you are studying only has a widely differing adaptation, you may want to consider just using clips of particularly appropriate scenes rather than the whole film.

Developing independence

Key to the studying of long novels is encouraging students to step up and take more of a lead over their own learning, rather than relying on you to give them the answers. As we have already discussed, they will have to do a substantial amount of independent reading and thinking outside of lessons in order to get the book read, and this independence should also filter through into your classroom practice.

'Flipped learning', where you give students the topic of the next lesson or sequence of lessons in advance and ask them to do some research and come prepared with material to contribute in class, is a fantastic way of giving students independence and of fostering debate. At Key Stage 5, where use of critical material is much more important, giving students critical essays to read and think about at home before studying them in class can lead to some brilliant discussions. Giving students the ability to come to the lesson already having knowledge and wanting to share it takes the onus of knowledge sharing from you and makes the classroom a much more democratic space. You can lead and guide the debates that come out of students' independent learning, but by empowering students to become the experts in their own line of enquiry, you engage them in the novel and its context much more fully and allow them to develop the ability to both analyse and evaluate a text independently, as well as construct a reasoned, evidenced argument to defend their views.

With long novels, there is far more scope for students to develop more original lines of thinking and to highlight areas of the story that speak to them. Encouraging students to present on the elements of the book they find most interesting, surprising, challenging or significant can be a wonderful way to develop critical skills alongside allowing them to be exposed to a range of different interpretations that you may choose to take further in subsequent lessons. Adopting an enquiry-based approach here, where students come up with their own research questions to answer, can have brilliant results, with students becoming much more engaged and intrigued by the text once they are given the responsibility of finding out something about it that matters to them.

Developing independence is very much about developing students' individual voices, and encouraging debate within your classroom is key to this. The more thematic approach to teaching long novels lends itself naturally to a more debate-focused classroom, and we think it is vital that wherever possible, you should allow students to talk through ideas and share them, to take a standpoint on an issue, to hear the views of others as to why their standpoint may differ, and to look at opposing viewpoints and evaluate which one they think has most value. This can be done at the beginning of lessons, allowing students to consider their feelings about a topic before you have studied it in depth together, and then revisiting the debate at the end of the lesson to see whether their opinion has changed now they have more information to base it upon. You can also use this as a way of developing students' essay-writing skills. Giving students essay-style questions to debate orally starts them on the process of formulating ideas and justifying arguments without the pressure of having to produce a long piece of written work. The more they get used to listening to the arguments of others, finding ways to add to, develop and challenge the comments of their peers, and locating specific textual evidence to support their views, the easier they will find it to move from talking through their ideas to writing those ideas down. Coming up with a range of ways to answer an essay question together purely through discussion can often be the most productive and enjoyable lessons, provided that everyone is given the opportunity to speak, and students are encouraged to make good notes to record their ideas as they go along. A good way of structuring these types of discussions is to pose a question and then draw a line on the board, with one end being 'completely disagree' and the other being 'completely agree'. Students then write their name on a post-it note and come and stick it on the line according to their personal viewpoint; you can then choose particular students to justify their place on the line, drawing students in to debate with one another, and then at the end of the lesson, ask students who think their mind has changed to come and move their post-it notes to reflect their new opinion. This can be quite a revealing exercise, and is a brilliant way for students to learn from one another and develop fresh perspectives to explore in their written work.

Socratic discussion is a fabulous way to develop independence in older learners and can be done as a whole class or in smaller groups, though smaller groups do tend to work better at ensuring everyone has a chance to speak. Key to all Socratic discussion is preparation of the text beforehand, which lends itself well to long novels, where students do so much work at home. Discussions of this nature can be incredibly helpful to consolidate ideas that come out of independent reading and enable students to test out ideas and learn from one another without having to take a risk in front of you or the whole class. There are plenty of online guides available to demonstrate the type of question structures that are most useful to stimulate conversation in a Socratic discussion, and as students become more comfortable, they can lead their own discussions and question one another quite effortlessly without your intervention, leading to much more interrogative and introspective thinking. You can use Socratic discussion as a tool for essay preparation, as a starter activity to stimulate ideas about a particular area of the text before the main teaching activity or as a basis for a group presentation activity. To add complexity, you can ask students to come up with their own topics and questions, or if you feel students need more guidance, you can set the parameters of the discussion in advance by providing some questions or key areas of text to look at.

A final tip for encouraging independence is to allow students to come up with their own essay questions, or to write several different essay questions and have students pick one out of a hat. With most students writing completely individual essays, you will therefore prevent them relying too much on peer support, and also encourage them to go down their own lines of individual enquiry. Reading out students' essays in class or allowing students to read each other's essays as part of a feedback session then becomes a way for them to amass a huge array of ideas about the novel as they are being exposed to so many different readings and approaches to the text at once. This also makes it much more interesting for you to mark a range of different essays rather than slogging through thirty identikit responses!

Summary

We hope that this chapter has shown you that teaching a long novel does not have to be a daunting task, and offers students a wonderful opportunity to challenge themselves and develop vital independent learning skills. By placing the onus on students to do much of the work, the learning experience becomes much more democratic and allows students to have a greater role in the direction of their lessons. Careful advanced planning and the use of creative visual aids, film and discussion activities help to create a rich and varied curriculum that allows students to deeply engage with and understand the novel they are studying just as well as they would a shorter text, while also building vital analytical and evaluative skills they can apply across all areas of their English studies. We really encourage you to give it a try!

6 Teaching nineteenth-century non-fiction

(continued)

Nineteenth-century non-fiction can be used in the classroom in so many different ways; as contextual information to support the teaching of fiction, as the basis for teaching persuasive writing techniques, as a stimulus for creative writing and drama tasks, as a point of comparison when looking at contemporary non-fiction, as a source for developing vocabulary and grammar skills – the list is endless! The bigger the bank of resources you build up, the more ways in which you'll find space for slotting nineteenth-century non-fiction into your lessons. The more frequently you use these resources, the more familiar with nineteenth-century language usage your students will become, demystifying it for them and enabling them to approach older texts with ever-increasing confidence.

Nineteenth-century non-fiction: a summary of its forms

The explosion of print culture in the nineteenth century is a phenomenon difficult for us to imagine today. From a handful of newspapers at the beginning of the century, by 1900, the array of magazines and newspapers available for readers of all backgrounds and interests numbered in the tens of thousands. The increase in leisure time amongst the middle classes, and the central importance of the home to middle-class life, was partly responsible for this, as was the rise in literacy and the development of investigative journalism, alongside the general improvement in technology and reduction in costs involved in mass-producing the written word.

Rather than the dry and factual newspaper reports of the early century, by the end of the Victorian era, newspapers were full of sensational accounts of murders and crimes, and many were fully illustrated, offering a tantalising glimpse of famous personages and exotic places. Newspaper sellers became a feature of city life, and newspaper lending clubs and libraries were set up for those who couldn't afford to buy their own copies. The increasing literacy of the working classes after the establishment of mandatory elementary education meant that many more people had access to the news, and newspapers began to diversify and specialise in order to meet the needs of an increasingly varied audience of readers.

However, it was the magazine (also referred to as a periodical) that really took hold in the latter half of the nineteenth century; published on a weekly, fortnightly or monthly basis, and often sold at Christmas in a bound edition of the whole year's publications, they were enormously popular. They contained a variety of articles on all manner of different topics, with, for example, essays on science, religion, book reviews, poetry, extracts from novels, commentary on political debates and tours of a new art gallery all rubbing alongside each other in the same issue. The Victorians did not compartmentalise knowledge in the way we do now, and there was a certain expectation that readers should and would be interested in a huge range of topics. Some magazines were very specific in their subject matter, of course, and tailored the content of their articles towards a particular audience, such as those catering for professions or for mothers, children, etc., but the major publications, such as *All the Year Round*, *The Strand* and *Cornhill Magazine*, were, to a modern eye, surprisingly polymathic in their choice of content.

The Victorian magazines that were most well known were those owned by publishing houses or authors, and which published, in serial form, the novels of the nineteenth century's most famous writers. Charles Dickens was the proprietor of two magazines, *Household Words* and *All the Year Round*, in which he first published his books on a month-by-month basis, writing each chapter in time for the next edition. The structure and style of Dickens' novels is much easier to understand and appreciate when you consider that he was under pressure to produce a certain number of words for each edition and provide a cliff-hanger at the end of every chapter. The same can be said for other serial writers such as Wilkie Collins and Arthur Conan Doyle. The publication of novels in magazines was a major reason why they were so popular; it might have taken up to two years to finish a whole book, but letters from the period suggest that readers loved the tension of the wait to find out the ending, and actively discussed and debated the characters and events with family and friends as they waited for the conclusion: much like we do with Netflix series these days! Moreover, new novels were incredibly expensive to buy throughout most of the nineteenth century, and most people relied on lending libraries to be able to read the latest releases. Having access to cheap fiction in the form of a magazine was, therefore, greatly appreciated by the burgeoning middle classes.

Finding non-fiction resources

Unfortunately, despite the fact that many nineteenth-century magazines and newspapers have been digitised, it is very difficult to gain access to the databases of these digitised copies outside of higher education institutions. If you do have access to a university library's online resource catalogue, you should be able to search the **Nineteenth-Century Newspapers** and **Nineteenth-Century Periodicals** databases and find original articles to print. If you are not able to do this, the **British Library's Newspaper Archive** is a reasonably priced searchable digital database of thousands of digitised newspapers, and it may be worth asking your school to invest in a membership, especially if other departments, such as Humanities, think they could find it useful, or if you could share a login across schools if you are part of a trust or alliance.

Outside of these databases, there are still plenty of free online sources of non-fiction (and fiction) texts where you can easily find extracts to use in the classroom. The **British Library** website is a great resource, and their Discovering Literature series of essays contains links to scans of original texts that you can print. For some of the major sensational events of the nineteenth century, such as the Jack the Ripper murders, there are websites created by enthusiasts with transcripts of newspaper articles, which can be easily edited for use in the classroom. The **Victoria and Albert Museum** also has several microsites dedicated to Victorian events, such as the Great Exhibition, the Boer War and the Crimean War, accompanied by photographs of original magazine covers and articles. Other major museum websites have similar microsites on Victorian topics, and most now have searchable online archives that can provide images of interesting non-fiction resources. A fantastic site that is free to use and constantly being updated is **archive.org**, which provides scanned-in copies of original texts that are located in libraries and archives around the world. There is plenty of non-fiction available, such as travel journals, diaries, letters, religious sermons, manuals and advice guides, and you can find all manner of nineteenth-century treasure on there. **Gutenberg.org** is another similar site that provides transcribed copies of out-of-print books, in a variety of different readable and printable formats, completely free of charge.

So, even though it may not be easy to find copies of the original publications, it is certainly not impossible, and a brief search online for nineteenth-century newspaper articles or a particular event or person you are interested in usually turns up something that can be used in the classroom. Keep an eye out also when you're in second-hand book or antique shops; often non-fiction books such as nineteenth-century volumes of autobiographies, letters and diaries are incredibly cheap, as are mouldering copies of Victorian newspapers. Having a few of these in your resource pile can be so helpful when you want to quickly photocopy a short extract to look at in class.

Using non-fiction as a way in to texts

Non-fiction can be a fantastic way to introduce the themes and context of a nineteenth-century novel. Looking at a range of historical sources such as newspaper articles, contemporary reviews of texts, advertising materials and transcripts of speeches before starting to read a novel for the first time gives students the opportunity to fully understand the world in which the book was written and appreciate the types of concerns the author is likely wishing to discuss within the text. This makes it much easier for them to spot contextual references and make more sophisticated connections between events and characters and wider themes and ideas once they start reading.

You don't necessarily need to spend a huge amount of time on this; two or three lessons of looking at non-fiction sources would be ample to give students a good contextual grounding. In addition, if this is the first time your students will have been expected to read a novel of this age, looking at non-fiction from the period before they start reading will give them a gentle introduction to linguistic and grammatical features of nineteenth-century English that should make any unfamiliar language features in the novel they are about to study much more accessible to them.

So, how should you choose appropriate non-fiction to share with your students? First of all, identify when the novel was written and when it is set; these could be different and it would be useful for you to think about why the novelist may have set their story during an earlier decade. How are they using the events of this earlier period to reflect on their current society? What parallels are they drawing? Use Chapter 1 to help you here; the timeline will allow you to pinpoint significant events and you can research these further if you feel any event not described in detail is of significance. If the novel is set at the time when it was written, you will want to consider whether the novelist makes specific reference to contemporary events, or avoids mentioning them. If they do avoid mentioning them, can you find evidence of them beneath the surface?

Once you've identified some events, people, discoveries or controversies that might be worth exploring further, you can start to look for some resources that will allow your students to learn about them while also being able to make the connection between this context and the novel they are studying. Think carefully about what you want the students to get from the non-fiction resources; do you want them to just understand the facts of an event, or do you want them to be able to interrogate the different attitudes towards a particular debate? Are there some key voices or perspectives they should hear, or will any newspaper article do? Once you've narrowed down your requirements, you can start hunting for the resources you will need.

For an example of what types of resources you could use to help students contextualise a novel, we'll use Charlotte Brontë's *Jane Eyre*. *Jane Eyre* was first published as a novel in three volumes in 1847. Something students often don't realise is that it was originally published with a subtitle – *Jane Eyre: An Autobiography*. This automatically tells us that the novel is not set in 1847, as it is told from the adult Jane Eyre's perspective and starts during her childhood. There is actually a fair amount of speculation amongst critics regarding when the events of the novel are supposed to have taken place, as unlike Emily Brontë, who meticulously dated the events of *Wuthering Heights*, Charlotte Brontë only gives one definitive pointer to a date: the fact that St. John gives Jane a copy of a 'new publication', Walter Scott's 1808 poem *Marmion*. For some time this was considered to be a reliable dating mechanism, but recent criticism from a variety of sources has raised questions due to the anachronisms in the novel. For example, John Sutherland in his book *Can Jane Eyre Be Happy? More Puzzles in Classic Fiction* (1997) points out that Adèle comes from France to England in a steam ship, which weren't in use for Channel crossings until the 1820s. He suggests that the key to the mystery is in Brontë's choice of language: she says 'new publication', not 'new poem'. As such he claims that the book in question is the new edition of *Marmion* published in 1834, not the original publication of 1808, which places the events of the adult Jane Eyre's life about a decade before Charlotte Brontë was writing. Even despite this convincing assessment, we can't be absolutely sure as Charlotte Brontë is deliberately vague about dates and there are still elements of the novel that don't quite add up with the 1834 dating. However, proceeding on the assumption that we're looking at a novel set during the 1820s–30s and written during the 1840s, we have a couple of key historical points to work with.

What we do know for certain is that the novel is not set during the reign of Queen Victoria and so is, technically, a historical novel. This is actually very typical of mid-nineteenth-century novels, most of which deal with events two decades or so removed from their own contemporary period, and are referred to as novels of the 'recent past'. Therefore, Brontë makes no reference to trains and all the journeys that take place are via carriage, and there is no telegraph system, either: students might like to think about how the use of the carriage rather than the train, and letters rather than telegraphs to deliver urgent news, contributes to the plot. The 1820s and 30s were characterised by agitation for political and social reform, as well as the abolition of slavery. Jane Eyre regularly refers to slavery in her narrative, using it as a point of comparison when considering her role in both the Reed and Rochester households. Many postcolonial critics have also discussed the fact that Bertha Mason Rochester comes from the West Indies, a site of many slave plantations, and that this could be an interesting allusion of Brontë's to the treatment of women as slaves by men.

Brontë was writing the novel during the 'hungry forties'; a time of economic depression and terrible famine across Europe – particularly Ireland – as a consequence of the failure of the potato crop. There was also growing restlessness at the inequality between rich and poor, and hunger and urban poverty mixed with the growth of new political ideas and agitation for reform contributed to a huge amount of tension, which ultimately erupted in the year of revolutions across mainland Europe in 1848. Charlotte Brontë lived in an area of the country that was heavily affected by rural poverty and she saw first-hand the desperate situations many people were living in, as her father, the local vicar, was often appealed to for help.

How do these contexts help us to decode the novel, and what sources could you use to communicate these to your students? Firstly, we could think about *Jane Eyre* from a feminist perspective, and explore the links between slavery and the treatment of women, and slavery and the role of the governess. Secondly, we could look at the text as a revolutionary, more Marxist story, with the punishment of Rochester the landowner for his sinful treatment of his 'slave' Bertha, and the way in which Jane Eyre rails against the blindness of the upper classes to the suffering of the poor in her depiction of the carelessness of Blanche Ingram and Rochester's other high-society friends.

So, if we want to think about these issues, we'll need to find some sources about slavery and the abolition movement, something to do with governesses and something to do with class conflict.

SOURCE 1: SLAVERY

From the *Leeds Mercury*, Saturday 25 May 1833

ABOLITION OF SLAVERY

In a county, which, to its lasting honour, has done so much to effect the liberation of the slave, every information that relates to that subject at this crisis of a fifty years' struggle, must be highly interesting. Having been placed during the present week in a situation to see and to observe the progress of this absorbing measure, we feel a pleasure too deep for any language to express, in saying that the clouds which seemed to darken one part of this hemisphere are gradually dispersing, and we trust will finally and entirely disappear. The Societies in London formed to effect the Abolition of Slavery, we mean the Anti-Slavery Society and the Agency Society, aided by the highly important services of the Delegates sent from various parts of the kingdom, are exerting a degree of zeal, and displaying a discriminating intelligence, which reflect honour upon themselves, and which cannot fail to produce essential benefit to the cause...

The friends of Negro Emancipation are, as far as we can observe, acting with the utmost cordiality, and one sentiment pervades all of their proceedings in London – a sentiment of gratitude for the immense benefits which the cause of liberty will obtain from the plan developed by Mr Stanley, in the House of Commons, on the 14th inst., mixed with deep disappointment that a measure so excellent in many of its parts should be deformed with a radical vice, which tends so much to detract from its intrinsic merits. To secure all the benefits of this plan, and to purify it from its great vice, is now the object of every friend to the negro, in every part of the United Kingdom. And here the question arises, how is this object to be best effected? We believe, by the Delegates from the country in London, and by the London Societies, supported by the voice of the constituent body in every part of the united empire, expressed through the legitimate organ of a well constituted and freely chosen Parliament. Amongst the members of the present Administration, every man, we believe, is an abolitionist, some more and some less ardent in their support; but they are all ready to end the most favourable ear to the cause of liberty.

This article was written about the Abolition of Slavery Act of 1833, which abolished the slave trade in the British Empire (the *state* of slavery had been abolished in 1807, but it was still possible to *trade* slaves), but did not immediately free slaves; they were expected to wait six years to be freed as part of an 'apprenticeship' programme. This caused an outcry amongst abolitionists who wanted slaves freed immediately, and it is this 'vice' that the article refers to.

The *Leeds Mercury* was a newspaper we know the Brontës had a subscription to, and Charlotte was living at home in 1833. Therefore she would almost definitely have read this article and have been fully up to date with the debates surrounding the Abolition of Slavery Act at the time when it was taking place. Obviously when she was writing *Jane Eyre*, this was some ten years in the past, but for Jane Eyre the character, presumably living during the 1830s, this would have been current events.

What might students take from this article, and apply to *Jane Eyre*? Who is a slave in the novel? What are they a slave to? How might Brontë be using the plight of slaves in the British Empire to draw parallels with her characters living in England?

SOURCE 2: GOVERNESS ADVERTISEMENTS

From *The Morning Post*, 25 March 1837

'GOVERNESS – A young Lady, aged 24, wishes for a Situation as GOVERNESS; she is competent to teach English and French (having been educated in France), flower painting, with the harp and guitar, if the young Ladies have masters*; she has been brought up in strict religious principles; would prefer junior pupils, and has no objection to the country.'

'GOVERNESS – A Lady, who has had 14 years' experience in tuition, and has resided many years on the Continent, desires a RE-ENGAGEMENT as RESIDENT or DAILY GOVERNESS; she lived four years in one family, and has finished the education of several pupils; she instructs in English, French, Geography, History, Writing, and Music, without masters*, and can give the most satisfactory references.'

*masters refers to professional male music teachers who were employed to teach pupils separately from the governess

The Morning Post was a national newspaper and its governess advertisements featured on a page advertising a host of other miscellaneous items such as clothes, books, etc. that the average reader might be interested in. Jane Eyre writes an advertisement for herself and sends it off to a newspaper when she decides it is time for her to leave Lowood; Mrs Fairfax reads it and responds, offering Jane employment at Thornfield.

The role of the governess was an incredibly difficult one, fraught with class anxiety that was felt keenly by both governess and employer. A governess was expected to be of good background and education, and by default was therefore invariably middle class. Usually they were the daughters of clergymen, or professionals, and occasionally of landowning gentlemen fallen on hard times. For most, their path would have been mapped out from a young age, as the education required to become a governess would need to be prepared for by providing appropriate schooling in the skills required. For middle-class fathers with limited financial means, it was a prudent course of action to ensure their daughters would be able to secure respectable employment and provide for themselves once they had reached young adulthood. School teaching or governessing were the only acceptable professions for a middle-class, unmarried woman without private means, and with most upper- and upper-middle-class families choosing to educate their children at home, they were in high demand. However, a governess was neither servant nor equal, and was not allowed to mix socially with the servants or with her employers, leaving her in a lonely and often miserable position. Often intelligent, cultured and used to a comfortable home, governesses frequently found themselves trapped in rural locations, in spartan quarters, with no intellectual equals for company, and forced to control spoiled children who had power over them as their social superiors. As the century drew on, the governess problem became a point of much discussion and collective anxiety, and her plight became a common feature of novels.

Charlotte Brontë was a governess and teacher for several years, so she was well aware of the tribulations of the teaching profession for middle-class women. Charlotte's depiction of Jane's positive experience of being a governess is shown to be highly unusual when we hear Blanche Ingram and her mother discussing Jane with disdain, and relating the terrible way in which the Ingrams treated their governesses when they were children. Jane is constantly aware of her lowly position and is surprised by the favourable treatment she receives from Rochester; understanding how governesses were usually treated is vital for students reading *Jane Eyre*, as this unlocks a huge amount of meaning within the text when considering Jane and Rochester's relationship.

What can be gained from reading these governess advertisements, then? Well, first of all, students can appreciate the knowledge governesses were required to have, as well as the knowledge they were expected to give. Governesses mainly taught girls, as most boys would have gone to school by the age of ten. What skills and knowledge were girls being taught, and why? What types of roles did this education equip them for? What does this tell us about the role of women in nineteenth-century Britain, and what does Brontë have to say about this in the novel?

Students can also consider the way in which the prospective governesses write about themselves, and what they say they would prefer in their new situation. How do they present themselves and what features do they clearly think will be important to employers? Who do they think has the most power: the governesses, or the employers? And what significance can they draw from the fact that the governess advertisements are on the same page as advertisements for clothes, books and other household items? What might this tell us about class in Victorian society, and what is Brontë using the role of the governess to say?

SOURCE 3: QUEEN VICTORIA'S DIARY

Saturday 13 August 1842

Mama [Victoria, Duchess of Kent] joined us at breakfast, after which we went out walking with Papa [Ernest I, Prince Albert's father] and showed him the Rockery and all our improvements, the Kennels, &c.

It is a pleasure to show him anything, as he is so easily pleased, and takes such interest in everything, being so worthy of all. We then drove to Frogmore, where we walked about with Mama.

Read and wrote, when I came home.

Both Children appeared at our luncheon. Papa thinks the Baby, so like Albert.

The accounts from Manchester are dreadful – such disturbances, as also in some other parts, near Sheffield, &c

Drove out with Papa & Alexandrine, Albert & Ernest, &c, riding. We drove to the Stud & showed Papa all the horses. We also looked at the Hunters. I never felt anything like the heat.

On returning, found Sir Robert Peel [the Prime Minister] & some of the other Ministers had come down for a Council, & I found a box from Sir Robert, in my room, in which he wrote that 3 Magistrates had come to Town this morning, giving an account of the bad state of things in Manchester, and expressing their anxiety that something should be done before the 16th inst, the anniversary of a great mob fight, which took place there in 1819 [the Peterloo Massacre], and some great explosion is dreaded for that day.

We saw Sir Robert Peel, and he said that the whole thing had arisen from Anti-Corn Law people & Chartists having closed their Mills, telling the people they might play for a while, by which they immediately jumped at the conclusion they were to cease working. They marched in procession into Manchester, where they forced all the other Manufacturers to join them. It is the horrid system of agitation pursued by several Members, which is responsible for this serious agitation. They might be prosecuted if it could be brought home to them. It is proposed to send a Battalion of the Guards tonight, by rail, to Manchester.

Then, held a Council, which was only for the Proclamation. The Duke of Wellington kissed hands, on being made Commander in Chief.

Ran up to the Nursery for a moment. Dinner the same as yesterday. We went a moment on the Terrace afterwards. Such tremendous heat, – quite wonderful!

Monday 22 August 1842

Dear "Pussy" [Victoria, Princess Royal; eldest daughter of the Queen] better, though still weak & languid, but otherwise there is nothing wrong with her.

I drove out with the Duchess of Norfolk, Albert riding, & the Ladies following. I found the Duchess very agreeable, & full of information. Papa, who had been to Kew, with Charles, met us, as we came home. It was again so hot.

Heard from Sir J. Graham that

> "the reports from the North are better this morning than on any former day, since the commencement of these disturbances. Some symptoms of disturbance have appeared at Merthyr Tydvil, but a demonstration of prompt military assistance has checked an outburst. In Birmingham the Civil Authorities have taken active measures to disperse a Chartist Meeting, which was summoned to assemble today, and ample military means are provided to aid the Civil Power in case of necessity. The Meeting summoned for this day at noon on Kensington Common, has been a signal failure. All the work-men, in the Metropolis are fully employed & although this evening an attempt to hold a Chartist Meeting, is anticipated, Sir J. Graham has made arrange-ments for dispersing it, & he is confident that the Public Peace will not be seriously disturbed."

We went up to the Nursery & found "Pussy" much better, and quite merry, in her bath.

Besides Mama, & Charles [the Queen's half-brother], & c, Lord Melbourne, and Lord and Lady Beauvale, (who stay till the 25th) dined.

Lord Melbourne is looking so well. Lady Beauvale is very pleasing, and speaks English, perfectly well; her German is very Prussian or Berlin German.

Talked to Lord Melbourne of our journey to Scotland, and he said that it would never do, not to go – it would have such a very bad effect, and that the late King's not going to the City, had had a deplorable effect. Unless anything very alarming or urgent, were to present us, we ought to carry out our project. He also, was glad to hear that the riots were better.

Queen Victoria's diaries and letters offer a glimpse of upper-class attitudes towards the working classes during the nineteenth century. In many ways Queen Victoria was a very sympathetic and compassionate woman, and it would be wrong to suggest that she had no feeling for the suffering of her people. However, she was very reliant on the advice given to her by older statesmen in the early years of her reign, who naturally presented a dim view of those agitating for change.

These two diary entries talk about Chartist activity in the summer of 1842, Chartism being a working-class campaign to reform the electoral system and allow working-class men to have a vote and a voice in government. The Chartists did a very good job of frightening the Establishment with their threat of riots and violence, but the reality was that they failed to garner enough support from working-class communities and the movement gradually petered out with little concrete success to report. It would take until 1867 to achieve the kinds of reform the Chartists were seeking.

What have these diary entries got to tell us about class conflict in the 1840s? The interest here actually lies in what Queen Victoria *doesn't* say. Encourage students to look at what the Queen writes about her day and the types of activities she enjoys, and then what she says about the Chartists. Does she seem to understand what they want, or show any sympathy for them? How much time does she spend talking about them versus the time she spends talking about the leisurely activities of her day? How might students apply this attitude of unthinking privilege to the attitudes of the Ingrams in *Jane Eyre*? And what about Rochester? It is tempting to read Rochester as a straightforward Byronic hero, but how does he treat the working classes? His torturing of Jane over Blanche Ingram could be looked at from a Marxist perspective as a way of Brontë exploring how the upper classes unthinkingly exploit the working classes. The enormous gulf shown in the diaries of Queen Victoria between the leisured lives of the rich and the gruelling, grinding poverty experienced by the poor can give students a much clearer idea of why there was so much discontent during the 'hungry forties'. *Jane Eyre* might not mention the Chartists specifically, but class conflict is very much alive beneath the surface of the text.

WHY NOT CONSIDER . . .?

Using nineteenth-century images, too. Posters, cartoons, illustrations and postcards used alongside non-fiction texts on the same topics and themes can be a great way of making complex contextual ideas clear. They can also be used as part of mix-and-match games — matching the article to the picture, the headline/caption to the picture, the theme or event to the picture; as stimulus for creative writing, and as materials for students to create posters/collages. A quick online search should yield plenty of images for you to use, from original advertising campaigns to satirical newspaper cartoons. Images from *The Illustrated London News* and *Punch* in particular are very easy to find online.

Using non-fiction to teach nineteenth-century vocabulary and syntax

Being able to understand nineteenth-century texts requires more than just appreciating the historical context of the period in which they were written. The vocabulary used by nineteenth-century writers, and their uses of grammar and sentence structure, can often be an impenetrable barrier for students. Nineteenth-century writing tends to feature very long sentences with multiple clauses, and a plethora of adjectives. Word order is often different, as are vocabulary choices, all of which can make students feel a bit like they're reading a foreign language. As such, some students will really need to have their confidence built up before they are asked to tackle an entire novel from the period, and a great way to do this is through the study of short, entertaining non-fiction texts that allow them to identify nineteenth-century language features quickly and easily. Over time, through looking at manageable pieces of non-fiction, they can build up a bank of commonly used vocabulary and become used to the rhythm and structure of sentences. Then, when they start to read fiction texts, they will be able to apply this existing knowledge, making the experience so much easier, and hopefully more pleasurable.

How you structure this type of learning process will depend on how you want to integrate nineteenth-century non-fiction into your curriculum. If you're planning on doing an entire unit on nineteenth-century non-fiction, you could choose particular pieces of non-fiction to highlight different language features and work on one language feature at a time. If you want to incorporate nineteenth-century texts into a unit of work on non-fiction that mainly focuses on contemporary writing, you may want to look at just a couple of nineteenth-century texts and draw as much from these as possible in one go. If you're going to use the method of introducing students to a novel through non-fiction first, then you might want to just spend a lesson looking at the texts through the lens of their linguistic construction before you start talking about them from a contextual perspective. Whichever way you do it, remember to be realistic about how much students can take on board in one go. Choose your articles carefully and provide summaries and glossaries wherever possible to smooth the process and enable your students to focus on what's important.

So, what should you be looking to guide your students towards when it comes to teaching them about the differences between nineteenth-century language usage and contemporary language usage? Let's look at an article to help us start to build a checklist.

'THE PLUMSTEAD GHOST' FROM *THE ILLUSTRATED POLICE NEWS*, 6 NOVEMBER 1897

In October 1897, many people saw a 'ghost' *flitting* about near St James's Church and school, Plumstead. Sensitive little girls had fainted when the white spectre approached them; some were still in bed, said the *Daily News*, suffering from **nervous exhaustion**. A timid **schoolmaster** had been frightened out of his wits when the 'Plumstead Ghost' suddenly grabbed hold of him from behind and shouted 'Boo-hah!' at the top of its voice. An old couple visiting the churchyard received a similar shock when the ghost *hailed* them from a tree, making use of the same *uncouth* outcry.

When another schoolmaster was taking an evening walk, he heard rustling in the hedges nearby, and a shout of 'Boo-hah!' He had brought with him a large Newfoundland dog, which he set on the spectre. Since the master distinctly heard the ghost give a yelp when the dog's fangs made contact with its *buttocks*, he became convinced that the Plumstead Ghost was **flesh and blood**. He spoke to both masters and schoolboys, asking them not to be fearful, but to teach the ghost **a hard lesson** if they came across it.

The *rowdy* schoolboys decided to do just that. <u>One evening, after scouts had reported that the ghost was at large, a troop of schoolboys, a hundred strong, stormed the churchyard</u>. Shouting and yahooing, they pelted the ghost with stones, but without scoring any hits on the *absconding* spectre. Instead, their missiles broke some valuable stained glass. Pursued by the Newfoundland dog, the ghost was seen to disappear into the hedges.

The schoolboys had been so rowdy that the police arrested two of the ringleaders and brought them to Woolwich, but after the masters had explained the extraordinary circumstances of their riot, they were both discharged. The evening after, the Plumstead Ghost was seen in the grounds of Mr J R Jolly. *Arrayed* in white *attire*, and wearing some kind of *grotesque* mask, the spectre was sitting in a tree, shouting its usual 'Boo-hah!' to frighten some female domestics. Mr Jolly was not at all amused: he sent for the police and the ghost was arrested. It turned out that the spectre's white *garb* had been torn, and his buttocks badly bruised, from his two encounters with the fierce Newfoundland dog. He turned out to be a local engineer. He was placed under restraint in an asylum, and the Plumstead Ghost was laid to rest.

Antiquated vocabulary – there are a fair few examples of interesting, antiquated vocabulary in this article that may prove a stumbling block for some students. You could approach this sort of problem in different ways; ask students to highlight words they don't know as they read the article, and then get them to use the dictionary to look up the words themselves, or pre-highlight and gloss words you assume they won't know. Depending on how much time you have and what skills you want the students to develop, you can choose the method that best suits you. Students can then start to make a list of useful nineteenth-century words in a separate book, or on a website such as Quizlet or vocabulary.com, where you can create a class list of words that students are tested on regularly. Encourage them to use these words in their speech and in their own writing, getting them to the point where these are not 'nineteenth-century words' but simply fantastic words to use!

Antiquated phrases/terminology – this article uses a number of phrases and terms that are no longer in common usage today. While the meaning of these isn't difficult for students to divine if they look at the context, they are interesting turns of phrase to remember when wanting to write their own nineteenth-century texts in order to insert an authentic touch.

Use of multiple clauses – nineteenth-century sentences tend to be much longer than modern-day ones, with multiple clauses and far more description. There's no definitive reason why this was the case, but it may well be that because of the lack of visual culture in nineteenth-century society, written language was more descriptive to allow people to imagine scenes more fully. Students should be encouraged to break down these clauses and work out which are the main and which the subordinate, in order to be able to identify the actual point of the sentence amidst what is often a lot of unnecessary description. Again, if you are getting them to produce their own nineteenth-century texts – an activity we would highly recommend to really cement their understanding of nineteenth-century language – then getting them to copy these longer sentence structures that often start with subordinate clauses will help them to not only develop the sophistication of their writing, but also decode the meaning of nineteenth-century sentences more quickly.

Another feature of nineteenth-century language usage worth noting, and not featured in the above article, is **syntactic inversion**. This is worth pointing out to students as an interesting quirk that can again add authenticity to their own writing. It very much creates the often overblown, hyperbolic nature of nineteenth-century prose that can come across as being excessively sentimental to the contemporary reader. Syntactic inversion usually consists of the inversion of the pronoun and verb, such as 'it was too late, said he, to send a letter; the last post was surely gone', but can also be seen in the inversion of the verb before the subject, such as 'weary were they as they laid their heads down to rest', or 'Came the rain in such sheets just at that moment that the walk had to be put off for another day'. Do be careful, however, to emphasise to students that they shouldn't use inverted syntax too liberally throughout a piece of writing, otherwise it will sound ridiculous!

WHY NOT CONSIDER . . .?

As a way of furthering students' understanding of language change, giving them a nineteenth-century newspaper article and a contemporary newspaper article on the same topic, and asking them to compare and contrast the styles of writing. They may be surprised by

(continued)

(continued)
how much is the same, but they should also be able to highlight differences that will enable them to add to their appreciation of how nineteenth-century language usage was different to today.

Using nineteenth-century non-fiction as a creative stimulus

The huge range of nineteenth-century non-fiction available, on all manner of topics, means that it should be possible for you to find an example to suit any subject you are working on. Rather than automatically going to a current newspaper or magazine to find an article, travel piece, celebrity interview, etc., to give students an engaging stimulus to respond to, why not use a nineteenth-century equivalent? The more you use nineteenth-century non-fiction, the more you are familiarising students with the vocabulary and grammatical structures of the period, as well as developing their understanding of nineteenth-century historical context, all of which is going to help them enormously when they come to studying nineteenth-century novels and poetry.

Chapter 7 provides a variety of non-fiction resources arranged by theme, along with ideas for how you can use each one in the classroom. There are endless ways of being creative: from getting students to write diary entries and letters in the voices of famous Victorians, to conducting interviews, holding murder trials and putting on plays, nineteenth-century non-fiction can provide a jumping-off point for any number of exciting and stimulating activities that introduce students of all ages to the language of the period in a non-threatening way. Why not experiment and see what fun you can have?

Summary

We hope that this chapter has shown you how useful non-fiction resources from the nineteenth century can be in teaching students across all stages of secondary education. From bringing the historical context of novels to life, to teaching students how to write using nineteenth-century vocabulary, they are a wonderful tool that adds variety to your teaching and opens students' eyes to a world that, in reality, wasn't much different to our own. The short length and often salacious content of Victorian newspaper articles are a gift when needing to engage reluctant students, and tackling nineteenth-century language in much smaller amounts means that students can build their confidence gradually. Our aim has been to encourage you to be creative and use non-fiction in ways you may not have thought of doing before: using the ideas here in conjunction with the bank of resources in Chapter 7 should, we hope, provide all the tools you need to give it a go.

7 Teaching resources

This chapter contains extracts from nineteenth-century fiction and non-fiction texts, arranged by theme, and with accompanying notes, comprehension questions and lesson ideas.

The extracts have been carefully chosen to be of interest to secondary-aged students in their subject matter, as well as to reflect the difficulty level and length students can expect when tackling unseen texts in public examinations.

These extracts can be used as exam practice for unseen texts, as an accompaniment to teaching nineteenth-century fiction in order to provide a wider sense of context, as part of thematic units on the media or particular fictional genres to widen students' exposure to nineteenth-century language, or as the basis of creative writing activities. Some are designed for older students, but many can be used to contribute to a rich curriculum at KS3.

GENDER

Extract taken from *The Women of England* by Sarah Stickney Ellis, first published in 1839

Sarah Stickney Ellis was a popular writer on women's place in society in the mid-nineteenth century. An evangelical Christian, much of her work revolved around proving the point that a woman's place was in the home and that her role in society was as a moral force of goodness on those around her. Stickney Ellis wrote to counteract the increasing calls for women to have access to education and other pursuits outside of the home – she believed that wishing to do so would cause nothing but trouble and alter the balance of society for the worse. A woman's role was to serve others – setting a good example that would influence the men around her rather than seeking to take on the role of men herself.

Woman, however, would but ill supply the place appointed her by providence, were she endowed with no other faculties than those of promptitude in action and energy of thought. Valuable as these may be, they would render her but a cold and cheerless companion, without the kindly affections and tender offices that sweeten human life. It is a high privilege, then, which the women of England enjoy, to be necessarily, and by the force of circumstances, thrown upon their affections, for the rule of their conduct in daily life. "What shall I do to gratify myself – to be admired – or to vary the tenor of my existence?" are not the questions which a woman of right feeling asks on first awaking to the avocations of the day. Much more congenial to the highest attributes of woman's character, are inquiries such as these: "How shall I endeavour through this day to turn the time, the health, and the means permitted me to enjoy, to the best account? Is any one sick, I must visit their chamber without delay, and try to give their apartment an air of comfort, by arranging such things as the wearied nurse may not have thought of. Is any one about to set off on a journey, I must see that the early meal is spread, or prepare it with my own hands, in order that the servant who was working late last night, may profit by unbroken rest. Did I fail in what was kind or considerate to any of the family yesterday; I will meet her this morning with a cordial welcome, and show, in the most delicate way I can, that I am anxious to atone for the past. Was any one exhausted by the last day's exertion, I will be an hour before them this morning, and let them see that their labour is so much in advance. Or, if nothing extraordinary occurs to claim my attention, I will meet the family with a consciousness that, being the least engaged of any member of it, I am consequently the most at liberty to devote myself to the general good of the whole, by cultivating cheerful conversation, adapting myself to the prevailing tone of feeling, and leading those who are least happy, to think and speak of what will make them more so."

Who can believe that days, months, and years spent in a continual course of thought and action similar to this, will not produce a powerful effect upon the character, and not upon the individual who thinks and acts, alone, but upon all to whom her influence extends?

COMPREHENSION QUESTIONS

1. Summarise, in three sentences, the main arguments of Sarah Stickney Ellis' article.

2. How does Stickney Ellis use language devices to persuade her audience of her argument?

3. What lexis does Stickney Ellis use to describe ideal female behaviour? What significance does this have?

4. Using evidence from the article, and drawing upon your own knowledge, what class of woman do you think Stickney Ellis is aiming the article at?

5. Describe in your own words, but using evidence from the article, the ideal woman, according to Stickney Ellis.

ADDITIONAL LESSON IDEAS

1. Use the article as a basis for practising letter writing by asking students to pose as either a nineteenth-century woman or modern-day woman, responding to Sarah Stickney Ellis' comments about what makes an 'ideal woman'. For some more fun, you could ask students to pose as the husband of a woman who doesn't meet Stickney Ellis' requirements, writing to her for advice. You can adjust the challenge for both of these options by giving students the chance to write using nineteenth-century vocabulary, in the style of Stickney Ellis, or allow them to write in contemporary formal English.

2. The article could provide a fantastic base for a creative writing task. Students could practise their descriptive writing skills by writing a day in the life of the type of ideal woman Stickney Ellis describes, or as a jumping-off point for a short narrative based around women's roles and the home in the nineteenth century.

3. Students could write a speech in support of/criticising Sarah Stickney Ellis, and take part in a whole-class debate about women's roles in nineteenth-century England. This could be part of a larger unit of work on nineteenth-century women writers, with students carrying out additional independent research on female roles in nineteenth-century Britain to help them develop their arguments.

Extract taken from 'The New Aspect of the Woman Question' by Sarah Grand, first published in *The North American Review*, 1894

Sarah Grand was a novelist who was considered to be one of the 'New Women' of the latter nineteenth century: women who were educated, independent and worked for a living. Many prominent men ridiculed these women and they were pilloried in the press. Sarah Grand's article was written as both a riposte to men for their attitude towards women wishing to live a life outside of the domestic sphere and a wake-up call to women to realise that they had allowed themselves to become manipulated by men and were partly to blame for their situation.

We must look upon man's mistakes, however, with some leniency, because we are not blameless in the matter ourselves. We have allowed him to arrange the whole social system and manage or mismanage it all these ages without ever seriously examining his work with a view to considering whether his abilities and motives were sufficiently good to qualify him for the task. We have listened without a smile to his preachments, about our place in life and all we are good for, on the text that "there is no understanding a woman." We have endured most poignant misery for his sins, and screened him when we should have exposed him and had him punished. We have allowed him to exact all things of us, and have been content to accept the little he grudgingly gave us in return. We have meekly bowed our heads when he called us bad names instead of demanding proofs of the superiority which alone would give him a right to do so. We have listened much edified to man's sermons on the subject of virtue, and have acquiesced uncomplainingly in the convenient arrangement by which this quality has come to be altogether practised for him by us vicariously. We have seen him set up Christ as an example for all men to follow, which argues his belief in the possibility of doing so, and have not only allowed his weakness and hypocrisy in the matter to pass without comment, but, until lately, have not even seen the humour of his pretensions when contrasted with his practices nor held him up to that wholesome ridicule which is a stimulating corrective.

Man deprived us of all proper education, and then jeered at us because we had no knowledge. He narrowed our outlook on life so that our view should be all distorted, and then declared that our mistaken impression of it proved us to be senseless creatures. He cramped our minds so that there was no room for reason in them, and then made merry at our want of logic. Our divine intuition was not to be controlled by him, but he did his best to damage it by sneering at it as an inferior feminine method of arriving at conclusions; and finally, after having had his own way until he lost his head completely, he set himself up as a sort of god and required us to worship him, and to our eternal shame be it said, we did so. The truth has all along been in us, but we have cared more for man than truth, and so the whole human race has suffered.

COMPREHENSION QUESTIONS

1. Summarise, in your own words, Sarah Grand's argument in this article.

2. List the faults of men, as described by Sarah Grand.

3. List the faults of women, as described by Sarah Grand.

4. What lexis does Sarah Grand use to describe men, and how does this compare with the lexis she uses to describe women? What significance does this have?

5. How does Sarah Grand use language and structural devices to create a powerful argument in this article?

ADDITIONAL LESSON IDEAS

1. Students could develop their article writing skills by continuing the article in the style of Sarah Grand, developing her argument to an appropriate conclusion. What might she suggest women do to improve their situation?

2. Have fun recreating Speakers' Corner in Hyde Park by having half the class continue Sarah Grand's article while the others write a counter-article in the voice of a man, critical of her comments. Students could then take it in turns to present their articles to each other, and deal with the jeers, shouts and questions from their nineteenth-century audience!

3. Show students some extracts from 'New Woman' novels, such as *Ann Veronica* by H.G. Wells, *The Romance of a Shop* by Amy Levy and *The Story of an African Farm* by Olive Schreiner, to help them understand further Sarah Grand's perspective. Students could then write their own short 'New Woman' story in response.

Extract taken from Rev. Sydney Smith, writing in *The Edinburgh Review*, c. 1830 (we have been unable to trace the original article)

Sydney Smith was a well-known intellectual, wit and clergyman who helped to found the *Edinburgh Review*, the nineteenth century's most prominent intellectual magazine, focusing on literary criticism. He was known as a champion of reform and had liberal values.

A great deal has been said of the original difference in understanding between men and women, as if women were more quick and men more judicious – as if women were more remarkable for delicacy of association, and men for stronger powers of attention. All this, we confess, appears to us very fanciful. That there is a difference in the understandings of men and the women we every day meet with, everybody, we suppose, must perceive; but there is none surely which may not be accounted for by the difference of circumstances in which they have been placed, without referring to conjectural difference of original conformation of mind. As long as boys and girls run about in the dirt, and trundle hoops together, they are both precisely alike. If you catch up one behalf of these creatures, and train them to a particular set of actions and opinions, and the other half to a perfectly opposite set, of course their understandings will differ, as one or the other sort of occupations has called this or that talent into action. There is surely no occasion to go into any deeper or more abstruse reasoning, in order to explain so very simple a phenomenon.

COMPREHENSION QUESTIONS

1. Summarise Sydney Smith's argument in two sentences.

2. How does Smith use opposition for effect in this article?

3. In what ways does Smith use language to persuade the reader of his opinion?

4. Why does Smith think the popular opinion of gender is 'fanciful'?

5. What does Smith not use in his article to support his opinion, and why do you think this might be?

ADDITIONAL LESSON IDEAS

1. Ask students to develop their persuasive writing skills by adding to Smith's article, improving his argument by adding in more persuasive writing techniques.

2. Students could put themselves in the position of someone opposed to Smith's unorthodox views, and write a strongly worded letter to the editor of the *Edinburgh Review* to discredit Smith's article. Students could also write an opposing article in response to Smith's, giving the opinion that men and women are not born equal. These tasks could be adjusted for difficulty by asking students to write using nineteenth-century vocabulary, or by allowing them to write in their own voice.

3. This article could be the basis for a research project on attitudes towards gender and nature v. nurture, culminating in a class debate – excellent practice for speaking and listening exams.

Extract taken from 'The Enfranchisement of Women' by Harriet Taylor Mill, first published in *The Westminster and Foreign Review*, 1850

Harriet Taylor Mill was a prominent intellectual and campaigner for women's suffrage. She was married to John Stuart Mill, the philosopher, who supported his wife in the fight for women to have equal rights in society. Taylor Mill wrote this article to report on the increasing movement in America calling for the enfranchisement of women, and specifically refers to a convention on this matter held in Ohio in 1850.

We deny the right of any portion of the species to decide for another portion, or any individual for another individual, what is and what is not their "proper sphere". The proper sphere for all human beings is the largest and highest which they are able to attain to. What this is, cannot be ascertained, without complete liberty of choice. The speakers at the Convention in America have therefore done wisely and right, in refusing to entertain the question of the peculiar aptitudes either of women or of men, or the limits within which this or that occupation may be supposed to be more adapted to the one or to the other. They justly maintain, that these questions can only be satisfactorily answered by perfect freedom. Let every occupation be open to all, without favour or discouragement to any, and employments will fall into the hands of those men or women who are found by experience to be most capable of worthily exercising them. There need be no fear that women will take out of the hands of men any occupation which men perform better than they. Each individual will prove his or her capacities, in the only way in which capacities can be proved – by trial; and the world will have the benefit of the best faculties of all its inhabitants. But to interfere beforehand by an arbitrary limit, and declare that whatever be the genius, talent, energy, or force of mind of an individual of a certain sex or class, those faculties shall not be exerted, or shall be exerted only in some few of the many modes in which others are permitted to use theirs, is not only an injustice to the individual, and a detriment to society, which loses what it can ill spare, but is also the most effectual mode of providing that, in the sex or class so fettered, the qualities which are not permitted to be exercised shall not exist.

COMPREHENSION QUESTIONS

1. Summarise Harriet Taylor Mill's argument in two sentences.

2. What is Taylor Mill's tone in this article? Use evidence from the text to support your views.

3. What is the significance of Taylor Mill's use of scientific and gender-neutral vocabulary? What effect does this have?

4. Why does Taylor Mill think that following her recommendations will benefit society?

5. Do you find Taylor Mill's argument persuasive? Explain your views.

ADDITIONAL LESSON IDEAS

1. Students could pose as journalists and write three questions for Harriet Taylor Mill, based on what she writes in this article. They could then work in pairs, groups or as the whole class to take it in turns to 'hot seat' Harriet Taylor Mill.

2. Students could imagine they were at the women's rights convention in Ohio that Taylor Mill mentions in her article, and write a diary entry describing their experiences there, or a newspaper article, reporting on the convention.

3. Students could design a leaflet or poster, agitating for gender equality, using some of the vocabulary from Taylor Mill's article.

EDUCATION

Extract taken from *Jane Eyre* by Charlotte Brontë (New York: Random House, 1949), p. 42

Charlotte Brontë's eponymous novel *Jane Eyre* is told as an autobiography, and details the childhood, youth and young adulthood of the narrator, an orphan, who becomes a governess in the home of Mr Rochester. Here Jane is remembering her time at Lowood school, a boarding school run by Mr Brocklehurst, a hypocritical and cold-hearted man who abuses the girls in the name of religion.

During January, February, and part of March, the deep snows, and, after their melting, the almost impassable roads, prevented our stirring beyond the garden walls, except to go to church; but within these limits we had to pass an hour every day in the open air. Our clothing was insufficient to protect us from the severe cold: we had no boots, the snow got into our shoes and melted there: our ungloved hands became numbed and covered with chilblains, as were our feet: I remember well the distracting irritation I endured from this cause every evening, when my feet inflamed; and the torture of thrusting the swelled, raw, and stiff toes into my shoes in the morning. Then the scanty supply of food was distressing: with the keen appetites of growing children, we had scarcely sufficient to keep alive a delicate invalid. From this deficiency of nourishment resulted an abuse, which pressed hardly on the younger pupils: whenever the famished great girls had an opportunity, they would coax or menace the little ones out of their portion. Many a time I have shared between two claimants the precious morsel of brown bread distributed at tea-time; and after relinquishing to a third half the contents of my mug of coffee, I have swallowed the remainder with an accompaniment of secret tears, forced from me by the exigency of hunger . . .

The Sunday evening was spent in repeating, by heart, the Church Catechism, and the fifth, sixth, and seventh chapters of St. Matthew; and in listening to a long sermon, read by Miss Miller, whose irrepressible yawns attested her weariness. A frequent interlude of these performances was the enactment of the part of Eutychus by some half-dozen of little girls, who, overpowered with sleep, would fall down, if not out of the third loft, yet off the fourth form, and be taken up half dead. The remedy was, to thrust them forward into the centre of the schoolroom, and oblige them to stand there till the sermon was finished. Sometimes their feet failed them, and they sank together in a heap; they were then propped up with the monitors' high stools.

COMPREHENSION QUESTIONS

1. How does Charlotte Brontë create pity for Jane and the students at Lowood school in this extract?

2. What impression do you have of the conditions of school life at Lowood?

3. What impression do you have of the adult Jane Eyre, from her description of her childhood at Lowood?

4. Choose a powerful example of imagery and explain why it is effective.

ADDITIONAL LESSON IDEAS

1. Ask students to continue the passage in the style of Charlotte Brontë, imagining what might happen next on a Sunday afternoon.

2. Students could write a diary entry in the voice of the child Jane Eyre, describing through her own eyes the experience of Sunday at school.

3. Students could write an exposé article on the cruelties of life at Lowood school, as discovered by a nineteenth-century school inspector.

Extract taken from *Hard Times* by Charles Dickens (London: Penguin, 2003), pp. 10–11

Charles Dickens wrote *Hard Times* as a parody of the fact-based Victorian education system. Here the teacher Thomas Gradgrind is putting his students to the test.

Thomas Gradgrind, sir. A man of realities. A man of facts and calculations. A man who proceeds upon the principle that two and two are four, and nothing over, and who is not to be talked into allowing for anything over. Thomas Gradgrind, sir – peremptorily Thomas – Thomas Gradgrind. With a rule and a pair of scales, and the multiplication table always in his pocket, sir, ready to weigh and measure any parcel of human nature, and tell you exactly what it comes to. It is a mere question of figures, a case of simple arithmetic. You might hope to get some other nonsensical belief into the head of George Gradgrind, or Augustus Gradgrind, or John Gradgrind, or Joseph Gradgrind (all supposititious, non-existent persons), but into the head of Thomas Gradgrind – no, sir!

In such terms Mr. Gradgrind always mentally introduced himself, whether to his private circle of acquaintance, or to the public in general. In such terms, no doubt, substituting the words 'boys and girls,' for 'sir,' Thomas Gradgrind now presented Thomas Gradgrind to the little pitchers before him, who were to be filled so full of facts. Indeed, as he eagerly sparkled at them from the cellarage before mentioned, he seemed a kind of cannon loaded to the muzzle with facts, and prepared to blow them clean out of the regions of childhood at one discharge. He seemed a galvanizing apparatus, too, charged with a grim mechanical substitute for the tender young imaginations that were to be stormed away.

'Girl number twenty,' said Mr. Gradgrind, squarely pointing with his square forefinger, 'I don't know that girl. Who is that girl?'

'Sissy Jupe, sir,' explained number twenty, blushing, standing up, and curtseying.

'Sissy is not a name,' said Mr. Gradgrind. 'Don't call yourself Sissy. Call yourself Cecilia.'

'It's father as calls me Sissy, sir,' returned the young girl in a trembling voice, and with another curtsey.

'Then he has no business to do it,' said Mr. Gradgrind. 'Tell him he mustn't. Cecilia Jupe. Let me see. What is your father?'

'He belongs to the horse-riding, if you please, sir.'

Mr. Gradgrind frowned, and waved off the objectionable calling with his hand.

'We don't want to know anything about that, here. You mustn't tell us about that, here. Your father breaks horses, don't he?'

'If you please, sir, when they can get any to break, they do break horses in the ring, sir.'

'You mustn't tell us about the ring, here. Very well, then. Describe your father as a horsebreaker. He doctors sick horses, I dare say?'

'Oh yes, sir.'

'Very well, then. He is a veterinary surgeon, a farrier, and horsebreaker. Give me your definition of a horse.'

COMPREHENSION QUESTIONS

1. What is the effect of Dickens' use of metaphor to describe Thomas Gradgrind in the second paragraph?

2. What impression do you have of Thomas Gradgrind? How would you describe him, in your own words?

3. How does Dickens use direct speech to create humour?

4. Choose an effective phrase from the passage and describe its effect on the reader.

ADDITIONAL LESSON IDEAS

1. Students could write and perform a short drama piece to bring the classroom of Thomas Gradgrind alive, making sure their speech echoes Dickens' style.

2. Students could write an advertisement for the school, explaining the benefits of the education Gradgrind offers, to potential parents.

3. Students could research Charles Dickens' attitudes towards education and child-hood, and use this knowledge, as well as the extract, to write a speech in the voice of Charles Dickens, explaining why he wanted to criticise the school system in nineteenth-century Britain.

Extract taken from *Tom Brown's Schooldays* by Thomas Hughes (London: Macmillan, 1904), pp. 116–117

Thomas Hughes' novel about the antics of Tom Brown and his friends at Rugby School, one of the new boys' public schools created in the nineteenth century, was the first in the genre of school stories and was a classic almost from its first publication in 1857. Here Tom is enjoying his first taste of school life.

The next day Tom was duly placed in the third form, and began his lessons in a corner of the big School. He found the work very easy, as he had been well grounded, and knew his grammar by heart; and, as he had no intimate companions to make him idle (East and his other School-house friends being in the lower fourth, the form above him), soon gained golden opinions from his master, who said he was placed too low, and should be put out at the end of the half-year. So all went well with him in School, and he wrote the most flourishing letters home to his mother, full of his own success and the unspeakable delights of a public school.

In the house, too, all went well. The end of the half-year was drawing near, which kept everybody in a good humour, and the house was ruled well and strongly by Warner and Brooke. True, the general system was rough and hard, and there was bullying in nooks and corners – bad signs for the future; but it never got farther, or dared show itself openly, stalking about the passages and hall and bedrooms, and making the life of the small boys a continual fear.

Tom, as a new boy, was of right excused fagging for the first month, but in his enthusiasm for his new life this privilege hardly pleased him; and East and others of his young friends, discovering this, kindly allowed him to indulge his fancy, and take their turns at night fagging and cleaning studies. These were the principal duties of the fags in the house. From supper until nine o'clock three fags taken in order stood in the passages, and answered any praepostor who called "Fag," racing to the door, the last comer having to do the work. This consisted generally of going to the buttery for beer and bread and cheese (for the great men did not sup with the rest, but had each his own allowance in his study or the fifth-form room), cleaning candlesticks and putting in new candles, toasting cheese, bottling beer, and carrying messages about the house; and Tom, in the first blush of his hero-worship, felt it a high privilege to receive orders from and be the bearer of the supper of old Brooke. And besides this night-work, each praepostor had three or four fags specially allotted to him, of whom he was supposed to be the guide, philosopher, and friend, and who in return for these good offices had to clean out his study every morning by turns, directly after first lesson and before he returned from breakfast. And the pleasure of seeing the great men's studies, and looking at their pictures, and peeping into their books, made Tom a ready substitute for any boy who was too lazy to do his own work. And so he soon gained the character of a good-natured, willing fellow, who was ready to do a turn for any one.

COMPREHENSION QUESTIONS

1. What do you understand to have been the role of a 'fag' in a boys' public school? Use evidence from the text to support your views.

2. What impression do you have of Tom Brown from this extract?

3. How does Thomas Hughes adapt his language to suit a young audience? Find examples to support your views.

4. What language techniques does Hughes use to bring Tom's experiences to life?

ADDITIONAL LESSON IDEAS

1. Ask students to write a diary entry in the voice of Tom, being careful to write using nineteenth-century vocabulary and schoolboy slang.

2. Allow students some time to research life in nineteenth-century public schools, then, using the extract as well as their research to guide them, ask them to write a 'survival guide' for new boys joining a public school for the first time.

3. Students could write an edition of 'The Rugby Magazine', creating the types of short stories, articles and letters a schoolboy readership might contribute to their school magazine.

Extract taken from *"Foodless, Friendless, in our Streets": Being a Letter About Ragged Schools; addressed to boys and girls* by Susanna Beever (Edinburgh: Johnstone and Hunter, 1853), pp. 5–7

This is an extract from a pamphlet designed to educate children about the purpose of Ragged Schools. These were set up from the 1840s, largely by Christian organisations, to educate the most destitute of children in Victorian cities. Alongside the basics of education, they were also provided with food and clothes, in the recognition that they could not learn anything until their basic needs were cared for. Ragged Schools were the only means by which the children of the poor could receive a free education until much later in the century, when primary schooling became compulsory and organised by central government.

Ask your friends to take you to see a Ragged School. There you will find poor children who have nobody at home to take care of them, or to teach them any thing that is good, boys and girls whose wicked parents teach them to lie and to steal, and to do every thing that is bad, and who beat them if they come home without having stolen something. How would you like to be thus treated? Or to be turned out of doors on a bitterly cold night, when the nipping frost benumbed you, or when pitiless snow-storms or pelting rain fell upon you? You would, I hope, be sorry if even your dog had to stay out on such a night! But just remember, that when you are going to your nice, warm, comfortable beds, after having had plenty of good food and clothing during the day, for which I hope you gratefully thank God before lying down to sleep in peace and comfort at night, that there are hundreds of poor children who have either no home to go to, or such an one as you would fear to enter; that many pass the night under arches, or on the steps of doors, or wherever they can – poor unhappy little beings! Oh! When you pray for yourselves, and ask God to bless your father and mother, your brothers and sisters, then do not forget to ask Him also to help the poor outcasts.

Now, Ragged Schools have been set on foot by kind and Christian people on purpose to do good to these unhappy children. They are brought to these schools, and there they have their torn, dirty clothes taken off, and after being washed, and made nice and clean, they have others put on to wear all day, but at night they are obliged to have their dirty ones put on again, because their parents are so wicked, that if they went home in good clothes they would take them from them and sell them, and spend the money on something to drink. Then they would send the children out again in miserable and filthy rags, or nearly without clothes at all; so the kind people at the schools take care of the clean clothing for them at night. The children stay at school all day and have food provided for them.

COMPREHENSION QUESTIONS

1. How does Susanna Beever use hyperbole for effect in this extract?

2. How does Beever adapt her language for children?

3. What aspect of the children's lives does Beever emphasise in her article? Why do you think she does this?

4. What impression do you have of life for the average Ragged School child?

ADDITIONAL LESSON IDEAS

1. Ask students to write a persuasive, informative article for children, entitled 'A Day in the Life of a Ragged School Child'.

2. Get your students to be as creative as they can when producing a charity campaign to raise money for a new Ragged School; they will need to produce leaflets, posters, adverts, a newspaper article and maybe even a promotional video!

3. Allow your students' creative juices to flow by giving them the title 'Ragged Child' and asking them to write a descriptive or narrative piece in response.

CRIME AND PUNISHMENT

Extract taken from 'Brutal Murder in Whitechapel' in *The Daily News*, 1 September 1888

This is an original report of the murder of Mary Ann Nichols, one of the first victims of the infamous serial killer, Jack the Ripper.

A murder of the most brutal kind was committed in the neighbourhood of Whitechapel in the early hours of yesterday morning, but by whom and with what motive is at present a complete mystery.

At a quarter to four o'clock Police Constable Neill, when in Buck's-row, Whitechapel, came upon the body of a woman lying on a part of the footway, and on stooping to raise her up, in the belief that she was intoxicated, he discovered that her throat was cut almost from ear to ear. Assistance was procured, a messenger being sent at once to the station and for a doctor. Dr. Llewellyn, of Whitechapel-road, whose surgery is not more than 300 yards from the spot where the woman lay, was aroused, and proceeded at once to the scene. He hastily inspected the body where it lay and pronounced the woman dead. The police ambulance from the Bethnal-green station having arrived, the body was removed there . . .

After the body was removed to the mortuary of the parish in Old Montague-street, Whitechapel, steps were taken to secure, if possible, identification, but at first with little prospect of success. The clothing on the body was of a common description. It was discovered that the skirt of one petticoat and the band of another article bore the stencil stamp of Lambeth Workhouse. The only articles in the pockets were a comb and a piece of looking glass. The latter led the police to conclude that the murdered woman was an inhabitant of one of the numerous lodging-homes in the neighbourhood.

As the news of the murder spread first one woman and then another come forward to view the body, and at length it was found that a woman answering the description of the deceased had lodged in a common lodging houses in Thrawl-street, Spitalfields. Women from that place were fetched, and they identified the deceased as "Polly" who had shared a room with three other women in the place on the usual terms of such houses – nightly payment of 4d. each, each woman having a separate bed. She had frequented the house for about three weeks past. When she presented herself for her lodging on Thursday night she was turned away because she had not the money. She was then the worse for liquor. A woman of the neighbourhood saw her later, she told the police – even as late as 2.30 on Friday morning – in Whitechapel-road, opposite the Church, and at the corner of Osborn-street, and at a quarter to four she was found within 600 yards of the spot murdered.

At about half-past seven last evening a woman named Mary Anne Monk, at present an inmate of Lambeth Workhouse, was taken to the mortuary, and identified the body as that of Mary Ann Nicholls.

COMPREHENSION QUESTIONS

1. How does the opening of the article create a sense of intrigue?

2. In what order is the information given in this article? What effect does this have on the reader?

3. What is the focus of the article? How might this reflect the concerns of a nineteenth-century audience?

4. What impression does the article give of the type of woman the victim was?

ADDITIONAL LESSON IDEAS

1. Depending on how much your class enjoy gore, encourage them to research the Jack the Ripper murders and the original newspaper articles detailing his crimes – these are freely available online. Ask students to give a presentation on what they've discovered, or, for a little more variety, prompt them to produce some more exciting oral activities, such as a witness interview, a court room scene, a conversation amongst newspaper reporters looking for the next Ripper scoop, etc.

2. Give students a contemporary newspaper article detailing a murder and ask them to compare and contrast with this one; how does the way we report murder differ from the nineteenth century?

3. Show students a short clip from the Jack the Ripper film *From Hell* (this is classified as a 15, so do exercise caution when choosing a clip if students are younger) and have them use this as inspiration to write a story set in Ripper's London.

Extract taken from 'Oscar Wilde and Taylor at Bow Street' in *The Illustrated Police News*, 20 April 1895

Oscar Wilde, the playwright and novelist, was at the height of his career when he was arrested for homosexuality, which was illegal in Britain until 1967. He had been having an affair with Lord Alfred 'Bosie' Douglas; when Douglas' father, the Marquess of Queensberry, discovered this, he publicly accused Wilde, causing his later arrest and imprisonment. The trial was a sensation, and the very public downfall of Wilde was chronicled closely in the press.

Oscar Wilde and Alfred Taylor were again placed in the dock at Bow Street Police Court on Thursday morning for further examination by Sir John Bridge on the charges preferred against them. When the accused arrived in the prison van the crowd outside the station assailed them with groans . . .

Wilde looked careworn and much older than he appeared when last before the Court. Taylor, on the other hand, looked all the better for his imprisonment. His cuffs and collar were spotlessly white; his face clean shaven, and his hair carefully brushed. Wilde's hair was not so carefully brushed as usual . . .

Frederick Atkins, a smooth-faced fellow twenty years of age, was next called. He said he was introduced to Wilde by Taylor at the Florence Hotel. They had dinner at which Wilde, witness Taylor, and two others were present . . . [w]itness explained that during the dinner Wilde asked him if he would like to go to Paris with him as his private secretary. He said, "Yes," and on the following day he actually went to Paris with Wilde, and stayed at the same hotel. Witness went on to describe what took place there, but the details are totally unfit for publication. Wilde told him to beware of women, as they ruined men. (Laughter.) One evening Wilde gave him a louis*, and told him not to go to a certain place of amusement, but he immediately went there. (Laughter.) At the hotel they had the "best dinners in the land." They stayed in Paris three days, and he then accompanied Wilde back to London. Wilde gave him £3 and a silver cigarette case. Witness afterwards saw Wilde at his house in Tite Street, where he attended in consequence of receiving a written invitation. As soon as he arrived Wilde asked him for the letter he had written, and he gave it up to him. He told witness to say nothing about their visit to Paris. On another occasion Wilde visited him at his lodgings. One night when they were at a hotel Wilde kissed the waiter. (Laughter.)

Mr Gill: What happened then?

He put his arm round my neck.

What else?

He put his arm round Douglas.*

Mr Gill (quickly): Never mind that. Keep to what he did to you.

*louis – a French gold coin
*Douglas – Lord Alfred 'Bosie' Douglas

COMPREHENSION QUESTIONS

1. In what ways could this article be said to be written more for entertainment than information?

2. What impression does the article writer give of Frederick Atkins?

3. Is this an unbiased article? Give your reasons why, using evidence from the text.

4. Is there anything that surprises you about this article? Explain your thoughts in as much detail as you can.

ADDITIONAL LESSON IDEAS

1. Ask students to rewrite the article from the perspective of wanting to provide a sympathetic view of Wilde and Taylor.

2. Give students some time to research the Wilde case and then ask them to write a report on their opinion of how Wilde was treated.

3. Students could write a diary entry in the voice of Wilde, explaining his feelings at falling from being the most fêted man in London to being the most reviled.

Extract taken from *Oliver Twist* by Charles Dickens (New York: The Century Company, 1911), pp. 406–407

This is taken from the end of Dickens' famous novel about the orphan Oliver Twist, when the notorious criminal Fagin is waiting to hear the verdict in his trial for murder.

The court was paved, from floor to roof, with human faces. Inquisitive and eager eyes peered from every inch of space. From the rail before the dock, away into the sharpest angle of the smallest corner in the galleries, all looks were fixed upon one man – Fagin . . .

He stood there, in all this glare of living light, with one hand resting on the wooden slab before him, the other held to his ear, and his head thrust forward to enable him to catch with greater distinctness every word that fell from the presiding judge, who was delivering his charge to the jury. At times, he turned his eyes sharply upon them to observe the effect of the slightest featherweight in his favour; and when the points against him were stated with terrible distinctness, looked towards his counsel, in mute appeal that he would, even then, urge something in his behalf. Beyond these manifestations of anxiety, he stirred not hand or foot. He had scarcely moved since the trial began; and now that the judge ceased to speak, he still remained in the same strained attitude of close attention, with his gaze bent on him, as though he listened still.

A slight bustle in the court, recalled him to himself. Looking round, he saw that the juryman had turned together, to consider their verdict. As his eyes wandered to the gallery, he could see the people rising above each other to see his face: some hastily applying their glasses to their eyes: and others whispering to their neighbours with looks expressive of abhorrence. A few there were, who seemed unmindful of him, and looked only to the jury, in impatient wonder how they could delay. But in no one face – not even among the women, of whom there were many there – could he read the faintest sympathy with himself, or any feeling but one of all-absorbing interest that he should be condemned . . .

He looked, wistfully, into their faces, one by one when they passed out, as though to see which way the greater number leant; but that was fruitless. The jailer touched him on the shoulder. He followed mechanically to the end of the dock, and sat down on a chair. The man pointed it out, or he would not have seen it . . .

Not that, all this time, his mind was, for an instant, free from one oppressive overwhelming sense of the grave that opened at his feet; it was ever present to him, but in a vague and general way, and he could not fix his thoughts upon it. Thus, even while he trembled, and turned burning hot at the idea of speedy death, he fell to counting the iron spikes before him, and wondering how the head of one had been broken off, and whether they would mend it, or leave it as it was. Then, he thought of all the horrors of the gallows and the scaffold – and stopped to watch a man sprinkling the floor to cool it – and then went on to think again.

At length there was a cry of silence, and a breathless look from all towards the door. The jury returned, and passed him close. He could glean nothing from their faces; they might as well have been of stone. Perfect stillness ensued – not a rustle – not a breath – Guilty.

COMPREHENSION QUESTIONS

1. How does Dickens create sympathy for Fagin in this scene?

2. Choose a phrase that you think is powerful in describing Fagin's feelings. How does Dickens use language for effect within this phrase?

3. What impression does Dickens give of the atmosphere within the courtroom?

4. How does Dickens contrast Fagin with the other people in the courtroom? What effect does this have?

ADDITIONAL LESSON IDEAS

1. Ask students to continue writing the scene: how does Fagin react to the guilty verdict?

2. Give students more information about the story of Oliver Twist and Fagin in particular, and then allow them, in small groups, to create their own courtroom and put Fagin on trial, with each member of the jury allowed to ask him questions about his conduct.

3. Show students a film version (or more than one if you can find them) of this scene and discuss how it has been brought to life. Students could then create their own storyboard for the scene and consider how they would bring it to life on screen or on the stage.

Extract taken from *The Spectator*, 18 August 1849

Maria Manning became a notorious mid-century murderer when she enlisted her husband to help her murder her lover, Patrick O'Connor, for his money. A Swiss former ladies' maid, Maria was determined to never live in poverty, and her greed led her to be hanged, alongside her husband, in 1849.

A murder was discovered in Bermondsey yesterday, which appears to have been planned and executed with a treachery singularly base and cold-blooded. The victim is Mr. Patrick O'Connor, a Customhouse-officer, who lived at No. 21 Greenwood Street, Mile-end Road; and was acquainted with one Manning, a person recently discharged from the service of the Great Western Railway, for supposed connexion with the late robberies on that line by Moore and Nightingale. Manning resided at the house No.3 Minerva Place, near the Leather Market, New Bermondsey; and with him lived a female of great personal beauty – said to be a Swede – who called him her "guardian."

Mr. O'Connor was frequently at Minerva Place, and was often seen with this "Swedish lady." On Thursday the 9th instant, Mr. O'Connor left his house near Mile-end Road early in the morning; in the afternoon of that day, he was seen by a friend, who spoke to him, near Manning's house in Minerva Place, and he said he was then going to Manning's: he was not seen alive again. By Monday his continued absence caused alarm at his lodgings, and the Police were called in: it was found that his boxes had been unlocked and rifled; and that Foreign Railway Bonds and other securities for money, to the amount of £4,000, with £300 in cash, had been carried away. Towards the end of the week, it was remembered that the Swedish lady had been to his rooms late on Sunday evening, and had access to his drawers and boxes, as had been her practice, with his permission, many times before. Manning had also been heard to use threats against Mr. O'Connor. The Police repaired to Minerva Place, and found Manning's house locked up. On forcing their way in, they found the place bare of furniture and deserted; and they discovered that Manning had left the neighbourhood on Tuesday last, having sold all his goods to a broker and manifested a desire to be off as soon as possible.

The house and garden at Minerva Place were searched for evidences of guilt; and at last, in the back kitchen, it was noted that one of the flag-stones of the floor appeared to have been recently lifted. On removing the pavement, the soil was found loose; and on digging, the body of the murdered man was found. "It was lying on the face, with the legs doubled up and tied to the haunches." A quantity of lime had been buried with the body, which was already corroded and decomposing. A surgeon who was brought in examined the body, and found that Mr. O'Connor had been shot: "two slugs were discovered near the temple." No report of fire-arms had been heard, and therefore it is suspected that an air-gun had been used. A number of the Detective Police have been despatched to the seaport towns; but no traces of Manning or his female companion have yet been discovered.

COMPREHENSION QUESTIONS

1. In what order is information given in this article? What effect does this have?

2. What type of information is dwelt upon? Why do you think this is?

3. What is the tone of the article? Find evidence for your ideas.

4. Is the article subjective or objective? Give evidence for what you say.

ADDITIONAL LESSON IDEAS

1. Ask students to dramatise the search for Mr O'Connor, writing a short story from the perspective of the police officers working on the case.

2. An activity more suited to younger students is creating a wanted poster; ask them to use the information in the article to create a wanted poster for Maria Manning. There are plenty of blank templates available online to make this easier!

3. Ask students to rewrite the newspaper article, making it more exciting and including quotations from neighbours and some potential witnesses.

TRAVEL

Extract taken from *Narrative of a Journey in Egypt and the Country Beyond the Cataracts* by Thomas Legh (London: J. Murray, 1816), pp. 82–83

Thomas Legh (1792–1857) inherited an enormous fortune and the estate of Lyme Park in Cheshire as a child. His wealth gave him the opportunity to indulge his passion for travel, which he did on a grand scale, becoming one of the first Europeans to travel up the Nile as far as Nubia, as well as exploring Greece, parts of Turkey and the Middle East. He wrote a detailed journal of his experiences, which included wrestling crocodiles, delighting nineteenth-century audiences with his depictions of a still as yet little-explored region of the world.

We left Dehr early in the morning of the 25th, and in an hour arrived at some ruins in the Desert . . . the remains of what was once a fine temple, since converted into a church by the early Christians. The hieroglyphics have been in consequence covered over with stucco, but where that has fallen off, the painted figures are to be observed in a state of wonderful preservation. The style of the building is rude, and not unlike that of the temple of Dehr, differing only in being built of stone instead of excavated in the rock. It is nearly buried in the sand, not more than the height of six feet remaining visible, and it is much disfigured by a number of mud houses built upon and around it.

On the 26th, we landed opposite to the ruins at Sibboi; while here, a Mameluke and several of his attendants came down to the Nile to water their horses. Our crew instantly hurried us on board. The Sheik's son, who had accompanied us from Essouan, was extremely alarmed, and instantly took off his caftan and gay turban to escape notice. He had fought against the Mamelukes in Upper Egypt, and was in great dread lest he should be recognized. Our boat's crew was also under considerable apprehension that we should be attacked and plundered.

On the following day, as we continued our voyage down the Nile, we perceived two Arabs mounted on camels, who . . . hailed us in Arabic. The fear of the Mamelukes still operating upon the minds of our crew, we rowed to the other side of the Nile, and were again hailed in Arabic. On this occasion we replied, and demanded what they wanted? To our great astonishment we were answered in English, and immediately recognized the voice of our friend Sheik Ibrahim, whom we had left in Siout, Upper Egypt, extremely well dressed after the Turkish fashion, and in good health and condition. He had now all the exterior of a common Arab, was very thin . . . he told us he had been living for many days with the Sekhs of the villages through which he had passed, on lentils, bread, salt and water, and when he came on board, could not contain his joy at the prospect of being regaled with animal food. The day before we had bought a lean and miserable sheep, for which the natives had demanded (an exorbitant price in that country) a dollar, and our friend contributed to our repast some excellent white bread which he had bought from Essouan. We smoked our pipes, congratulating each other on our good fortune in having met, and communicating our different plans and adventures.

COMPREHENSION QUESTIONS

1. What impression does Thomas Legh give of the native peoples of Egypt? Use quotations to explain your views.

2. Choose an example of how Legh exoticises Egypt. Explain the effect of this.

3. How does Legh tailor his description to suit the interests of a western audience? Use quotations to explain your answers.

4. What does Legh's description suggest it is like for a westerner to travel through Egypt? Use quotations to support your views.

ADDITIONAL LESSON IDEAS

1. Ask students to imagine they are a nineteenth-century traveller in Egypt and write a short travelogue of their experiences, based on Legh's descriptions.

2. Get students practising their descriptive writing skills by choosing a vivid moment from the passage and describing it in detail (the temple, the Nile, etc.).

3. Have students imagine they are Legh, just returned to England from his exciting travels. He has been asked to give a presentation about his experiences; students should write the text of this speech and then present it to the class.

Extract taken from *Recollections of a Happy Life: The Autobiography of Marianne North*, ed. J. Addington Symons (London and New York: Macmillan, 1892), pp. 58–59

Marianne North (1830–90) was born into a wealthy and well-connected family. She always enjoyed painting from nature, and after her father's death when she was forty, she decided to use her inheritance to travel the world independently, painting the flora she came across in their native environments. Her intrepid adventures received much attention, and she could count Charles Darwin amongst her acquaintances. Her paintings enabled many new species to be identified, and allowed British audiences to see vividly the exotic environments of far-flung countries. Marianne North established an eponymous gallery in Kew Gardens in 1882, which remains open today and displays 832 of her fascinating botanical paintings.

The falls far outstretched my grandest ideas. They are enormous, the banks above and below wildly and richly wooded, with a great variety of fine trees, tangles of vine and Virginian creeper over them, dead stumps, skeleton trees, and worn rocks white with lichens; the whole setting is grand, and the bridges are so cobwebby that they seem by contrast to make the falls more massive. From my home I could walk along the edge of the cliff over the boiling green waters all the way to the falls, and if they had not been there at all I would willingly have stayed to paint the old tress and water alone. Mr Rosli gave me wonderful accounts of the falls in winter, when great masses of ice came down from Lake Erie, got jammed between the rocks and banks, and gradually froze the water between them, then more ice slipped under and it was lifted up like a bridge; he said it was a most marvellous sight, and he had known carriages driven across on the ice under the bridge, but that did not often happen. It is much milder at Niagara than in Lower Canada, grapes and peaches ripen better; the old arbor-vitae trees are splendid, as scraggy as any old silver firs, and the oak trees are drawn up into grand timber, the trunks rising without a branch for over fifty feet. It was difficult to choose out of so many subjects where to begin. The Horseshoe Fall tempted me much, standing close to its head, with the rapids like a sea behind, and the rainbow dipping into its deep emerald hollow; the tints were endless in their gradations, and delicious, but I got wet through in the mist.

Another tempting bit was below my home, looking down on the whirlpool, where the savage green boiling water seemed piled up in the centre like some glacier; there were foregrounds of great arbor-vitae trees almost hanging in the air like orchids, with long twisted bare roots exposed against the edge of the cliff, from which all the earth had been washed. The rapids about Goat Island on the American side were also full of wonders. One day it blew such a gale that I had to sit down and hold on tightly to the bars of the bridge on returning; no carriages attempted it that day.

COMPREHENSION QUESTIONS

1. Choose two examples of description from this passage and explain why they are effective.

2. Choose two examples of figurative language and explain why they are effective.

3. How does Marianne North reveal that she is a painter in her description of this scene? Use quotations to evidence your ideas.

4. What impression does North give of the Niagara region? Use quotations to explain your opinion.

ADDITIONAL LESSON IDEAS

1. Students could write a letter home in the voice of Marianne North, telling her sister of all her experiences in America.

2. Marianne North's description could form the basis of a travel brochure, advertising the Niagara region to nineteenth-century tourists: students could use their imagination to fill in the gaps that North's article leaves.

3. Students could write a series of questions to ask Marianne North, then write up the imagined answers as a magazine interview.

Extract taken from *A Lady's Life in the Rocky Mountains* by Isabella Bird (London: Virago, 1982), Letter 7

Isabella Bird (1831–1904) was a pioneering world traveller who was also a keen naturalist. In later life she trained in medicine, founding a hospital in India. Her lively travel writing earned her fame in her own lifetime, when to travel widely was unusual, let alone being a female travelling abroad alone. She travelled across Asia, India, Australia, Africa and America, and delighted in the sights she experienced; most of her published writings consist of letters sent home to family and friends, which were later reproduced in journals and magazines for public consumption.

From the dry, buff grass of Estes Park we turned off up a trail on the side of a pine-hung gorge, up a steep pine-clothed hill, down to a small valley, rich in fine, sun-cured hay about eighteen inches high, and enclosed by high mountains whose deepest hollow contains a lily-covered lake, fitly named "The Lake of the Lilies." Ah, how magical its beauty was, as it slept in silence, while THERE the dark pines were mirrored motionless in its pale gold, and HERE the great white lily cups and dark green leaves rested on amethyst-coloured water! From this we ascended into the purple gloom of great pine forests which clothe the skirts of the mountains up to a height of about 11,000 feet, and from their chill and solitary depths we had glimpses of golden atmosphere and rose-lit summits, not of "the land very far off," but of the land nearer now in all its grandeur, gaining in sublimity by nearness – glimpses, too, through a broken vista of purple gorges, of the illimitable Plains lying idealized in the late sunlight, their baked, brown expanse transfigured into the likeness of a sunset sea rolling infinitely in waves of misty gold.

The gloom of the dense, ancient, silent forest is to me awe inspiring. On such an evening it is soundless, except for the branches creaking in the soft wind, the frequent snap of decayed timber, and a murmur in the pine tops as of a not distant waterfall, all tending to produce EERINESS and a sadness "hardly akin to pain." There no lumber-er's axe has ever rung. The trees die when they have attained their prime, and stand there, dead and bare, till the fierce mountain winds lay them prostrate. The pines grew smaller and more sparse as we ascended, and the last stragglers wore a tortured, warring look. The timber line was passed, but yet a little higher a slope of mountain meadow dipped to the south-west towards a bright stream trickling under ice and icicles, and there a grove of the beautiful silver spruce marked our camping ground.

Hereafter, when I call up memories of the glorious, the view from this camping ground will come up. Looking east, gorges opened to the distant Plains, then fading into purple grey. Mountains with pine-clothed skirts rose in ranges, or, solitary, uplifted their grey summits, while close behind, but nearly 3,000 feet above us, towered the bald white crest of Long's Peak, its huge precipices red with the light of a sun long lost to our eyes . . . soon the afterglow came on, and before it faded a big half-moon hung out of the heavens, shining through the silver blue foliage of the pines on the frigid background of snow, and turning the whole into fairyland.

COMPREHENSION QUESTIONS

1. How does Isabella Bird create mood and atmosphere in this extract?

2. Choose two examples of figurative language from the extract and explain their effect.

3. What impression does Bird give of the Rocky Mountains? Use quotations to explore your views.

4. What lexis does Bird use in the extract and what effect does this have?

ADDITIONAL LESSON IDEAS

1. Give students the title 'A Lady's Life in the Rocky Mountains' and ask them to write their own short story or descriptive piece in response, either in their own voice or using nineteenth-century vocabulary.

2. Ask students to imagine they are Isabella Bird, and that they have been asked by the Rocky Mountains Tourist Board to write an article to persuade people to visit the area. They should try to replicate Bird's voice in their article.

3. Have students use this extract along with Marianne North's and Fanny Trollope's to create a travel brochure for would-be nineteenth-century tourists to America.

Extract from *The Domestic Manners of the Americans* by Fanny Trollope (London and New York: Whittaker, Treacher and Co, 1832), pp. 38–39

Frances 'Fanny' Trollope (1779–1863) was a popular novelist. Now she is mostly remembered as being the mother of novelist Anthony Trollope.

The town of Natches is beautifully situated on one of these high spots; the climate here, in the warm season, is as fatal as that of New Orleans; were it not for this, Natches would have great attractions to new settlers. The beautiful contrast that its bright green hill forms with the dismal line of black forest that stretches on every side, the abundant growth of pawpaw, palmetto and orange, the copious variety of sweet-scented flowers that flourish there, all make it appear like an oasis in the desert. Natches is the furthest point to the north at which oranges ripen in the open air, or endure the winter without shelter. With the exception of this sweet spot, I thought all the little towns and villages we passed, wretched looking, in the extreme. As the distance from New Orleans increased, the air of wealth and comfort exhibited in its immediate neighbourhood disappeared, and but for one or two clusters of wooden houses, calling themselves towns, and borrowing some pompous name, generally from Greece or Rome, we might have thought ourselves the first of the human race who had ever penetrated into this territory of bears and alligators. But still from time to time appeared the hut of the wood-cutter, who supplies the steam-boats with fuel, at the risk, or rather with the assurance of early death, in exchange for dollars and whiskey. These sad dwellings are nearly all of them inundated during the winter, and the best of them are constructed on piles, which permit the water to reach its highest level without drowning the wretched inhabitants. These unhappy beings are invariably the victims of ague, which they meet recklessly, sustained by the incessant use of ardent spirits. The squalid look of the miserable wives and children of these men was dreadful, and often as the spectacle was renewed I could never look at it with indifference . . . I never witnessed human nature reduced so low, as it appeared in the wood-cutters' huts on the unwholesome banks of the Mississippi.

It is said that at some points of this dismal river, crocodiles are so abundant as to add the terror of their attacks to the other sufferings of a dwelling there. We were told a story of a squatter, who having "located" himself close to the river's edge, proceeded to build his cabin . . . [t]his was done; the wife and five young children were put in possession of their new home, and slept soundly after a long march. Towards daybreak the husband and father was awakened by a faint cry, and looking up, beheld relics of three of his children scattered over the floor, and an enormous crocodile, with several young ones around her, occupied in devouring the remnants of their horrid meal. He looked round for a weapon, but finding none, and aware that unarmed he could do nothing, he raised himself gently on his bed, and contrived to crawl from thence through a window, hoping that his wife, whom he left sleeping, might with the remaining children rest undiscovered till his return. He flew to his nearest neighbour and besought his aid; in less than half an hour two men returned with him, all three well armed; but alas! they were too late! the wife and her two babes lay mangled on their bloody bed.

COMPREHENSION QUESTIONS

1. How does Fanny Trollope create a sense of the 'other' in this extract? Use quotations to support your views.

2. How does Trollope use emotive language for effect in this extract?

3. What impression does Trollope give of the south of America in this extract?

4. Choose an example of how Trollope creates a vivid sense of place and explain its effect.

ADDITIONAL LESSON IDEAS

1. Ask students to write a newspaper article, reporting on the death of the family killed by the crocodile.

2. Students could pose as an inhabitant of the region Trollope is writing about, and write a letter to their local newspaper, complaining about Trollope's depiction of their home.

3. Get students practising their creative writing by asking them to write a story entitled 'The Crocodile'.

SCIENCE AND TECHNOLOGY

Extract taken from *Dombey and Son* by Charles Dickens (London: Hazell, Watson and Viney, 1935), p. 60

This novel, written between 1846 and 1848, offers one of the only passages in Victorian fiction to describe the experience of a railway line being built. The 1840s were the years of the 'railway mania', when railway lines and new stations sprung up all over England.

The first shock of a great earthquake had, just at that period, rent the whole neighbourhood to its centre. Traces of its course were visible on every side. Houses were knocked down; streets broken through and stopped; deep pits and trenches dug in the ground; enormous heaps of earth and clay thrown up; buildings that were undermined and shaking, propped by great beams of wood. Here, a chaos of carts, overthrown and jumbled together, lay topsy-turvy at the bottom of a steep unnatural hill; there, confused treasures of iron soaked and rusted in something that had accidentally become a pond. Everywhere were bridges that led nowhere; thoroughfares that were wholly impassable; Babel towers of chimneys, wanting half their height; temporary wooden houses and enclosures, in the most unlikely situations; carcasses of ragged tenements, and fragments of unfinished walls and arches, and piles of scaffolding, and wildernesses of bricks, and giant forms of cranes, and tripods straddling above nothing. There were a hundred thousand shapes and substances of incompleteness, wildly mingled out of their places, upside down, burrowing in the earth, aspiring in the air, mouldering in the water, and unintelligible as any dream. Hot springs and fiery eruptions, the usual attendants upon earthquakes, lent their contributions of confusion to the scene. Boiling water hissed and heaved within dilapidated walls; whence, also, the glare and roar of flames came issuing forth; and mounds of ashes blocked up rights of way, and wholly changed the law and custom of the neighbourhood.

In short, the yet unfinished and unopened Railroad was in progress; and, from the very core of all this dire disorder, trailed smoothly away, upon its mighty course of civilisation and improvement.

But as yet, the neighbourhood was shy to own the Railroad. One or two bold speculators had projected streets; and one had built a little, but had stopped among the mud and ashes to consider farther of it. A bran-new Tavern, redolent of fresh mortar and size, and fronting nothing at all, had taken for its sign The Railway Arms; but that might be rash enterprise – and then it hoped to sell drink to the workmen. So, the Excavators' House of Call had sprung up from a beer-shop; and the old-established Ham and Beef Shop had become the Railway Eating House, with a roast leg of pork daily, through interested motives of a similar immediate and popular description.

COMPREHENSION QUESTIONS

1. Choose three examples of effective description and explain how Dickens uses these to bring the scene to life.

2. What impression is given of Dickens' response to the railway, from the language he uses?

3. What does Dickens suggest this neighbourhood now resembles? Use quotations to support your views.

4. How does Dickens use different structural features in his writing for effect?

ADDITIONAL LESSON IDEAS

1. Ask students to imagine they are one of the residents of the neighbourhood destroyed by the coming of the railway. How do they feel? Write a diary entry in their voice.

2. Have students imagine what the neighbourhood might look like after the railway comes, and write a description of the scene.

3. Students could pretend to be a member of the railway board, advertising for new businesses to come to the area once the railway has been built; they should write a prospectus for new investors, telling them all about the benefits of investing in this area and what it will look like in the future.

Extract taken from *On the Origin of Species* by Charles Darwin (London: John Murray, 1859), pp. 126–128

Charles Darwin (1809–82) was a British naturalist who revolutionised Victorian society when he wrote the culmination of decades of research, *On the Origin of Species*, which, for the first time, rationally explained the link between primitive and developed species. Darwin's vision of the world was that of chaos rather than order, competition rather than harmony, and chance rather than choice. All living organisms were in competition with one another, and only the fittest would survive. His brutal, atheistic vision of the world rocked the foundations of a society still built around Christian morals and principles, and led many to lose their faith in God altogether. Darwin was arguably the greatest influence on Victorian thought and changed the way in which many nineteenth-century intellectuals viewed themselves and the world around them.

If during the long course of ages and under varying conditions of life, organic beings vary at all in the several parts of their organisation, and I think this cannot be disputed; if there be, owing to the high geometrical powers of increase of each species, at some age, season, or year, a severe struggle for life, and this certainly cannot be disputed; then, considering the infinite complexity of the relations of all organic beings to each other and to their conditions of existence, causing an infinite diversity in structure, constitution, and habits, to be advantageous to them, I think it would be a most extraordinary fact if no variation ever had occurred useful to each being's own welfare, in the same way as so many variations have occurred useful to man. But if variations useful to any organic being do occur, assuredly individuals thus characterised will have the best chance of being preserved in the struggle for life; and from the strong principle of inheritance they will tend to produce offspring similarly characterised. This principle of preservation, I have called, for the sake of brevity, Natural Selection. Natural selection, on the principle of qualities being inherited at corresponding ages, can modify the egg, seed, or young, as easily as the adult. Amongst many animals, sexual selection will give its aid to ordinary selection, by assuring to the most vigorous and best adapted males the greatest number of offspring. Sexual selection will also give characters useful to the males alone, in their struggles with other males.

Whether natural selection has really thus acted in nature, in modifying and adapting the various forms of life to their several conditions and stations, must be judged of by the general tenour and balance of evidence given in the following chapters. But we already see how it entails extinction; and how largely extinction has acted in the world's history, geology plainly declares. Natural selection, also, leads to divergence of character; for more living beings can be supported on the same area the more they diverge in structure, habits, and constitution, of which we see proof by looking at the inhabitants of any small spot or at naturalised productions. Therefore during the modification of the descendants of any one species, and during the incessant struggle of all species to increase in numbers, the more diversified these descendants become, the better will be their chance of succeeding in the battle of life.

COMPREHENSION QUESTIONS

1. Summarise Darwin's theory about 'Natural Selection' in three sentences.

2. In five bullet-points, outline the stages of Darwin's theory.

3. How does Darwin make his theories intelligible to a non-expert reader?

4. How does Darwin use language to persuade his readers of his findings?

ADDITIONAL LESSON IDEAS

1. Show students a short video (plenty are available on YouTube) outlining Darwin's theories and a little more context about his work before having them read the extract above. Students could then write a newspaper article detailing Darwin's findings and the response from the public to his book.

2. Students could design a newspaper advert for *On the Origin of Species*, with a blurb about the book designed to make it appeal to nineteenth-century audiences.

3. Show students Matthew Arnold's poem 'Dover Beach' and have them imagine how Darwin's theory might have contributed towards Arnold's feelings about his faith, before analysing the poem together.

Extract taken from 'The Transatlantic Cable' in the *Freeman's Journal*, 5 September 1857

The first attempt to lay a transatlantic cable between Britain and America was in 1857. A highly complex task, it was tried three times before it was successful, with the first transatlantic message being sent in 1858. However, within a month, the signal failed. It took another six years before a permanent connection was formed between the countries, revolutionising worldwide communication.

Though the first attempt to connect Europe and America by the electric wire has not succeeded, we may draw sufficient encouragement from what has been accomplished to predicate a speedy renewal of the effort to bring the two great continents into instantaneous communication. The thing to be done is so stupendous in character, so marvellous, so far surpassing the most brilliant idea of the most vivid imagination . . . that had it met with repeated failures instead of a single check we would still urge perseverance in the attempt. But when we consider the vast importance of its accomplishment to the most civilised portions of the human race we cannot but congratulate the enterprising men who have undertaken the great work, that nothing has yet occurred to show the impossibility of the undertaking. A few years since the man who should have proposed to fathom the vast depths of the Atlantic with the electric cable would have been regarded as a fit candidate for Bedlam*. The depths of the Atlantic were then unsounded, the strength of the undercurrents untested. All was mysterious as the ocean itself. Now we know that a plateau of land covered with minute, unbroken, yet brittle shells, runs in a direct line from near Ireland to Newfoundland, at a mean depth of about two miles, as if to invite to the enterprise. These unbroken shells show that the cable when submerged will be far more secure from danger than if placed in shallower water; once laid down little or no danger is to be apprehended from ocean currents. The tempest may rage above in all its fury; in these vast depths all is calm, and no force exists sufficiently strong to injure the delicate brittle shell. The only apprehensions of mischief from the storm exist at the two extremities of the line, where the cable must rest in shallow water . . .

   We now approach the failure, for the present at least, of this grand experiment . . . a quarter to four on the morning of the 11th . . . [the cable] snapped asunder, and 835 miles of cable were submerged. The accident arose from a cause which, though deeply to be deplored, can be carefully guarded against for the future. The care and watchfulness, as well as the necessity of having all hands ready for any emergency during the trying period of the cable's descent into the rapidly increasing depths, during the previous day and night, had completely exhausted the staff of skilled mechanics. The engineer, finding all going on well, allowed them to take their rest . . . during this temporary absence, the breaks were left, as the event unfortunately proved, in the charge of a man not sufficiently skilled in their management . . . An accident like this may be prevented for the future by having a sufficient staff of skilled mechanicians to allow them to take necessary rest from labour by relays.

*a hospital for those certified insane

COMPREHENSION QUESTIONS

1. How does the writer of the article create a sense of wonder and awe around the topic of the transatlantic cable? Use quotations to evidence your views.

2. Explain in your own words why the laying of the cable failed.

3. What is the effect of the hyperbole in the article?

4. What does the author of the article think about what will happen regarding the cable in future?

ADDITIONAL LESSON IDEAS

1. Students could write a letter from the ship's captain home to his family, explaining what he has seen and experienced on the ship, and his feelings about the failure of the cable-laying process.

2. Have students imagine a world without the internet and all the things they would not be able to do without it. They should then create a presentation on the impact the internet has had on the world, and share it with the class.

3. Students could imagine that they are the founder of the Transatlantic Cable Company. What dreams and ambitions might the founder have had, and what might his hopes be for the future in a world of transatlantic communication? After planning their ideas, students could write a rousing speech for the founder to give at the opening ceremony of the new cable, and deliver it to the class.

Extract taken from 'Fatal accident to Mr Huskisson' in *Sheffield Independent*, 18 September 1830

The opening of the world's first passenger railway, the Liverpool and Manchester Railway, took place on 15 September 1830. Trains full of dignitaries, including the war hero the Duke of Wellington, left Liverpool station to make the journey to Manchester, as part of the ceremony to open the new line. One of the dignitaries was a prominent MP, William Huskisson. When the trains stopped to take on extra water for the steam engines, some of the dignitaries, despite being told not to, got off their train to speak to one another. On the parallel track, the steam engine Rocket was advancing towards the party, and when warned, all the other men either got back onto their carriages, or left the tracks to make way for the Rocket. William Huskisson, however, panicked, and could not get out of the way in time; he was run over and died from his injuries, becoming the first ever victim of a passenger train service.

We have the melancholy satisfaction of being enabled to give a more detailed account than has hitherto appeared, of the fatal accident which has deprived the country of one of its most able and liberal statesman: –

On the stoppage at the station, a number of gentlemen descended from their carriages, to converse with their friends, in other parts of the procession, and, amongst them, Mr Huskisson alighted from the front part of the Duke's carriage, in which he had been seated, and whilst he was passing to speak to some of the ladies, the Duke of Wellington perceived him, and gave him a cordial recognition and shake by the hand. He then advanced towards Mrs Huskisson, who was sitting amongst a group of ladies near the Duke; and in order that he might the more freely communicate with her, he opened the carriage door, which was unfortunately very wide. The line of rails on which this carriage stood was that to the south of the road, and immediately a cry was raised, that the Rocket, with its train of carriages, was approaching on the north line of the railway. Before the Rocket came directly opposite the Duke's carriage, Prince Esterhazey and Mr Littleton, the Member [of Parliament] for Staffordshire, were pulled into the carriage, and several voices exclaimed – "Come in." – "Take care of Mr Huskisson." Alas! the admonition was vain. The fatal engine arrived, and, striking the open door of the car which Mr Huskisson held in his hand, that gentleman was violently thrown down before the engine, his body being under the Rocket, and one of his legs lying across the inner rail; the wheels of the engine, and one wheel of the first carriage attached to it, passed over the limb, and taking a diagonal direction over the upper part of it, crushed the thigh to within three or four inches of the body. The scene of horror was the work of an instant – the Rocket was stopped, unhappily too late. A loud and simultaneous shriek issued from all the witnesses of this appalling catastrophe, and the unfortunate gentleman lay stretched upon the ground, bleeding most profusely. Mrs Huskisson, overwhelmed by her feelings, sunk into a state of insensibility, from which she was aroused only to witness the reality of her most fearful apprehensions. The Right Hon. Gentleman was raised from the ground by the Earl of Wilton and Mr Joseph Parkes, of Birmingham, to whom he exclaimed, "I have met my death – God forgive me!"

COMPREHENSION QUESTIONS

1. How does the writer of the article create a sense of tension and foreboding in the article?

2. How does the final part of the article create a sense of drama?

3. Choose a phrase from the article that you find particularly effective and explain its effect.

4. Summarise in your own words the circumstances of the accident.

ADDITIONAL LESSON IDEAS

1. Ask students to imagine they witnessed the accident; have them write a letter or diary entry, detailing their thoughts and feelings about what they saw. Encourage students to draw a contrast between the excitement of the railway opening and the tragic ending to the day.

2. For those students who enjoy drama, ask them to script a short play outlining the events of the day and perform it to the class.

3. Give students the title 'The Railway Accident' and have them write a short narrative in response, drawing on the information given in the article.

Appendix I
Mansfield Park unit plan

Week	Learning objectives	Resources	Suggested activities
1	L/O: To explore the context of the novel L/O: To sequence the novel (2 lessons) L/O: To watch the film of the novel	Video Images PowerPoint Worksheet Worksheet	Starter: students watch short video on Jane Austen: www.youtube.com/watch?v=LlYiThAyY8s. Main: students look at a range of images relating to Regency Britain (slavery, French Revolution, newspapers, urban lifestyle) and discuss what these might have to do with the novel. Plenary: students to then complete mix-and-match worksheet activity to link events of the novel to contextual factors. Starter: what is the most important event in the book? Discussion. Main: students to work in pairs to fill in chapter, quote and character summary sheets to sequence the novel. Plenary: repeat starter – do we still have the same opinion? Watching the film. Students to have 5 minutes at the end of the lesson to note any differences to the novel or any points to discuss.
2	L/O: To watch the film of the novel L/O: To explore characterisation L/O: To analyse a character's presentation in the novel	A3 paper Extract from the novel	Watching the film. 10-minute discussion at the end to discuss talking points. Starter: who's your favourite character and why? Pair and share discussion. Main: students work in groups of 3 on an allocated character – create an A3 poster detailing the character's personality, relationships, key events, themes and purpose in the novel. Key quotes should also be found. Plenary: students present their posters to one another and hand them in for reproduction **Homework: Annotate a character extract and find three main points to say about the character's presentation.** Starter: recap writing features through projecting an extract on the board and asking students to just say what they see. After a group attempt, put a list of techniques on the board. Main: teacher to model response to a character presentation extract question through going systematically through the extract and explaining features. Students to then have a go at writing their own using the annotated extract they did for homework. Plenary: peer assessment. Students to hand in work for marking.

(continued)

(continued)

Week	Learning objectives	Resources	Suggested activities
3	L/O: To analyse the structure of the novel L/O: To explore the settings of the novel L/O: To analyse the significance of the theme of wealth and poverty	Post-it notes Images of the settings Setting worksheet	Starter: what are the key turning points of the novel? Students to write their key moments on post-it notes and come and put them on the board. Teacher to discuss and then put them on a visual timeline. Main: students to be shown each of the key events and discuss their significance, with teacher support to draw out the presentation of the event, how it moves the plot forward and from whose perspective we see it. Students to consider why each event is portrayed in the way it is. Plenary: students to draw a timeline and plot the key events on it, finding a key quotation for each event, before writing a sentence to summarise each event and why it is so important. Starter: Students to look at images/clips of the main settings. How are they portrayed in the novel? Students to fill in worksheets with quotations and adjectives to describe each place. Main: students to work in groups to look at a key location in the play, creating a poster that explores the significance of the setting – how is it described, who likes it/doesn't like it, what happens there, etc. Students to swap after 15 minutes to look at what another group has done and see if they can add anything to their work. Plenary: students to present their original poster, with additions – teacher to draw out any insights missed. **Homework: Write a descriptive passage about Mansfield Park.** Starter: students to come up with as many examples as they can of how wealth and poverty are portrayed in the novel. Who/what is contrasted to show the difference? Who speaks about wealth and poverty? What significance does it have? Main: students to work in pairs on finding contrasts between wealth and poverty in the novel, with teacher guidance (i.e. Mansfield Park v. Portsmouth, characters – Lady Bertram and Mrs Price, Fanny's room v. rest of Mansfield Park) – what do these contrasts tell us about Austen's attitudes towards the two states? Students to then think about characters' attitudes towards wealth and poverty – what effect does money have on the characters and does having wealth necessarily make you a better person? What is more valuable – financial wealth, or moral wealth? Plenary: students to write a short analysis of the significance of Austen's contrast of wealth and poverty in the novel, with students pushed to use relevant terminology and quotations to support their views. **Homework: Extract question: Portsmouth and how it is represented.**
4	L/O: To analyse the significance of slavery to the novel L/O: To analyse the significance of the theme of gender and power to the novel	Print-out of article Double gingerbread man	Starter: students to watch this short introductory video to slavery in the UK: www.youtube.com/watch?v=_WiIznET63U. Students to look at some relevant Regency images of slavery. Discussion of what significance this has to the novel. Main: students to consider how the novel uses slavery as a device: what significance does it have that Sir Thomas' fortune is built upon slavery? What metaphorical slavery exists within the novel? Students to read this article: www.telegraph.co.uk/culture/books/1098704048/Mansfield-Park-shows-the-dark-side-of-Jane-Austen.html and discuss their ideas. Plenary: students to summarise the main points of the article in 250 words.

L/O: To analyse the significance of the theme of love, sexuality and marriage to the novel

Starter: students to watch this short film on gender and morality: www.bl.uk/romantics-and-victorians/videos/jane-austen-gender-and-morality. How does this make us feel? How does the portrayal of Fanny and Mary fit Kathryn Sutherland's view on what Austen felt about women? Main: students to create a list of the powerful characters in the novel. Why are they powerful? What kind of power do they have? Students to then create a list of the least powerful characters. Why are they lacking power? How does this affect their lives? Students to then consider female characters who try and take power – Mary Crawford, Maria Rushworth, Mrs Norris – what is the outcome of this and what does this tell us? How is our view on this perhaps different to the viewpoint of someone reading the novel in Austen's time? Plenary: students to find a quotation that expresses gender and power in the novel.

Starter: watch short video on marriage from Discovering Literature: www.bl.uk/romantics-and-victorians/articles/courtship-love-and-marriage-in-jane-austens-novels. Main: students to come up with a list of features of a bad husband and a bad wife, and then a good husband and a good wife. Students to then consider how these qualities reflect the marriages in the novel. Who has a 'good' marriage and who a 'bad'? Why? What role does love have in the novel? Students to choose a married couple of their choice and complete a double gingerbread man to explore the qualities of each of the partners in the marriage before writing a short paragraph to explain what type of marriage they have and why they think Austen portrays it in the way she does. Plenary: students to present their work.

Homework: Extract question: Tension/discomfort – Fanny and Mary/Henry.

Homework: Research the slave origins of your London street (see www.ucl.ac.uk/lbs).

5

L/O: To analyse the significance of the theme of nature v. nurture to the novel

L/O: To analyse the significance of the theme of social status/class and morality to the novel

Photocopies of passages

Starter: students to consider the question: are we inherently made a particular way? Or are our lives dictated by our upbringing? Main: students to consider the depiction of the Ward sisters, the Bertram siblings and the Price siblings. How are they different and how are they similar? Students to then look at the passages about Mrs Price and Lady Bertram (p. 460) – what is Austen trying to say here about what someone's surroundings can do? Was Fanny inherently 'better' than her siblings, or was she made better by the world in which she was brought up? And how did Fanny grow so different from Maria and Julia? What is the impact of who nurtures and supports us as we grow? What wider significance could we draw from this? Plenary: students to write a paragraph to explore their views.

(continued)

Week	Learning objectives	Resources	Suggested activities
	L/O: To compare and contrast the presentation of Fanny and Edmund and Mary and Henry	Print-outs of Burke's peerage and navy lists Post-it notes Photocopies of passages	Starter: students to look at images from Burke's Peerage (on Discovering Literature website) and from the Navy – what do these tell us about status in Regency society? Main: students to work together to 'rank' the characters of the novel by social status on the board. Students to then see what would change if the characters were ranked by their moral integrity as opposed to their social class. What might Austen be telling us about society's values through challenging the accepted status quo of rank = value? Students to then consider the Bertrams: why do they have status as a family? What affects their moral status? What might Austen be saying here? Plenary: write a letter from Sir Thomas to Burke's Peerage, describing what he should have included in his entry (directed writing). Starter: who do you like best – Fanny and Edmund or Mary and Henry? Why? Class debate. Main: students to work in small groups to look at passages describing the characters and their fates. Close text analysis – how does Austen present these characters? How are we shown the moral value of their outlook on life? (Through characters or through narration?) Is it clear who Austen wants us to favour? Does she manage to do this successfully? Why and how are these characters different? How have their lives differed to make them so contrasting – why do the Crawfords have such loose values? What contextual factors could we link this to? Plenary: write a diary entry in the voice of one of the characters.
6	L/O: To analyse different elements of the writer's craft L/O: To understand how to plan, structure and write an analytical essay (2 lessons)	Photocopy of passages	Starter: students to be given a passage of text from the novel and to find as many interesting features using terminology that they can. Teacher-led analysis to follow on the board, using students' ideas. Main: students to complete their own written analysis of a different passage. Can work in pairs if struggling. Plenary: peer assessment of analyses with teacher highlighting examples of good practice (reference to English Language and writer's craft). Spend two lessons going over planning, structuring and writing of non-passage-based essay questions. **Homework: Writing an essay.**
7	L/O: To assess essay writing skills L/O: To revise the novel L/O: To complete a timed essay		Students to receive marked essays back, and teacher to give general feedback on areas where improvement can be made. Teacher to use (with consent) sections from students' essays and model how they could be improved. Students to then take a paragraph from their essay and rewrite it based on the feedback received. Students to play Mansfield Park Pictionary to revise the novel. Students complete a timed essay in preparation for the mock.

Appendix 2
Mansfield Park
summary sheet

	What happens?	Key quotes	Key characters
Volume I	We are introduced to the main characters. Sir Thomas goes to Antigua, leaving Mansfield Park in the charge of Mrs Norris. Maria becomes engaged to Mr Rushworth and the Crawfords arrive. A day out at Sotherton, Mr Rushworth's home, proves that Maria is unhappy and a flirtation develops between her and Henry Crawford. Meanwhile, Edmund is falling for Mary Crawford, and the relationship between these characters develops further when the play *Lover's Vows* is rehearsed at Mansfield Park, much to Fanny's distress. Volume I covers a period of around eight years, with the main events taking place over the rough two-year period Sir Thomas is away in Antigua.	**Mrs Norris** – 'I suppose, sister, you will put the child in the little white attic.' **Mrs Norris** – 'she would learn to be good and clever from them [her cousins].' **Sir Thomas** – 'they cannot be equals' (speaking of Fanny and his children) 'Nobody meant to be unkind, but nobody put themselves out of their way to secure her comfort.' 'The kindness of her cousin Edmund gave her better spirits' 'Edmund's friendship never failed her . . . he encouraged her tastes, and guided her judgment.' 'Tom's extravagance had . . . been so great . . . the younger brother must help pay for the pleasures of the elder.' **Mrs Norris** – 'Sir Thomas's means will be rather straightened, if the Antigua estate is to make such poor returns.' **Fanny on Edmund** – 'She regarded her cousin as an example of everything good and great.'	**Fanny Price** 'She was small for her age . . . exceedingly timid and shy.' **Sir Thomas Bertram** 'had . . . a general wish of doing right.' **Lady Bertram** 'a woman of very tranquil feelings, and a temper remarkably easy and indolent.' **Mrs Norris** 'it would be totally out of Mrs Norris's power to take any charge of her.' **Edmund Bertram** **Tom Bertram** **Maria Bertram** **Julia Bertram** **Mr Rushworth** **Mary Crawford** **Henry Crawford**
Chaps 1–4	Introduction of the Ward sisters and their various fates. Fanny is taken to live at Mansfield Park with her aunt and uncle Sir Thomas and Lady Bertram; after initial discomfort, she settles in, largely thanks to the kindness of her cousin Edmund. By the end of chapter 3, some years have passed and Sir Thomas takes his dissolute son Tom with him to his plantation in Antigua, for at least a year. Maria, the eldest Bertram daughter, becomes engaged to the rich but dull Mr Rushworth, and the Crawfords, siblings of the new Rector's wife, arrive to stay at Mansfield.		

| Chaps 5–8 | The intimacy between the Bertrams and the Crawfords grows. We see that Henry is a flirtatious and handsome young man, who soon charms both Bertram sisters, much to Fanny's distaste, especially as Henry seems to be enjoying flirting with Maria rather too much. Edmund, despite having misgivings about Mary's character, is irresistibly attracted to her and spends an increasing amount of time with her. Mr Rushworth announces a scheme of improvement for his nearby house, Sotherton, and by the end of chapter 8, the Bertrams, Crawfords and Fanny arrive to see the house for themselves. | Mary Crawford – 'Of Rears and Vices, I saw enough. Now do not be suspecting me of a pun, I entreat.'
 Edmund and Fanny – 'Having formed her mind and gained her affections, he had a good chance of her thinking like him.'
 Edmund – 'He was in a line of admiration of Miss Crawford.' | Mary Crawford
 'lively dark eye, clear complexion, and general prettiness.'
 'Nothing ever fatigues me, but doing what I do not like.'
 Henry Crawford
 'the most agreeable young man the sisters had ever known.' |
| Chaps 9–11 | The party arrives at Sotherton and are given a tour of the house, during which they separate. Mary is sarcastic and dismissive of the clergy and Church until she realises that Edmund is to become a Rector, and is then horrified at her mistake. Henry continues his now obvious flirtation with Maria, absconding with her in the grounds of Sotherton. It is clear that Maria is regretting her engagement, and Julia is jealous of Henry's attentions to her sister. Edmund becomes increasingly attracted to Mary, despite their obvious differences, shown through Mary's often flippant treatment of religion, which horrifies Fanny, and Fanny finds herself alone and miserable at seeing Edmund charmed by Mary, by the time they return to Mansfield. | 'Miss Crawford . . . had only the appearance of civilly listening, while Fanny . . . attended with unaffected earnestness.'
 Mary Crawford – 'Everybody likes to go their own way'
 Mary Crawford – 'She looked almost aghast. . . . "Ordained! . . . what, are you to be a clergyman?"'
 Mary on Edmund – 'You really are fit for something better.'
 Maria – 'that iron gate, that ha-ha, give me a feeling of restraint and hardship. I cannot get out, as the starling said.'
 Maria – 'it was a gloomy prospect' (her marriage) | Mary Crawford
 Henry Crawford
 Edmund Bertram
 Maria Bertram |

(continued)

	What happens?	Key quotes	Key characters
Chaps 12–18	Tom arrives back at Mansfield Park, but Mary has no interest in him now and is decidedly attached to Edmund. Henry Crawford briefly returns to his own estate, much to the pining of Maria and Julia. The arrival at Mansfield Park of a friend of Tom's, Mr Yates, who is a fan of acting, leads to the group deciding to perform a play themselves. Edmund is opposed to the idea, thinking his father wouldn't like it, but he is overruled, and the play *Lover's Vows* is chosen. This highly inappropriate play, enabling the women to behave in a sexual manner, is considered particularly dangerous considering Maria's status as a newly engaged woman, but she ignores her brother's concerns and revels in playing opposite Henry, highlighting the falsity of her behaviour towards Mr Rushworth. Mr Rushworth is shown to be a fool in his almost slapstick portrayal. Despite Edmund's misgivings, he is eventually persuaded to perform the role of Miss Crawford's romantic partner, a vicar – the similarity to their own situation makes this especially uncomfortable for Fanny, who can't understand Edmund's poor judgement when it comes to Mary. By the end of chapter 18, the play is having its final rehearsal – Fanny is about to be forced into reading a part meant to be played by the absent Mrs Grant – when Sir Thomas unexpectedly arrives home, bringing everything to an abrupt end.	'Maria . . . missed Mr Crawford grievously . . . Julia . . . even more.' **Fanny on Henry** – 'she could never see Mr Crawford with either sister without observation, and seldom without wonder or censure.' **Tom to Edmund** – 'Don't act yourself, if you do not like it, but don't expect to govern everybody else.' **Edmund** – 'I think it exceedingly unfit for private representation.' **Fanny** – '"You must excuse me, indeed you must excuse me," cried Fanny, growing more and more red from excessive agitation, and looking distressfully at Edmund.' **Mrs Norris** – 'I shall think her a very obstinate, ungrateful girl, if she does not do what her aunt and cousins wish her – very ungrateful indeed, considering who and what she is.' 'Mrs Norris, having stipulated for there never being a fire in it on Fanny's account.' 'Edmund so inconsistent . . . Alas! It was all Miss Crawford's doing.' **Fanny** – 'Her spirits sunk under the glow of theirs.' (Edmund and Mary's)	

Volume 2	This volume of the novel is largely concerned with the relationships between Henry and Mary Crawford and Fanny Price and Edmund Bertram. William, Fanny's brother in the navy, comes to stay and a ball is thrown by Sir Thomas. By the end of the volume, Henry has proposed to a horrified Fanny after securing her brother's promotion, and Edmund is hopelessly in love with Mary, whose feelings are still not yet clear.	**Sir Thomas Bertram** **Henry Crawford** **Maria Bertram** **Mr Rushworth**
Chaps 1–3	Sir Thomas' return brings about great change at Mansfield as he restores benevolent but unwelcome order to his house. The play is cancelled, and Henry Crawford leaves, much to the disappointment of Maria, who really thought he would save her from marriage to Mr Rushworth. Sir Thomas' kind treatment of Fanny highlights Mrs Norris' cruelty, and his surprise at her good looks shows how she has grown into an attractive young woman in his absence. The silence that greets Fanny's inquiry into the slave trade suggests a discomfort of the family to acknowledge the source of their wealth. Sir Thomas is shown to be a kind father in speaking to Maria and reassuring her that she can break with Rushworth if she wants to – abandoned by Henry and not wanting to give him the satisfaction of further pain, she denies her unhappiness and marries Rushworth anyway, preferring married independence to life under her father's roof.	'It was a moment of absolute horror' (Sir Thomas' return) **Maria** – 'Henry Crawford's retaining her hand at such a moment . . . was worth ages of doubt and anxiety.' **Sir Thomas** – 'he was grown thinner and had the burnt, fagged, worn-out look of fatigue and a hot climate.' **Mrs Norris** – 'she was ashamed to confess that she had never seen any of the impropriety which was so glaring to Sir Thomas.' 'Maria was in a good deal of agitation. It was of the utmost consequence to her that Crawford should lose no time in declaring himself.' 'Henry Crawford was gone . . . and so ended all the hopes his selfish vanity had raised in Maria and Julia Bertram.' 'Under his government, Mansfield was an altered place.' **Edmund on Fanny** – 'Your uncle thinks you very pretty . . . You must really begin to harden yourself to the idea of being worth looking at.'

(continued)

What happens?	Key quotes	Key characters
	Fanny – 'Did you not hear me ask him about the slave trade last night? … but there was such a dead silence!'	
	'Advantageous as would be the alliance, and long standing and public the engagement, her happiness must not be sacrificed to it.'	
	'It was an alliance which he could not have relinquished without pain.' (Sir Thomas on the Rushworth marriage)	
	'Henry Crawford had destroyed her happiness, but he should not know that he had done it; he should not destroy her credit, her appearance, her prosperity, too.'	
Chaps 4–7	Fanny grows in consequence in the absence of her cousins, and much to Mrs Norris' horror, becomes a favourite at the Crawfords, even being invited to dine out. She still cannot like Mary, and continues to be bemused and jealous of Edmund's interest in her, an interest that Mary obviously shares despite knowing Edmund will not have a fortune and will be a Rector. Mary's feelings are certainly much stronger and genuine than her brother's, who decides to make Fanny fall in love with him for fun, though as time goes on, he does start to realise that he likes her more than he expected to. In chapter 6, much to Fanny's delight, her naval brother William arrives to stay at Sir Thomas' invitation, and proves to be a well-liked and respectable young man who Fanny hasn't seen since she left Portsmouth. Henry Crawford finds Fanny even more attractive and worthy of respect when he sees how much she loves her brother, and his attempts to attract her approval increase.	'Fanny's consequence increased on the departure of her cousins.'

'Fanny went to her (Mary) every two or three days; it seemed a kind of fascination; she could not be easy without going, and yet it was without loving her, without ever thinking like her'

Mrs Norris – 'people are never respected when they step out of their proper sphere. Remember *that*, Fanny.'

Mrs Norris – 'Remember, wherever you are, you must be the lowest and last.'

Henry Crawford – 'With a significant smile, which made Fanny quite hate him, he said "So! Rushworth and his fair bride are at Brighton, I understand – happy man!"'

Fanny on Henry – 'he can feel nothing as he ought.' | |

Mary on Edmund – 'It was plain that he could have no serious views, no true attachment, by fixing himself in a situation which he must know she would never stoop to.'

Henry – 'My plan is to make Fanny Price in love with me.'

Henry – 'I only want her to look kindly on me, to give me smiles as well as blushes, to keep a chair for me by herself wherever we are, and be all animation when I take it and talk to her; to think as I think, be interested in all my possessions and pleasures, try to keep me longer at Mansfield, and feel when I go away that she shall never be happy again.'

Mary – 'without attempting any further remonstrance, she left Fanny to her fate.'

Henry – 'It would be something to be loved by such a girl . . . she interested him more than he had foreseen. A fortnight was not enough. His stay became indefinite.'

'Edmund at this time was particularly full of cares . . . He knew his own mind, but he was not always perfectly assured of knowing Miss Crawford's.'

'Fanny still resisted, and from her heart. The gift was too valuable.'

'Fanny, in great astonishment and confusion, would have returned the present instantly.'

'Miss Crawford, complaisant as a sister, was careless as a woman and a friend.'

Chaps 8–10	Sir Thomas plans to throw a ball for Fanny, on the occasion of her brother being at Mansfield. Edmund is tortured by his ongoing love for Mary as he prepares for his ordination. He can no longer see her faults, much to Fanny's distress. Henry continues to further his suit with Fanny, enlisting Mary's help in giving Fanny a necklace that she does not realise has been given as a gift from him. At the ball, Henry tries all his charms on Fanny and fails, though Sir Thomas notices and is delighted that Henry is in love with his niece, and plans to encourage the match. Edmund and Mary only succeed in upsetting each other as Mary tries to resist her true feelings.

Fanny Price
Henry Crawford
Mary Crawford
Edmund Bertram
Sir Thomas Bertram

(continued)

	What happens?	Key quotes	Key characters
		'But he was deceived in her; he gave her merits which she had not; her faults were what they had ever been, but he saw them no longer.' **(Fanny on the ball)** – 'To be placed above so many elegant young women! The distinction was too great!'	
Chaps 11–13	Henry's affection for Fanny increases to the point where he determines to marry her. His sister encourages him in this. To further his suit, he uses his influence with his naval uncle to secure William Price a promotion, which delights Fanny, though his proposal does not, leaving her in great confusion and distress.	'You must be aware that I am quite determined to marry Fanny Price.' 'I will make her very happy, Mary, happier than she has ever been herself.' 'His last journey to London had been undertaken with no other view than that of introducing her brother in Hill-street, and prevailing on the Admiral to exert whatever interest he might have for getting him on.' 'Offering himself, hand, fortune, everything to her acceptance.' '"No, no, no," she cried, hiding her face, "This is all nonsense. Do not distress me . . . I know it is all all nothing."'	**Henry Crawford** **Fanny Price**
Volume 3	In this final volume, all of the plot is brought to a close. With Henry Crawford and Maria Rushworth's elopement, the falsity of the Crawfords is made clear, and all thought of marital alliances between them and the Bertrams is over. The consequences of a poor moral education for his daughters is revealed to Sir Thomas, who sees that Fanny is greater than his own children ever were. Edmund finally sees Fanny's worth and marries her; they live happily ever after and the Bertrams have had a lesson in the importance of moral over financial worth.		

| Chaps 1–4 | Sir Thomas, Lady Bertram and Henry Crawford all try to persuade Fanny to accept Henry's proposal, but Fanny is determined that she cannot marry him. Henry's insistence only makes him worse in Fanny's eyes, and Sir Thomas' inability to see Fanny's perspective makes him tell her that she is being thoughtless and ungrateful. When Edmund returns, he too tries to convince Fanny that he would be a good match, showing his own lack of judgement when it comes to the Crawford family. | 'If Mr Crawford would but go away! That was what she most earnestly desired.'

'I – I cannot like him sir, well enough to marry him.'

'Her ill opinion of him was founded chiefly on observations, which, for her cousins' sake, she could scarcely dare mention to their father.'

'You think only of yourself' (Sir Thomas on Fanny's refusal to marry Henry)

'She was miserable forever. She had no one to take her part, to counsel, or speak for her.'

'A fire! It seemed too much; just at that time to be giving her such an indulgence.'

'She told him, that she did not love him, could not love him, was sure she never should love him.' | **Sir Thomas Bertram**
Fanny Price
Henry Crawford |
| | These chapters also contain Sir Thomas' shock that Fanny has never been given a fire – his ordering of a fire for her shows his warmth towards her, but this incident also shows how little control he has had over his own house and his foolishness in handing over authority to Mrs Norris for so long. | 'Now she was angry. Some resentment did arise at a perseverance so selfish and ungenerous. Here again was a want of delicacy and regard for others which had formerly so struck and disgusted her.'

Lady Bertram to Fanny – 'And you must be aware, Fanny, that it is every young woman's duty to accept such a very unexceptionable offer as this.'

Henry – 'By that right I do and will deserve you.' | |

(continued)

	What happens?	Key quotes	Key characters
Chaps 5–9	Henry, Mary and the Bertrams continue to try and persuade Fanny to marry Henry, and though his feelings seem very honourable, Fanny is determined that she can't love him. As a way to try and show her what she'll be missing by not marrying a man of fortune, Sir Thomas devises a plan to send Fanny back to Portsmouth for a visit to her family, hoping the contrast will make her realise that a sensible marriage is her best option. Fanny is horrified by what she finds in Portsmouth, but this does not drive her any further towards Henry, and she spends much of her time thinking about Edmund, and whether his planned proposal to Mary will have been successful.	'The promised visit from her "friend", as Edmund called Miss Crawford, was a formidable threat to Fanny, and she lived in continual terror of it.' **Fanny** – 'I cannot think well of a man who sports with any woman's feelings.' **Fanny on Mary** – 'She might love, but she did not deserve Edmund by any other sentiment.' **Sir Thomas** – 'Her father's house would, in all probability, teach her the value of a good income; and he trusted that she would be the wiser and happier woman, for all her life, for the experiment he had devised.' 'Yet she thought it would not have been so at Mansfield. No, in her uncle's house there would have been a consideration of times and seasons, a regulation of subject, a propriety, an attention towards everybody which there was not here.' 'She soon learned to think with respect of her own little attic at Mansfield Park.' 'It was the abode of noise, disorder and impropriety.' **On Mrs Price** – 'She might have made just as good a woman of consequence as Lady Bertram, but Mrs Norris would have been a more respectable mother of nine children, on a small income.'	**The Prices**

| Chaps 10–13 | Henry Crawford travels from London to Portsmouth to see Fanny, and she remains insistent that she won't marry him, despite starting to see that he is not the man she thought he was. She waits with trepidation for a letter from Edmund, who she believes to be on the brink of proposing to Mary. Edmund has, however, returned to Mansfield from London without proposing, fearful of being rejected though unable to stop loving Mary. Fanny continues to despise Mary and longs to be back at Mansfield, away from her indifferent parents and their raucous household. At the end of chapter 13, Fanny receives a letter from Lady Bertram, detailing Tom's dangerous illness. | **Fanny on Henry** – 'She was willing to allow he might have more good qualities than she had been wont to suppose. She began to feel the possibility of his turning out well at last; but he was and must ever be completely unsuited to her, and ought not to think of her.'

'It often grieved her to the heart – to think of the contrast between them – to think that where nature had made so little difference, circumstance should have made so much, and that her mother, as handsome as Lady Bertram, and some years her junior, should have an appearance so much more worn and faded, so comfortless, so slatternly, so shabby.'

Edmund on Mary – 'She is the only woman in the world whom I could ever think of as a wife.'

Fanny on Mary – 'she loves nobody but herself and her brother.' | **Fanny Price**
Edmund Bertram
Henry Crawford
Mary Crawford |

(continued)

	What happens?	Key quotes	Key characters
Chaps 14–17	While still in Portsmouth, Fanny receives a letter from Mary, detailing how finances still prevail in her marital decisions. The next day she receives a further letter from Mary, hinting at some scandal between Maria and Henry; it soon transpires that they have eloped together, as has Julia with Mr Yates. Edmund comes to take Fanny back to Mansfield Park, with her sister Susan, and with the truth about the Crawfords finally out, all thought of Edmund marrying Mary and Fanny marrying Henry is quite over. Maria, divorced by Rushworth, is banished with Mrs Norris to a cottage at some distance from Mansfield, and by the end of the novel, Edmund has realised Fanny's worth and they marry, taking up the living of Thornton Lacey together.	'Portsmouth was Portsmouth. Mansfield was home.' **Mary** – 'Varnish and gilding hide many stains.' 'Edmund would be forgiven for being a clergyman, it seemed, under certain conditions of wealth.' 'If there was a woman of character in existence, who could treat as a trifle this sin of the first magnitude, who could try to gloss it over, and desire to have it unpunished, she could believe Miss Crawford to be the woman!' **Edmund on Mary** – 'the charm is broken. My eyes are opened!' **Edmund** – 'How I have been deceived! Equally in brother and sister deceived!' **Sir Thomas** – 'the anguish arising from the conviction of his own errors in the education of his daughters, was never to be entirely done away.' 'He had meant them to be good, but his cares had been directed to the understanding and manners, not the disposition; and of the necessity of self-denial and humility, he feared they had never heard from any lips that could profit them.' 'Edmund did cease to care about Miss Crawford, and become as anxious to marry Fanny, as Fanny herself could desire.'	**Maria Rushworth** **Henry Crawford** **Mary Crawford** **Edmund Bertram** **Fanny Price** **Sir Thomas Bertram**

Bibliography

Austen, Jane, *Mansfield Park* (London: Penguin, 2003)

Austen, Jane, *Pride and Prejudice* (Ware: Wordsworth, 1999)

Barrie, J.M., *Peter Pan* (London: Collins, 2013)

Beecher Stowe, Harriet, *Uncle Tom's Cabin* (Ware: Wordsworth Editions, 2002)

Braddon, Mary Elizabeth, *Lady Audley's Secret* (London: Penguin, 2012)

Brittain, Vera, *Testament of Youth* (London: Virago, 2018)

Brontë, Anne, *Agnes Grey* (London: John Murray, 1922)

Brontë, Anne, *The Tenant of Wildfell Hall* (London: Penguin, 1996)

Brontë, Charlotte, *Jane Eyre* (New York: Random House, 1949)

Brontë, Emily, *Wuthering Heights* (London: Penguin, 2003)

Bunzl, Peter, *Cogheart* (London: Usborne, 2016)

Carroll, Lewis, *Alice's Adventures in Wonderland* (London: Macmillan Classics, 2014)

Collins, Wilkie, *No Name* (London: Penguin, 1994)

Collins, Wilkie, *The Moonstone* (London: Penguin, 1986)

Collins, Wilkie, *The Woman in White* (London: Penguin, 2003)

Conan Doyle, Arthur, *The Hound of the Baskervilles* (London: Vintage, 2004)

Conan Doyle, Arthur, *The Sign of Four* (London: John Murray, 1966)

Conrad, Joseph, *Heart of Darkness* (Oxford: Oxford University Press, 2008)

Darwin, Charles, *On the Origin of Species* (London: John Murray, 1859; London: Vintage, 2009)

Darwin, Charles, *The Descent of Man* (London: Penguin, 2004)

Dickens, Charles, *A Christmas Carol* (London: Wordsworth Editions, 1993)

Dickens, Charles, *Bleak House* (London: Penguin, 1996)

Dickens, Charles, *David Copperfield* (London: Penguin, 1996)

Dickens, Charles, *Dombey and Son* (London: Hazell, Watson and Viney, 1935)

Dickens, Charles, *Great Expectations* (London: Penguin, 2004)

Dickens, Charles, *Hard Times* (London: Penguin, 2003)

Dickens, Charles, *Nicholas Nickleby* (London: Penguin, 1999)

Dickens, Charles, *Oliver Twist* (New York: The Century Company, 1911)

Dickens, Charles, *Our Mutual Friend* (London: Penguin, 1997)

Dickens, Charles, *The Signalman; A Tale of Two Cities* (London: Penguin Classics, 2000)

Doherty, Berlie, *Street Child* (London: HarperCollins, 1995)

Eden, Emily, *The Semi-Attached Couple and the Semi-Detached House* (London: Latimer House Limited, 1943)

Eliot, George, *Daniel Deronda* (Oxford: Oxford University Press, 1984)

Eliot, George, *Middlemarch* (London: Penguin, 2003)

Eliot, George, *Silas Marner* (London: Wordsworth Editions, 1993)

Eliot, George, *The Mill on the Floss* (London: Penguin, 2003)

Ferguson, Rachel, *Alas, Poor Lady* (London: Persephone Books, 2006)

Gaskell, Elizabeth, *Mary Barton* (London: Penguin, 1996)

Gaskell, Elizabeth, *North and South* (London: Penguin, 1996)

Gaskell, Elizabeth, *Ruth* (London: Penguin, 1996)

Gissing, George, *New Grub Street* (Oxford: Oxford University Press, 2016)

Gissing, George, *The Nether World* (Oxford: Oxford University Press, 2008)

Gissing, George, *The Odd Women* (Oxford: Oxford University Press, 2008)

Grossmith, George and Weedon, *Diary of a Nobody* (London: Wordsworth Editions, 1994)

Haggard, H. Rider, *King Solomon's Mines* (London: Penguin, 2007)

Hardy, Thomas, *Tess of the D'Urbervilles* (London: Penguin Classics, 1998)

Hepworth Dixon, Ella, *The Story of a Modern Woman* (London: Broadview Press, 2004)

Hodgson Burnett, Frances, *A Little Princess* (London: Puffin, 2014)

Hodgson Burnett, Frances, *The Secret Garden* (London: Wordsworth Editions, 1993)

Hughes, Thomas, *Tom Brown's School Days* (London: Macmillan, 1904)

Kilvert, Francis, *Kilvert's Diary* (London: Vintage, 2012)

Kingsley, Charles, *The Water Babies* (Oxford: Oxford University Press, 2014)

Kipling, Rudyard, *Kim* (London: Vintage, 2010)

Lyell, Charles, *Principles of Geology* (London: Penguin, 1997)

Malory, Thomas, *Morte d'Arthur* (London: Penguin Classics, 1986)

Mayhew, Henry, *London Labour and the London Poor* (Oxford: Oxford University Press, 2012)

Meade Falkner, J., *Moonfleet* (London: Vintage, 2011)

Morrison, Arthur, *A Child of the Jago* (Oxford: Oxford University Press, 2012)

Nesbit, E., *The Railway Children* (London: Wordsworth Editions, 2018)

Oliphant, Margaret, *Chronicles of Carlingford* series (London: Virago, 1986)

Pullman, Philip, *The Ruby in the Smoke* (London: Scholastic, 2004)

Shelley, Mary, *Frankenstein* (London: Penguin, 2012)

Smiles, Samuel, *Self-Help* (Oxford: Oxford World's Classics, 2008)

Stevenson, Robert Louis, *The Strange Case of Dr Jekyll and Mr Hyde* (New York: Signet Classics, 2012)

Stevenson, Robert Louis, *Treasure Island* (London: Penguin, 2000)

Stickney Ellis, Sarah, *The Women of England* (London: Forgotten Books, 2012)

Stoker, Bram, *Dracula* (London: Penguin Classics, 1993)

Sutherland, John, *Can Jane Eyre Be Happy? More Puzzles in Classic Fiction* (Oxford: Oxford University Press, 1997)

Thackeray, William Makepeace, *Vanity Fair* (London: Wordsworth Editions, 2001)

Trollope, Anthony, *Barchester Towers* (London: Vintage, 2015)

Wells, H.G., *Ann Veronica* (London: Penguin, 2005)

Wharton, Edith, *The House of Mirth* (Oxford: Oxford University Press, 2008)

Wilson, Jacqueline, *Clover Moon* (London: Doubleday, 2016)

Wilson, Jacqueline, *Hetty Feather* (London: Doubleday, 2009)

Wollstonecraft, Mary, *A Vindication of the Rights of Woman* (London: Penguin, 2004)

Poems

Arnold, Matthew, 'Dover Beach', in *Dover Beach and Other Poems* (New York: Dover Publications, 1994)

Barrett Browning, Elizabeth, Sonnet 29, 'I Think of Thee', in *AQA GCSE Literature Poetry Anthology* (Manchester: AQA, 2015)

Blake, William, 'A Poison Tree', in *The Complete Poems* (London: Penguin Classics, 1977)

Browning, Robert, 'The Pied Piper of Hamelin', in *The Oxford Book of Narrative* (Oxford: Oxford University Press, 1983)

Byron, Lord, 'When We Two Parted', in *AQA GCSE Literature Poetry Anthology* (Manchester: AQA, 2015)

Hardy, Thomas, 'Neutral Tones', in *AQA GCSE Literature Poetry Anthology* (Manchester: AQA, 2015)

Patmore, Coventry, 'The Angel in the House', in *The Oxford Book of Victorian Verse* (Oxford: Oxford University Press, 1987)

Rossetti, Christina, 'Goblin Market', in *The Oxford Book of Narrative* (Oxford: Oxford University Press, 1983)

Tennyson, Alfred Lord, 'The Charge of the Light Brigade', in *AQA GCSE Literature Poetry Anthology* (Manchester: AQA, 2015)

Tennyson, Alfred Lord, 'The Lady of Shalott', in *The Oxford Book of Narrative* (Oxford: Oxford University Press, 1983)

Wilson Gibson, Wilfrid, 'Flannan Isle', in *Fires* (New York: The Macmillan Company, 1912)

Wordsworth, William, 'Composed Upon Westminster Bridge', in *Selected Poems* (London: Penguin Classics, 2004)

Index